F.A. Campbell

**A Year in the New Hebrides, Loyalty Islands, and New Caledonia**

F.A. Campbell

**A Year in the New Hebrides, Loyalty Islands, and New Caledonia**

ISBN/EAN: 9783337319274

Printed in Europe, USA, Canada, Australia, Japan

Cover: Foto ©Andreas Hilbeck / pixelio.de

More available books at **www.hansebooks.com**

# A YEAR IN THE
# New Hebrides, Loyalty Islands,
## AND NEW CALEDONIA.

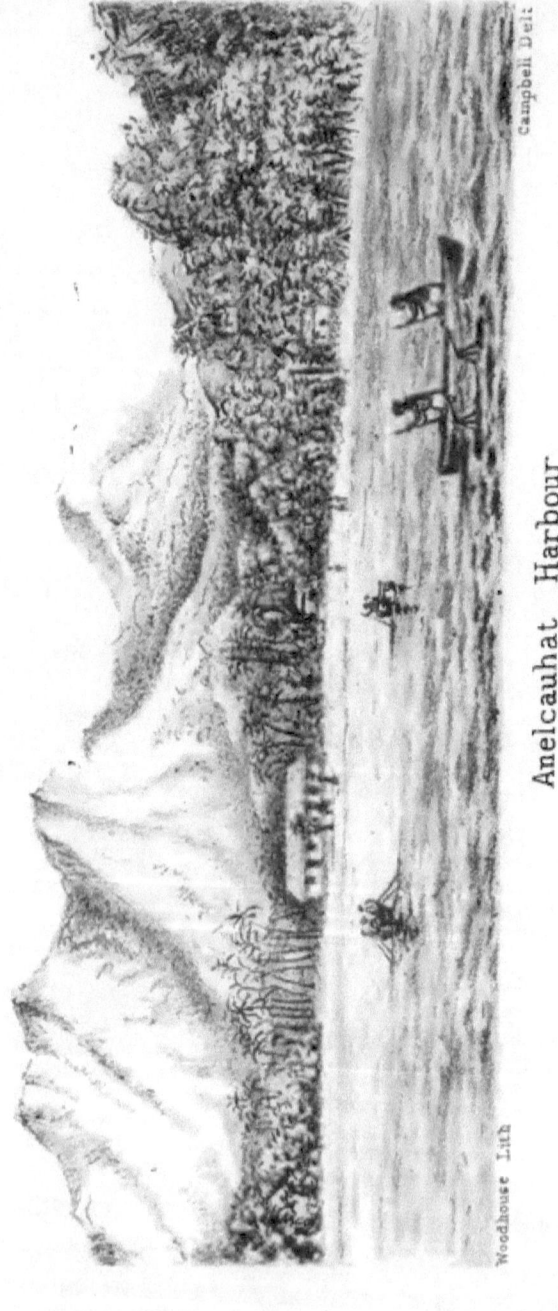

Anelcauhat Harbour
Aneityum

# A YEAR IN THE NEW HEBRIDES,

LOYALTY ISLANDS,

## NEW CALEDONIA.

### BY F. A. CAMPBELL.

WITH

AN ACCOUNT OF THE EARLY HISTORY OF THE
NEW HEBRIDES MISSIONS,

BY A. J. CAMPBELL, GEELONG;

A NARRATIVE OF THE VOYAGES OF
THE "DAYSPRING,"

BY D. M'DONALD, D.D.;

AND

AN APPENDIX, CONTAINING A CONTRIBUTION
TO THE PHYTOGRAPHY OF THE
NEW HEBRIDES,

BY BARON VON MUELLER, C.M.G., M.D., PH.D., F.R.S.

ILLUSTRATED.

GEELONG:
GEORGE MERCER, MALOP STREET.
MELBOURNE:
GEORGE ROBERTSON.

PRINTED BY
George Mercer, Malop Street,
GEELONG.

# PREFACE.

IT is a hundred years since Cook visited and described the New Hebrides; and his account of them has not been entirely superseded, even to this day.

Captains of the Navy and Christian Missionaries have given us Sketches of the People, and of their Ways, and of their Island Homes. But their narratives have been fragmentary in their intelligence, and many of them fugitive in their form.

The present volume cannot claim to be much more than its predecessors. It is a contribution merely to the physical, social, and religious history of this interesting and important group.

It has been prepared, mainly, with the desire of giving the many friends of the New Hebrides Mission some clear notion of the kind of places where their Missionaries are labouring, and the kind of work which they are trying (with God's help) to do.

It consists of Four Parts :—

I. An account of the beginning of the Presbyterian Missions in 1848, when the London Missionaries of Samoa introduced Dr. Geddie to Aneityum,—and of the early progress of the work. The facts related in Chapters III.—VI. have been gathered from Mr. Murray's interesting volume on Polynesia.

II. The story of the " Dayspring," from its building in Nova Scotia to its loss on Aneityum. This paper has been furnished by Dr. McDonald of Melbourne, to whom the Mission stands a debtor for this final labour, and for many that have gone before. It is a valuable document, showing that the Mission Ship—though a costly appliance of an Island Mission—is, in present circumstances at least, an indispensable one.

III. A series of Letters from the Islands—written by a young Voyager, who went there in quest of health. Having taken upon myself the responsibility of recommending their publication, I think it right to say that, whatever may be their literary qualities, I believe them to be faithful representations of what they describe; and this statement I wish to be extended to the views of island scenery—which were taken by him upon the spot with much care, and were reproduced here under his own eye.

One of these Letters (the XVI.) treats of the Labour traffic, which has its chief seat of operations in the New Hebrides. It deals with the very important question of the Results to the natives of their deportation and three years' residence on the plantations, and entirely demolishes Mr. Anthony Trollope's justification of the trade on the ground of its civilizing and christianizing effects. The writer, it is true, speaks only of what came under his own observation; but if corroborative or additional evidence that these are the invariable results of the trade is required, it can be furnished to any extent. And really this State of the Case ought to settle the question. Regulation of the traffic will not avert the cruel wrong—nothing short of its suppression will.

IV. An Appendix, containing a phytological description of the Plants collected by Mr. F. Campbell. This paper will possess a special interest to the lovers of botanical study; while Baron Von Mueller's established reputation carries with it an ample guarantee of the scientific accuracy of his contribution.

A. J. C.

St. George's Manse, Geelong,
  *December, 1873.*

# Contents.

## I.

## AN ACCOUNT OF THE EARLY HISTORY OF THE NEW HEBRIDES MISSIONS.

|   |   | Page |
|---|---|---|
| I. | The Ground of Missionary Duty | 1 |
| II. | The Pioneer | 5 |
| III. | The Mission Field | 10 |
| IV. | The Work | 14 |
| V. | The Work Continued | 19 |
| VI. | The Fruit | 25 |
| VII. | Progress of the Work | 32 |
| VIII. | Prospects of the Mission | 36 |

## II.

## THE "DAYSPRING."

History of the "Dayspring" ... 41

## III.

### A YEAR IN THE NEW HEBRIDES, &c.

#### LETTER I.

The voyage from Melbourne to Aneityum, and First Impressions of that Island .. .. .. .. .. .. .. .. .. .. *Page* 69

#### LETTER II.

The New Hebrides—Their Discovery—Aneityum—Its Characteristics—Inhabitants—The Mission Station at Anelcauhat—Rambles along the Shore and Inland—A Marriage—Native Service .. .. 74

#### LETTER III.

The Mission Station at Anamé—Fotuna—A Day Ashore—Aniwa—The Cocoanut Palm—Tana—Appearance of the Volcano—Port Resolution—Depopulation—Black Beach .. .. .. .. .. 87

#### LETTER IV.

Eramanga—Its Appearance and Characteristics—Dillon's Bay—Whaling Establishment—Efaté—Its Natural Features—Pango Bay—The Islets of Fili and Melé, and their Inhabitants—Visits paid to them .. .. .. .. .. .. .. .. .. .. .. .. 100

#### LETTER V.

Havannah Harbour—Trading Establishments—Vessel grazes a Reef—Nguna—Two Hills—Arrive at Santo .. .. .. .. .. 111

#### LETTER VI.

History of the Discovery of Santo—Its Appearance—Bartering with the Natives—The Queen's Birthday—Mau and its People—Visit Ashore—Return to Aneityum .. .. .. .. .. .. .. 117

#### LETTER VII.

The Mission Conference—Settlement of Mr. Robertson at Dillon's Bay, Eramanga—Settlement of Mr. McDonald at Havannah Harbour, Efaté—Visit to Ambrim .. .. .. .. .. .. .. .. 126

## LETTER VIII.

The Loyalty Islands—Their Nature, Characteristics, and **People—Maré**—The Mission Station of Mr. Jones—A Ride across the **Island**—A few Remarks about the Natives and their Houses—The **Vessel** Sails again for the **New** Hebrides .. .. .. .. .. .. 133

## LETTER IX.

The Natives **of the** New Hebrides—Their Personal Appearance—Diversity of Language—Remarks as **to their Probable Origin,** 141

## LETTER X.

Varieties of Life on Aniwa—Corals—Remarks on the Formation of these Islands .. .. .. .. .. .. .. .. .. .. 148

## LETTER XI.

Cross over to Tana—Death of a Bull—The Breakers—The Forest—The Tanamen and their Wars—Yam Cultivation—Amusements—Kava Drinking—Religion .. .. .. .. .. .. .. .. .. 158

## LETTER XII.

Residence at Port Resolution—Ascent of the Volcano—What we Saw from the Edge of the Crater—The Descent—Something about the Manners and Customs of this Volcano .. .. .. .. .. 172

## LETTER XIII.

The Industries carried on in the New Hebrides—Cotton Growing—Cobra—Arrowroot—Whaling—What might be done here—Mode of Reaching the Islands, and Outfit—The Disadvantages connected with Residence here .. .. .. .. .. .. .. .. 180

## LETTER XIV.

The New Hebrides Missions—Attacks on Missions generally—Mission Work on the Group—Benefits to Science and Commerce rendered by Missionaries—The Native Teachers .. .. .. .. .. 188

## LETTER XV.

Leave Tana for Aneityum—The Hurricane—The Wreck—A Sale by Auction—Life of the Shipwrecked Party Ashore—The Earthquake .. .. .. .. .. .. .. .. .. .. .. 197

## LETTER XVI.

The Labour Traffic—The Two Great Evils connected with it—The Mischief done by the Procurers of Labour—The Bad Effects of their Residence Abroad upon the Natives—Depopulation of the Islands ... .. .. .. .. .. .. .. .. .. .. 206

## LETTER XVII.

Leave Aneityum for New Caledonia in the "Sea Witch"—Appearance of the Shores of that Island—A Brief Account of its Characteristics—Life at Noumea—Leave for Sydney .. .. .. .. 213

# IV.

## PHYTOGRAPHY OF THE NEW HEBRIDES, &c.

(APPENDIX.)

# ILLUSTRATIONS.

## LITHOGRAPHS.

|  |  |  |
|---|---|---|
| I. | Anelcauhat Harbour, Aneityum | *Frontispiece.* |
| II. | Port Resolution, Tana | 32 |
| III. | The "Dayspring" (full sail) | 43 |
| IV. | Fotuna | 89 |
| V. | Mau and Pele | 124 |
| VI. | Dillon's Bay, Eramanga | 128 |
| VII. | The Crater of the Volcano | 176 |
| VIII. | East Coast of Tana | 192 |
| IX. | Wreck of the "Dayspring" | 198 |

## WOOD CUTS.

|  |  |  |
|---|---|---|
| I. | Dr. Geddie's Monument | xvi. |
| II. | Line of March | 74 |
| III. | Mission House, Aniwa | 95 |
| IV. | Huts on Fili Island | 108 |
| V. | Native Drums on Fili Island | 111 |
| VI. | Native Church on Maré, Loyalty Islands | 137 |
| VII. | Mission House at Kwamera, Tana | 159 |
| VIII. | Banyan-Tree and Kava-House on Tana | 167 |
| IX. | Mont D'Or, New Caledonia | 220 |

## MAP OF THE NEW HEBRIDES,

Shewing their relative position with Australia, New Zealand and Fiji .. .. 69

# AN ACCOUNT OF THE EARLY HISTORY

## OF THE

# NEW HEBRIDES MISSIONS.

BY

A. J. CAMPBELL,

GEELONG.

# In Memoriam.

## JOHN GEDDIE, D.D.

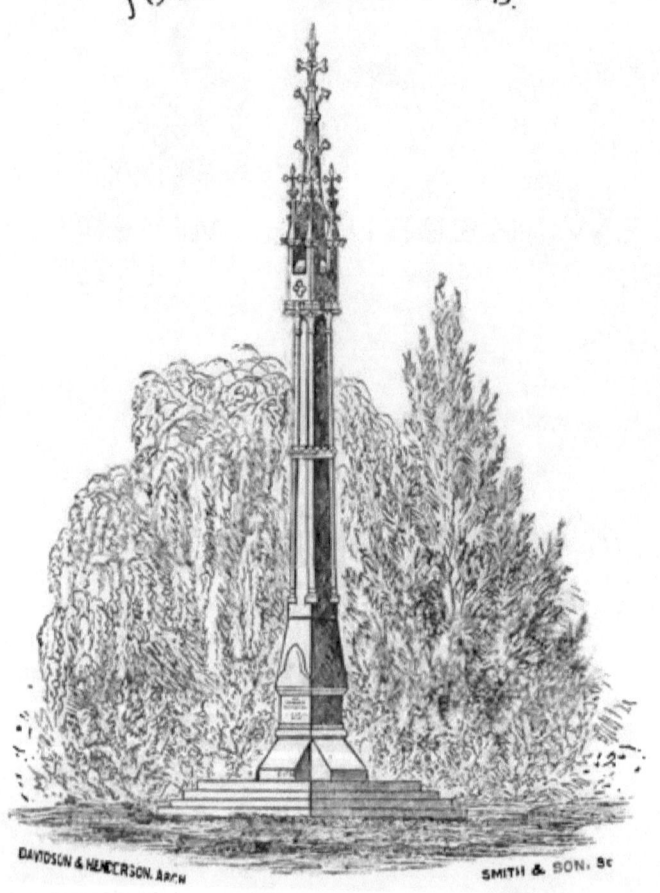

GEELONG CEMETERY.

## I.

### THE GROUND OF MISSIONARY DUTY.

"AS truly as I live, all the earth shall be filled with the glory of the Lord."

That is to be the final destiny of this sin-cursed, God-loved world.

And therefore while other men are looking wistfully into the gathering Night, and are asking "What *is* to become of this poor world?" let Christian men briefly reply, "THIS is what is to become of it: It is to be filled with the glory of the Lord."

And let no strangeness nor darkness of the night; no scoffs of ungodly men; no declensions of the Church, and no miscarriages even, in their own missionary efforts abate the absolute confidence with which they repose on that most ancient and, (looking at the circumstances of its utterance,) most extraordinary of all those Words on which God has caused them to hope.

In the Desert of Sinai, when His people refused to follow Him into Canaan, God came down to judge and punish them. First, He stripped them of the high vocation which they had despised; and then He doomed them to perish in the wilderness.

And now it seemed as if His great purpose of mercy had been defeated. His chosen nation, to whose custody He had entrusted it, had gone, like a gallant ship, to pieces on the rocks of unbelief. But God's purpose cannot fail.

On the field of that disaster He raised this ground and pillar of Hope. Standing amid His weeping people, now awakened to a sense of their disfranchisement, and degradation and doom, He uttered those mighty words, by which He detached the Promise from that wrecked nation, and fixed it to the rock of His own indestructible existence.

"The world's Hope shall no longer be tied to your life, but to Mine. It is not—as truly as you live, but as truly as I live. You may perish, but I remain. And I have sworn by myself that the whole earth shall be filled with my glory."

JESUS CHRIST IS THE GLORY OF GOD. And that promise of the desert began to blossom when He was planted in Judea, and it reached its perfection when He ascended up on high that He might fill all things.

For then the two great hemispheres—Heaven and Earth—so long parted, came together in His hand; and the power of both was given Him, that He might rule them both on the same principles of righteousness and fill them both with His glory.

No sooner was He clothed with this all-power in Heaven and Earth than He set in motion the machinery which He had already prepared. "Go ye, therefore," He said to His disciples, "and teach all nations.—Go ye into all the world, and preach the Gospel to every creature."

These were—these still are, the Church's "MARCHING ORDERS." She has no alternative but to obey them.

And when Christian men and women go forth to encounter the dangers of missionary enterprise, and to place themselves in contact with the pollutions of heathenism, it is not to be concluded that they are actuated by the mere impulses of humanity, or the love of sacrificing themselves. But the heathen belong to Christ. He has asked and obtained them as His inheritance and possession, and has commanded His disciples to claim them and christianise them for Him. For His sake, and for the glory of His name, they will seek their good. Obedience and Love to Christ, then, are the chief grounds and motives of missionary duty.

Men who decline the authority of Christ will, of course, act on a very different principle. The heathen are nothing to them beyond what they can get from them in the way of pleasure or trade; and as their persons are more valuable than their productions, they will buy and sell them—kidnap and kill them as it suits them to do so.

And if we believed that they were less than men—that they had no part in man's sin and no share in Christ's salvation, if they had been exempted from His Possession and excluded from our Commission, we would not feel that we had any serious duty toward them. But they are under the empire of Sin and Death, even as we are—and by special grant have been included in the Kingdom of Christ. Therefore, of whatever character or condition they may be—lovely or unlovely—a noble race or a very contemptible one—because Christ does not despise them we dare not; because He says "Go to all nations," and "Preach the Gospel to every creature," we cannot rest till we have finished that work given us to do.

And although the faults and shortcomings which are laid at the door of Christian missionaries were true, and although they were multiplied a thousandfold, that would not alter our duty, nor affect our determination to do it by God's help.

But these charges (charges chiefly of indolence and uselessness, and hypocritical washing black men white) are not true. They are not true to any appreciable extent. I feel bound to speak on this subject. And having had long acquaintance with the missionaries of the present generation—beginning with John Williams and Alexander Duff—I must be permitted to offer them the tribute of a humble but very sincere admiration. They are among the Church's foremost men.—They are among her greatest benefactors; for while they have been advancing the lines of light upon the frontiers,—more than most men they have been wakening up and fanning into vigour the flame of Christian love at Home.

And I am persuaded, dear reader, that when you have read the following sketch of one of these labourers you will not refuse to rank him among that goodly company of Christian men, who have not counted their lives dear to them, that they might fulfil their Master's high command, and earn the servant's coveted reward—their Lord's welcome and well-done.

## II.

### THE PIONEER.

THE South-Sea Islanders have no history. We found them in their beautiful homes a hundred years ago; but whence they came or how they got there, they cannot tell us. Since then, however, there has grown round them a history of a singularly interesting though sadly chequered kind. Not a national but a Christian history. For while the nations of Europe and America have been struggling for empire, or urging on their great commercial enterprises, there has been going on throughout these Islands an incessant warfare in the name of the Prince of Peace, and a succession of conquests—not always bloodless in their course, but always beneficent in their consequences.

I say not a national history; for these Islands of the Pacific, although grouped together on the bosom of the sea as the stars are grouped together in the constellations of the skies, can not be expected to take any rank among the kingdoms of the world; any more than the counties of England, if separated by fifty or a hundred miles of ocean, could be expected to coalesce and keep together as a nation.—But a Christian history, in which Christ, the Lord of Life, has made a conspicuous display of his power to destroy the works of the Devil, and to lift up men from the dunghills of heathenism and set them in the pure and wholesome light of the kingdom of heaven.

Among the events of that missionary history the following are not to be forgotten.

1769: May 1, Captain Cook landed on Tahiti, erected an observatory, and, amid the solemn silence of the natives, watched the transit of Venus across the Sun's disc.

1796: Captain Wilson carried the first band of christian missionaries, sent out by the London Society, to Tahiti, in the ship "Duff."

1812: After sixteen years' seemingly fruitless labour, and while the missionaries were absent from the Island—driven away by war—a few of the natives met to pray; and when the missionaries returned they found the people prepared to abandon idolatry and embrace christianity.

1817: John Williams joined the mission.

1827: The first missionary ship, the "Messenger of Peace," was built by John Williams at Raiatea.

1838: The first British missionary ship, "The Camden," was built in England.

1839: November 19, John Williams paid the first missionary visit to the New Hebrides, and placed native teachers on Tana. On the following day he landed at Eramanga, and was murdered.

1848: May 28, Mr. and Mrs. GEDDIE landed at Aneityum.

My story opens at the last of these dates, and will narrate the labours of the last-named missionary. But first I shall say a few words about his previous career.

JOHN GEDDIE was born in 1816, in the quaint old town of Banff on the shores of the Moray Firth. His father followed the honourable occupation of a goldsmith. He was a much-respected citizen and a devout christian. He had come to be much interested in the London Society's South-Sea enterprise, and was anxious to help on God's work in the world. Robert Morrison, China's great missionary, was his apprentice—whom he released from a profitable indenture that he might equip himself for higher service. And when this child was born his parents gave him up in a silent dedication to God, for such mission work at home or abroad as He might be pleased to appoint for him. Their wishes in that matter were abundantly gratified.

Shortly after his birth, his mother's health demanding a change of climate, the family crossed the Atlantic and settled in Pictou in Nova Scotia. There, amid the the rich fresh scenes of that new land, they nursed their boy; and as he grew up they suffered him to follow the bent which his own mind took very early towards the work of the ministry. He was just twenty-one when he presented himself before the Presbytery, and asked to be licensed to preach the gospel of the blessed God. Immediately after receiving license he was settled at Cavendish, in Prince Edward's Island; and having contracted marriage with Miss McDonald of —————, he spent eight busy, useful, happy years there.

But he was ever turning from that pleasant labour-field to the thick darkness that covered the earth—out of which there seemed to come a voice, which he could not mistake, calling him to enter that darkness and work there. The Church of Scotland was now—under Alexander Duff's loud trumpet blasts—awakening to its long-forgotten evangelistic duty; while the people of England were listening with startled and delighted interest to John Williams's reports of what he had seen and heard in the South Seas. And so it came into the heart of this young minister—not indeed to offer himself for service in India or in Tahiti, but (which was unspeakably better) to seek to rouse his adopted church to engage in mission work. She might be the least among the thousands in Israel—yet not too little, surely, to serve Him who has told us that the little children are the great ones of the kingdom of heaven.—Then why should not the Church of Nova Scotia send her contingent, however small, into the field? He succeeded in his task, and when the question was raised, "Whom shall we send?" and "Who will go for us?" He replied, "If you count me worthy, send me."

Then he learned for the first time, from his widowed mother, of his early dedication to God's service—a discovery which greatly fortified his purpose; which was strengthened on the other side by the hearty concurrence in it of his beloved partner. To her, with four little children round her knees, the work could have slight attraction of romance; but she would venture all for Christ.—*He* was worthy for whom they should do this.

While they were waiting for their commission in Halifax, two of these little children died. If they had been looking for a sign from Heaven, this dark sorrow might have staggered and stopped them. Perhaps they did find an interpretation of it afterwards—" You are going forth among the perils of the deep, and the perils of the heathen; entrust these little ones to ME."

The commission which they received was very vague. Under the guidance of God's good Spirit they were to seek a field of labour somewhere in the South Seas. They wisely betook themselves to the missionary brethren in Samoa, and craved advice as to their future movements.

Their arrival was hailed with joy. There was a field of labour waiting for them.

Ever since John Williams's death his coadjutors had been longing to embrace the New Hebrides within the scope of their labours. They had frequently revisited them; they had sought to win the confidence of the natives, and had succeeded in planting christian teachers on five of them. The work, however, had made little effective progress; indeed, at the date of Mr. Geddie's arrival at Samoa it seemed desperate. Only upon the island of Aneityum was there a gleam of hope. On the last occasion of the missionaries' visit to that island they found the teachers sadly disheartened, and anxious to be removed. They were received on board, and sailed round to Anelcauhat. While lying at anchor there, one of the missionaries, deeply sorrowing at the prospect of leaving this fair island under the powers of darkness, said to the teacher Simeono,

"What a pity it is to leave this fine place without a teacher, and let go our hold upon it. What would you think of staying and giving it another trial?" He said he would, if another teacher would stay with him. Another was quickly found. These two teachers were landed and left behind; and thus the door was kept open. And by that open door Mr. and Mrs. Geddie now entered upon their mission work.

## III.

### THE MISSION FIELD.

ANEITYUM with its three thousand souls would have seemed to Dr. Chalmers a well-defined and manageable parish; and the young missionary, if he had an eye for beauty, must have been captivated with its exceeding loveliness. I shall leave the description of its physical aspects to my son, and ask you to look at its inhabitants. The condition of a people may be gauged on the one side by looking at their HOMES; on the other by looking at their TEMPLES. In what kind of gods do they believe? In what family-order do they live? Their Worship and their Home-ways determine their character and social state.

I. The principal Deity of Aneityum was Nugerain. He had a name above every name. Like God's great name "Jehovah," which the Jews refuse to utter, no one dare use his name unless he belonged to the highest caste. To this god they ascribed the origin of their island. He went out fishing one day, and having hooked some very ponderous thing, he hauled it up. It turned out to be Aneityum. Of their own origin they knew nothing. They had a vague tradition of the Fall, however. On account of some act of wickedness, they said that their ancestors were doomed to die; otherwise they would have lived for ever.

Nugerain was supposed to have a numerous progeny. These were called Natmases. They filled the earth, the air, and the sea—each race ruling over its own realm. The sun and moon were also deified, and worshipped with many honours. Human sacrifices were sometimes offered to their deities, but not frequently. When animals were offered, the priest first partook of the flesh, and then the people were allowed to feast upon it. The people stood greatly in awe of their imaginary gods, and never engaged in any undertaking without invoking their assistance or propitiating their favour. Among all the multitude of them there was not one of them whom they believed to be a purely good being. They were quick-sighted, capricious, and vindictive beings, exercising a reign of terror over men in the flesh. Almost more dreaded than their gods, were the disease-makers—men who arrogated to themselves the power of inflicting diseases, and levied large contributions from the friends of sick people. When a man fell sick, a conch shell was blown, which was meant as an appeal to the disease-maker to cease the burning which was supposed to cause the disease; and this was followed by presents more or less costly, according to the violence of the attack. These men—with the rain-makers, thunder-makers, fly and mosquito-makers, &c.—were the true gods of Aneityum. For an Idol is nothing in the world; but these men were a very terrible Something in Aneityum.

They believed in a future state—a paradise, full of all sensual delights; and a place of punishment. To the latter they consigned all murderers and all *stingy* persons. In their code of morals stinginess was the crowning vice—generosity the cardinal virtue. This virtue was expected to display itself in large offerings of food at the public feasts. Poor people would starve themselves for weeks beforehand that they might fatten up the consecrated pig, and be credited with having presented the finest.

The oppressive influence of these superstitious beliefs, and the formidable barrier which they opposed to the entrance of God's Word, will appear in the progress of our story. We turn now to their Homes.

II. The family order is of God; and the foundation of it is the law of marriage, which He ordained "in the beginning," and which Christ re-enacted,—marriage between one man and one woman. Wherever the integrity of that ordinance is violated the home loses its glory, and becomes a scene of discord and a nursery of vice. Aneityum furnished in its heathen times a pregnant proof of this. Polygamy was practised without limit. A woman, instead of becoming a wife by marriage, became a servant. Indeed the Aneityumese had no word for wife—they called a married woman "Naheca," which means a slave. She was treated with less humanity than we treat our beasts of burden. She had no rights, no rest from toil, no sweet happiness of home. While her husband was fighting or feasting, she was doing the work of the house or the plantation. So darkly and heavily did life press upon her, that not unfrequently she flung herself from some beetling cliff into the sea. Even the death of her husband did not loose the woman from the law of her husband. When she was married, instead of the wedding ring being put upon her finger, the wedding cord was put round her neck—which she must always wear; for when her husband died—before his body was cold—she would be strangled with that cord, and sent swiftly after him to serve him in the other world and be his slave for ever. Alas! poor woman, who must work as well as weep—who, living or dying, must be your husband's Slave.

"This practice," says Mr. Murray, "had a strange hold upon the people. They clung to it with most determined pertinacity. The strangler was always the woman's own son, if he was old enough; in some cases it was done by a *daughter!* And it *must* be done, else the whole family would incur lasting disgrace."

While the wife was working, her husband was fighting. He had no other serious occupation, except feasting. When the fight was over he and his companions sat down to feast—too often on the dead bodies of their slaughtered enemies.

Infanticide and parricide were also practised. The mother might not forget her sucking child, but it was often wrested from her—especially if it was a girl—and cast out into the bush or on the sea-beach to die; and the old man, who should have been his children's glory, was buried alive by them.

Such were the religious beliefs and social practises of the Aneityumese before the Dayspring from on high visited them. Let the reader ask himself what kind of a life these poor people could have. Could it possibly be a happy life—a gentle life— a noble life? And yet there are persons among us who would have stopped Mr. Geddie as he went, Lamp-in-hand, into that thick darkness, and entreated him not to interfere with these children of Nature: not to interfere with their religion—it was *their* religion, and therefore good for them; not to interfere with their ways—they were *their* ways, and therefore the best for them.

## IV.

### THE WORK.

WE have looked at Mr. Geddie's parish—the "cure of souls" which he got from his Master's hands. What did he propose to do with them?—To civilize them?—to teach them?—But can these savages learn? He meant to solve a far more important question—Can these souls live? He believed that the Gospel is the power of God unto salvation; and, relying on that power, he stepped on shore and began his work at Anelcauhat.

The little frame-house which he brought from Samoa was soon put up, and alongside of it a House of God. They were lowly buildings; but the one was a Christian HOME, and the other a Christian TEMPLE—dwelling-places of God, in whose Name he thus took possession of the land. In a few weeks he was able to speak a few words to the natives in their own tongue; and having made a circuit of the island, he planted down a teacher in each of the four maritime districts.

The peace was soon broken, however. One day he observed that the chapel was almost deserted, and an angry scowl was resting on the faces of those present. He found on enquiry that he had committed three great crimes. In the first place he had pulled some cocoanuts from his own trees, which having been tabued for a feast, were sacred. Secondly, he had taken some coral from the reef and burned it for lime. The Natmas of the Sea had smelt it burning, and been made very angry. Thirdly,—He was erecting a fence round the chapel, which would cut off the path by which the Natmases were accustomed to pass from the mountain to the sea. The missionary pleaded ignorance—gave up his cocoanuts, promised to take no more coral, and agreed to leave a path open for the perambulations of the Natmases—a very wise mode of procedure, although it might have been construed into an admission of the reality of those beings.

Another storm gathered round him a few months afterwards. A severe hurricane swept round the harbour, devastating the gardens and levelling the fruit trees. Thua—a neighbouring chief, a thunder-maker—was supposed to have caused the disaster. War was proclaimed against him, and the hostile tribes met to fight. Mr. Geddie resolved, if possible, to prevent bloodshed. It was a bold undertaking, but by God's blessing he succeeded; and thus, for the first time, Peace was made on Aneityum—made, shall I not say, by the blood of the cross.

Towards the close of that year (1849) Mr. Geddie was cheered by some faint rays of light shining through the darkness. About forty persons attended the Sabbath service; families were beginning to worship God; a class of enquirers came weekly for instruction; and three of the natives had volunteered to assist him in his journeys.

He had, however, during the whole of that year, a hand-to-hand fight with the cruel customs of the people—in which he was often beaten—but not always. For example: Having heard that a married man was dying, he hastened to his house. He found a number of the wife's relatives there, waiting to perform the horrid deed as soon as her husband breathed his last. After expostulating with them he returned home, leaving two or three friendly natives on watch. When the man died the stranglers were going to begin their bloody work. Waihit—one of the watchers—calling upon his companions to be courageous, said to the heathen, "If you kill that woman we will kill you." The men were overawed, and desisted; but the woman threatened that if they didn't kill her she would run to the bush and kill herself. Waihit stationed himself at the door, and began to talk kindly to her. It was a talk against time; for the thought of the people is that if the wife does not get into the other world nearly as soon as her husband she will never be able to overtake him; and so half-an-hour's talking put this woman beyond danger.

Another bloodless battle was fought in 1850. The Natmases were becoming very wrathful at the slights and neglects which the christianly-disposed natives were putting upon them; and so, one Sabbath evening, a messenger arrived to inform Mr. Geddie that the mission station was to be attacked next day. He immediately went to Nohoat, the hostile chief, to ascertain the cause. He was told to give himself no concern—he would be saved, but some of his people must die. Mr. Geddie told him that all the Christian party were ONE, and that if he lifted a weapon against any of them he would remove to another island. Nohoat, on whose territory Mr. Geddie resided, felt that this would be a great loss to him, and agreed, after much talk, to change the combat from a war of blows to a war of words. "Then leave your weapons behind." "Our spears we will leave, but not our clubs." The chief gave him his hand, however, that he would not fight. On returning to his own people Mr. Geddie was delighted to find that they had resolved not to fight—rather to die. Next day the battle came off: during two hours Nohoat beat the air with a vehement harangue, bewailing the decay of the ancient religion, and accusing the white man's God of invading their hereditary rights. The other side kept silence, or uttered only a few soft words. And so when Nohoat had exhausted his power of speech, the war of words came to a sudden end. And thus the reign of Peace was consolidated.

In 1851 the missionary gained another triumph. A christian

woman fell from a cocoanut tree and was killed. Her husband wished her to have christian burial, and not to be cast into the sea; but the relatives came in force, demanding her body. The christian people were inclined to resist them; but Mr. Geddie, having first cased the body in a shroud, placed it before them, and, in a kindly way, told them that it mattered nothing to the poor woman where she was buried, and that, although he hated the practice of throwing their dead into the sea, if they insisted on having it they might take it. The heathen party were divided. Their division grew into a quarrel. "Let him bury it," some cried out. "Is that your decision?" he asked. There was no answer. And so the body was borne to the grave, and in the presence of her heathen relatives prayer was offered. And thus the first christian burial took place on Aneityum.

On the 24th April of this year Mr. Geddie wrote: "Our prospects are beginning to brighten a little. We have been sowing in tears, but, we have some reason to hope, not in vain. Some of the natives are apparently in a thoughtful state, and I have had some applications for baptism—a man notorious for his opposition to Christianity having placed himself under instruction. He says he is tired of the old system, and wishes to learn the truth. He is one of the greatest sacred men in the district, and has lived by the superstitions of the people." "Among the number of enquirers," he wrote again, "is Kopaio, a brother of Nohoat—a thorough savage, notorious for his wickedness. He is a violent hater of all white men. He has lately commenced attending our services. When we first came to the island he regarded us as liars (he says) and used to steal our property; but having narrowly watched our conduct, he was convinced of the truth of our religion and the falseness of his own."

After Kopaio became a Christian he divulged a story, which if it startled Mr. Geddie in its recital, filled him with a delightful sense of God's fatherly care. For a long time this savage had sought an opportunity of assassinating the missionary. It seems a wonder that he did not succeed, as he lived within half-a-mile of the mission station. It happened, however, that Mr. Geddie had become aware that his life was in danger, and seldom went beyond his own premises. Disappointed in his hope of meeting him, Kopaio came several evenings after dark to his garden, armed with his club, in the hope that Mr. Geddie would go outside the house. He was a very powerful man, and one well-directed blow would have done the work. Mr. Geddie did go out one night, and passed close by the bush under which Kopaio was concealed. Now the critical moment was come—the long-desired opportunity. Kopaio grasped the club, that he might spring upon his victim and fell him to the ground. But lo! his hands had forgot their cunning—they were powerless. A strange sensation came over him, and all thoughts of injuring the man of God were at an end. Was it conscience that arrested him? or did he hear that voice that has been heard so often through the ages, "Touch not mine anointed, and do my prophets no harm." However it was, the good missionary failed not to acknowledge that the Keeper of Israel had kept him in that dark hour of unconscious danger.

## V.

### THE WORK CONTINUED.

THE righteous is as bold as a lion. Certainly Mr. Geddie was, and I suppose that we should all be so if we really believed that God was taking such care of us as he was evidently taking of him. Mr. Geddie, I may inform my readers, was not a formidable man to look at; there was nothing lordly in his presence. And yet he faced the rude savages without fear, and managed them like children. One morning Nohoat's son told him that his little brother was dying, and that so soon as he died Nohoat was going to strangle his mother. Mr. Geddie sought him out, and taxed him with his wicked intention. But all in vain. He then cut the matter short by telling him that he was going to take the child and his mother to his own house, where Nohoat might come and see them if he liked. He took them. They were pursued by the chief, but got safely inside the mission house. Two days afterwards the child died. The poor father, catching up the lifeless body and pressing it to his bosom, rolled on the earth in unutterable grief. Then he turned to Mr. Geddie and asked, "What has become of my boy?—where has he gone?" He—greatly touched with the father's sorrow—told him that the little one was in the arms of the Good Shepherd. When Mr. Geddie asked what was to be done with the body, "Let it be buried," he said. And the mother—there was no more talk of strangling her. This incident reveals the height to which the Power of the Gospel was rising, and how skilfully the missionary was using it in pulling down the strongholds of Satan.

Nohoat had a brother-in-law—Topoe—next in dignity to himself. In 1850 he gave a great feast, and the following year the chiefs who had been his guests resolved to return the compliment. It occurred to them at the same time that they might take this opportunity of annihilating the mission. Small and insignificant as it was, they could not conceal from themselves the fact that it was daily growing in vigour. If it should overspread the land, what would become of their poor Natmases? and as they were all chief men, and makers of diseases, &c., what would become of their revenues? So they determined, under cover of this feast, to destroy or drive away the missionary. This plot came to Mr. Geddie's ears. He found the danger to be a very real one. Round the festive board there would assemble some of the chiefs who had defied his influence, and who were thirsting for the blood of his little flock. But the Lord brought the counsel of the heathen to nought. Topoe, it seems, had intimated his intention of joining the christian band as soon as this feast was over. He thought he could not, as a christian, keep a heathen feast. But God helped him to take a nobler course. He and his followers abandoned heathenism, and openly joined the christian interest before the feast. It would have been contrary to savage etiquette, I suppose, for the givers of the feast to assassinate their guests. At all events, they didn't do it. And so this storm passed away, leaving a clearer sky, and a wider horizon round the rejoicing inmates of the mission house. A month after, Mr. Geddie wrote, "We have had many accessions of late." "Nohoat professes a great desire for religious instruction. At his own request I send a native every evening to conduct family-worship." This was the chief who was going to strangle his dying child's mother. The house of the murderer is becoming a christian home.

The heathen were discomfited by Topoe's apostacy—but not conciliated. They showed their enmity against every christian native who fell into their hands—spearing, clubbing, and sometimes killing them; and in November they resolved to bring the matter to a crisis. On Monday, the 24th day of that month, a number of the Christian natives started on an evangelistic tour. Mr. Geddie providentially remained, intending to follow them next day. A little after midnight, Mrs. Geddie was roused by the sound and smell of fire; and on looking up, saw that the roof was in a blaze. She escaped with her two children, and gave the alarm. With much labour the fire was got under, before any very extensive damage was done. Mr. Geddie immediately sent for Nohoat, who burst into tears when he looked on the smouldering roof. He immediately set himself to ascertain the guilty parties. He found that the plot had been fully organised; and afraid that the attempt might be repeated, a guard was set on the premises. Nohoat himself slept in Mr. Geddie's house every night for two months, that he might share the danger with him. And thus the Lord made this last device of the heathen folk of none effect. It rallied the native christians round them in bonds of strong affection. "If," said Nohoat to Mr. Geddie, "Lucy and Elizabeth had been burnt, and *my coat* (a military one which he kept at the mission) we would not have listened to words of peace; there would have been many persons killed to-day." The children thus mercifully preserved have consecrated their lives to the mission work, and are labouring on the Islands with their husbands—Mr. Nelson of Tana and Mr. McDonald of Efate.

At the end of this year Mr. Geddie could record many unequivocal proofs of progress. The sacred groves were disappearing. The fear of the false gods and their crafty priests was dying away. And next year opened with the removal from the island of the most violent opponent of the mission—a white man, who delighted in wickedness. From that hour the Word of God had free and rapid course. Some of the diseasemakers came to the mission house and delivered up their apparatus. These were contained in bags, the contents of which were curious. A little black earth—chewings of a sacred leaf—human hair—a shred of calico, &c. When a disease-maker wished to make a person sick, he procured something that belonged to him, and put it with these chewings into a charming-pot, which he placed on the fire, and prayed to his Natmas to inflict the disease. And then came the extortionate demand for release. One can understand with what delight these poor people would turn from these cruel makers of disease, to the Great Healer of it, and contrast the mighty compassion of Jesus with their oppressive greed.

Thus encouraged, Mr. Geddie began to direct his lines of operation more upon the inland tribes. He found them wonderfully prepared to listen to the gospel; and in a very short time he had the pleasure of driving their Natmases into the region of non-existence. But he was overtaxing his strength. For the first time he was assailed by an enemy that often returned—a slow fever, like the well-known jungle fever of India, the violence of which was encouraged by the want of suitable food. Let those who talk of the luxurious lives of missionaries read the next sentence. "The most of my nourishment during my sickness was a bit of toasted musty bread and a few pieces of hard biscuit, which a poor shipwrecked sailor was kind enough to send me out of his weekly allowance. May God repay him."

A few weeks after this illness he had the inexpressible pleasure of welcoming the *John Williams*, with the Rev. J. P. Sunderland—who tells us, in his account of his visit, with what joyful surprise he witnessed the change that had taken place during these three years. There was now at Anelcauhat a congregation of one hundred persons; a daily school of eighty; a christian class of sixty ; and forty who had learned to read. On the occasion of his visit a christian church was formed, and thirteen persons partook of the Lord's Supper. It was the first celebration of that ordinance in Western Polynesia, and was a season of thrilling interest. " Let the friends of missions," he says, " take courage, and let the God of missions be magnified who has given this pledge of ultimate and complete success."

1852 was signalised by another token of God's gracious purpose to bless these islands. On the 1st July the much-esteemed Bishop Selwyn arrived in his schooner the *Border Maid*, bringing with him the Rev. John Inglis and Mrs. Inglis, of the Reformed Presbyterian Church of Scotland, who were now to join Mr. Geddie in his work. They came unexpectedly, and if they had come down from Heaven they could not have got a warmer welcome. On the 4th of July, under a brilliant sky, in the presence of a crowded congregation, Mr. Inglis was introduced to his charge at Aname, on the opposite side of the island.

And now the transition from darkness to light proceeded with an astonishing rapidity; and incidents were continually occurring which proved the reality of the change. Here is one : " 19th September, chapel crowded to excess. Mr. Inglis came round from his station, bringing with him an influential chief named Iata, formerly a great warrior and notorious cannibal. In the house of God he met another chief—Nimtiwan. They were deadly foes. The last time they met was on the field of battle. I wondered how they would act now. And Oh ! how delighted I was to see these two men come out of the house of God with their arms round each other. I could not help calling the attention of Mr. Inglis to the scene, and saying. 'See what the Gospel has wrought.'"

The next year we learn that the congregation had risen to 350; that there were seventy-five native assistants, who were carrying the truth over the whole face of the island ; and twenty-five schools, with 1400 persons under instruction, *being the half of the whole population*. For their use Mr. Geddie had prepared, with infinite labour, a version of the Gospel of Mark, which was printed in Sydney, and 3000 copies brought to Aneityum in the *John Williams*.

And now the little church, having attained stability and strength, put forth its first missionary effort. Two teachers—Waihit and Josefa—were sent forth to the neighbouring island of Fotuna, and shortly afterwards two more to Tana.

In 1854 a church was opened at Aname, and the Lord's Supper was observed with nine native christians. The multitude of hearers who assembled was nearly a thousand. Such a gathering had never been seen in the island since the world was; for the people lived in such hatred and fear of each other that they seldom crossed the narrow boundaries of their own tribes. The church at Anelcauhat was also rebuilt this year, and made capable of containing 900 persons. Mr. Hardie, of the London Missionary Society—who visited Aneityum in October of that year — tells us that 2000 of the natives had openly renounced heathenism and embraced christianity; thirty schools were in operation, and everything indicated the most cheering progress. "The christian party," he writes, "has gained a very decided ascendancy all over the island; the ancient customs are everywhere on the wane. War, cannibalism and heathen orgies may be now reckoned among the things that were. The Natmases are everywhere being cast away or neglected, and for eighteen months no case of strangling has occurred."

## VI.

### THE FRUIT.

MANY persons wonder exceedingly how the missionary who has enjoyed the high pleasures of refined christian society can go down among the low-living people of heathen lands, and bring up his children among them with any cheerfulness and comfort of life. They can understand a man conducting an expedition, and heading an assault upon the strong places of heathenism; for there is an infinite pleasure in overthrowing the works of darkness. But should there not be a still greater pleasure in building up the works of righteousness, and goodness, and truth? True, it is much slower work; and when it is accomplished, what has been gained? Mr. Geddie didn't add to the low stature of the Aneityumese—nor organise them into a political body—nor make fine creatures of their women. I suppose that he would have told us that these were not the things he tried to do. But he tried to put down the murderous propensities and practices of the people—to make them truthful, honest, chaste—with a reverent fear of God about them, and loving obedience to Christ. He would have told us, moreover, that it was the delightful consciousness that God's Spirit was breathing on the dry bones of Aneityum and making them live, that sustained him and his wife in their long years' toil; and the delightful proofs that were meeting him every day, of the quiet happiness which the kingdom of Heaven was diffusing over the homes of the people. Every one, who has helped any poor sunken fellow-creature out of the misery and mire of sin into the pureness and calmness of the christian faith and the christian life, will readily understand this. He will understand what a joy it must have been to the missionary when (for example) he liberated the whole people of a district from the fear of their chief, Yakanua. He was a sacred man, a great disease-maker, and a voracious cannibal. The first teachers who were settled in that district found very few children there.—The explanation was that Yakanua had killed them and eaten them. The old people, too, lived in great fear for their lives. He used to lie in wait for his victims, and spring upon them and murder them. His sacred character shielded him from all reprisals—so that he went about among them like a ravening beast of prey. Towards the close of 1854 he was carried with the stream into the profession of christianity—with what good to himself I do not know; but with very decided good to the people of the district, who declared that *now they would be able to sleep in peace.* To tame that child-devouring savage, and let fathers and mothers sleep in peace, was surely a blessed work; and then to set before them that good Saviour, who would give them the everlasting rest, and would suffer them to bring their children to Him that He might lay His hands on them and bless them.

Let us take, as further samples of the redeeming power of the Gospel, the two chiefs of Anelcauhat—Waihit and Nohoat. The first was the ruler of the sea, the other of the land. Waihit was as much dreaded as Yakanua. His club was always in his hand, and many a poor woman's bones were broken by it. He was one of the first earnest listeners to the gospel, and by-and-bye took his stand beside the missionary as a christian. The change in his conduct gave very gratifying proof of the change in his character. He began to tell his countrymen that he was ashamed of his old evil ways, and wished them to serve the living and true God. He became the object of deadly hatred. Many a spear was hurled at him.

But he met all oppositions with a brave heart, and took meekly wrongs which he would have visited with death when he was a heathen. One Sabbath he went to Ametch, to speak to the people about God. There had been a severe storm, the blame of which they put upon him, and drove him away with their clubs. Next Sunday, however, he insisted on returning—when the people admiring his boldness, received him kindly. On another occasion, while going to Ametch, a man who had concealed himself near the path came upon him—armed with a club —and, in great anger, threatened to kill him. Ten days before, the tide had overflowed this man's garden, and destroyed his taro. He believed that Waihit had sent that destructive tide. He told him that he was no ruler of the sea now—God was. But the man would not listen to him. "Well," said the chief, "I will not run away from you. You can kill me if you will— I am not afraid to die." By this time some of the people came up, on their way to the service, and interfered. This exhibition of gentleness on the part of this once-fierce chief, I need scarcely say, gave him mighty power as a preacher of the gospel, and fitted him for going forth, in 1853, to Fotuna, the first-fruits of Aneityum unto Christ in the field of evangelistic work.

Nohoat—the ruler of the land—was perhaps less savage, but was more crafty, than Waihit. He welcomed the first missionaries' visits because he expected temporal good from them; especially his heart was set upon getting some pigs from them with long ears; and whenever he met them he put his hands to his ears to remind them of his wish. When Mr. Geddie landed he professedly gave him a welcome; but he told his people they might get rid of him by stealing from him. Finding, however, that the residence of the missionary increased his importance, he afterwards extended to him (as we have seen) a very effectual protection. The turning point in his history seems to have been the death of his child, when Mr. Geddie saved him from murdering its mother. From the missionary's own pen we have the following sketch of him :—

"He took the side of christianity at the time that the mission was in its greatest trials. His previous hostility had been so marked, that his sincerity was for some time doubted; but he soon gave satisfactory evidence of it, by giving up many heathenish customs. All his influence was now exerted in favour of christianity. I shall never forget his kindness to myself and my family when our lives were threatened. For more than two months he slept in my house, for our safety, and said that the heathen must kill him before doing any injury to us. Indeed, had not this man been raised up to befriend the mission, it is questionable if it could have risen above the opposition aimed against it. After Nohoat embraced christianity he became a humble disciple at the feet of Jesus. Though sixty years of age, he attended school regularly every morning, and his seat in church was never vacant. It was not to be expected that a man who had been under the influence of a degrading heathenism till far advanced in life, would become an intelligent and in all respects a consistent christian. He was naturally proud, passionate, and deceitful; but, with all his infirmities, I believe that he was a good man. No man did more for christianity on this island than Nohoat, and yet none suffered so much from the change. The class of chiefs to which he belonged were regarded with religious veneration while they lived, and were worshipped when they died. But when christianity divested him of his sacred character he was no longer dreaded; and having been an unpopular man in the days of his heathenism, he lost much of his influence, which he never recovered. When the mission to Tana was undertaken he rendered valuable aid, as he could speak the Tanese language. On one of his visits to that island, he had undertaken to conciliate a tribe that were approaching for a fight. It was a dangerous embassy; for the enemy, knowing his powers as a peacemaker—'if he gets among us we shall have no fight,' they said—fired two or three shots at him before he reached them. He pressed on, however, and succeeded in stopping the war. He was on a visit to Tana when he was seized with his last illness, which carried him off in about three weeks after his return. The last interview I had with him was two days before his death. Mrs. Geddie had several very interesting conversations with him. He confessed the wickedness of his life, but expressed a humble hope of salvation, through Jesus Christ. I have lost in him a sincere and valuable friend."

Alongside this sketch let me place another—of a native girl, Mary Anne. She was a little princess in rank—a pleasant child, but very thoughtless. Her parents, afraid of her falling into the hands of white men, brought her to Mrs. Geddie, entreating her to take her into her boarding establishment, which she did. But she was a restless bird, flying away, and after a few days returning. "One evening," Mrs. Geddie wrote, " I called her and her companion into my bedroom, and had a long conversation with them. I told them I was sadly grieved to see them so thoughtless; that I had left my home that I might teach them the word of God ; and that I had just parted with my own child, who was very dear to me (she had gone to school at Walthamstow) in order that I might remain among them. I said that I would never regret leaving my home and friends and parting with my child, if I were to have the happiness of seeing them seeking the Saviour ; and that now, as my daughter had left me, they should try as much as possible to fill her place to me. They both cried very much, and said they knew what I told them was true, and that they were very bad and dark-hearted. From this time I could see an evident change in them both. Dear Mary Anne became quite a changed girl, and, we have every reason to believe, a decided christian. She tried in every way to please me, and to be a daughter to me. We all loved her very much, and never, as far as I remember, had reason to reprove her." After she left the school she was married to one of the christian teachers in Mr. Inglis's district, but kept up a regular correspondence with Mrs. Geddie. "What would I have been," she used to say, "if you had not taken care of me? You are my mother—and although I love my parents, I love you and Mr. Geddie better." Shortly after her marriage she was seized with a mortal sickness, and was removed to her father's, close to the mission. "In as gentle a manner as possible I told her that the doctor thought her very ill, and was very doubtful whether she would recover. I was surprised to hear her say, with the greatest calmness, that she did not expect to recover, and that she felt very happy at the thought of going to her Saviour. Her parents, sisters, husband, were overwhelmed with grief—she alone remained composed. She talked a great deal to her parents and others, urging them to be zealous in Christ's service. She spoke very earnestly to her eldest sister, who often quarrelled with her own husband, telling her how happily she and her husband had lived together. Taking her husband's hand into hers, and looking affectionately at him, she said, 'William, I feel very sorry for you; great is my love for you, and I would like to live for your sake—but my desire to be with Jesus is greater.' A few days after this she passed away, in the peace and joy of believing. I have never met with a native who had the same ideas of modesty and propriety that Mary Anne professed. After she became decidedly pious, her views appeared quite above those of a young person brought up in heathenism."

Mary Anne's companion joined her in her faith and love of Christ. She became the wife of Lathella, the son and successor of the chief Nohoat. She died in 1861, leaving behind her the remembrance of a pure and loving life.

Let these slight sketches explain to my readers the substantial joy which rewards the missionary's self-sacrifice. He leaves home, and friends, and other pleasant things of this world : but he receives an hundredfold when he sees the dark prisoners of Satan coming out of the bondage of corruption ; and the tide of deep warm love to the Lord of Life springing up in their hearts—a love which purifies them—which makes them tenderhearted, forbearing and forgiving, and clothes them with those graces of christian gentleness and humility which render them amiable and lovable. Let them explain also one of the chief secrets of the missionary's success. Mrs. Geddie, when she had lost her own daughter, said to Mary Anne, " You must take her place ; you must be a daughter to me, and love me and help me ; and I will be a mother to you, and will love and help you." This was not a piece of sentiment. It was a true outgoing of christian love to that dark child. And it was this tender love, growing up between Mr. and Mrs. Geddie and their children in the Lord, that bound them to their island home for twenty-two years, and sustained them through that long isolation. That love of their children and that joy of the Lord were their strength.

## VII.

### PROGRESS OF THE WORK.

I AM not going to follow Mr. Geddie through the various labours of his life between 1854 and 1872. For as the mission spread itself over other islands it embraced the labours of many workmen—concerning whom and their work we shall hope to have some connected and detailed information when Mr. Inglis or some other Father of the Mission has leisure to give it. I shall simply indicate the progress of the work, by continuing the Missionary Calendar (see § II.) down to the present date.

1852 : Mr. and Mrs. Inglis (Reformed Presbyterian Church of Scotland) settled at Aname in Aneityum, where by the help of God they have continued to this day.

1854 : A large majority of the Aneityumese having abandoned heathenism, Aneityum is to be regarded henceforth as a christian land.

1857 : Mr. and Mrs. Gordon (Church of Nova Scotia) settled on Dillon's Bay, Eramanga.

1858 : Mr. and Mrs. Paton and Mr. Copeland (both of Reformed Presbyterian Church of Scotland) and Mr. and Mrs. Matheson (of Church of Nova Scotia) settled on Tana.

1859 : Mr. and Mrs. Johnston (Church of Nova Scotia) settled on Tana. Mrs. Paton and child died.

1861 : Mr. Johnston died.

1862 : Tanese mission broken up. Mr. Paton visited Australia, and pleaded the cause of the mission and the mission ship. Mrs. Matheson died on Aneityum, and Mr. Matheson on Lifu. Mr. and Mrs. Gordon murdered at Eramanga. First

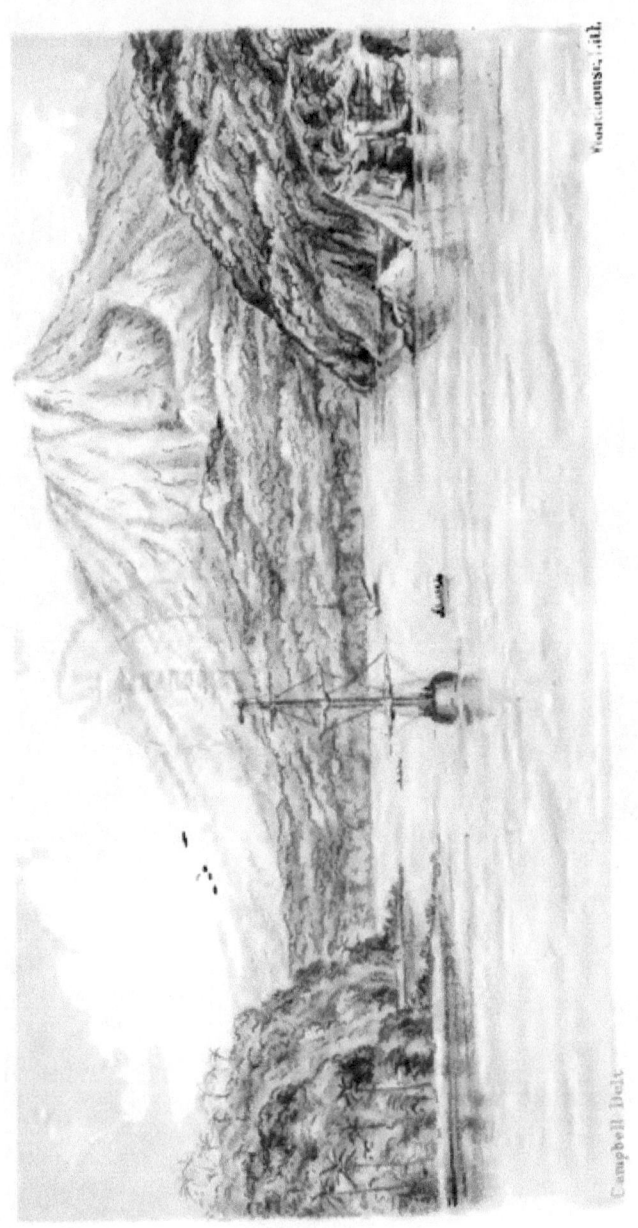

edition of the New Testament translated by Mr. Geddie, printed in London by the British and Foreign Bible Society, under the superintendence of Mr. Inglis.

1863: The *Dayspring* mission ship arrived in Melbourne, bringing Mr. and Mrs. Morison, Mr. and Mrs. McCullagh, and Mr. James Gordon (from the Church of Nova Scotia); the first of whom was settled on Efate, and the last at Portinia Bay, Eramanga.

1864 and 1865: Mr. and Mrs. Geddie revisited Nova Scotia, and addressed the Presbyterian congregations of the Lower Provinces and of Canada.

1866: Mr. Geddie returned to the islands with Mr. and Mrs. Cosh, Mr. and Mrs. Neilson (both of Reformed Presbyterian Church of Scotland) and Mr. and Mrs. McNair (of Free Church of Scotland) Mr. Cosh was settled at Pango on Efate; Mr. McNair at Dillon's Bay, Eramanga; Mr. Copeland on Fotuna; and Mr. Paton on Aniwa. The Queen's university of Canada conferred the degree of D.D. on Mr. Geddie.

1868: The mission on Tana re-established, under the care of Mr. Neilson.

1869: Mr. Watt (Reformed Presbyterian Church of Scotland) joined Mr. Neilson on Tana. Mr. Morison died in New Zealand.

1870: In consequence of Mrs. Cosh's ill-health, Mr. Cosh resigned. Mr. and Mrs. Milne (Free Church of Scotland) settled on Nguna, and Mr. and Mrs. Goodwill (Presbyterian Church of Canada) on Santo. Mr. McNair died.

1872: Mr. James Gordon murdered at Eramanga. Mr. and Mrs. McKenzie (Church of Nova Scotia) settled at Pango on Efate; Mr. and Mrs. Murray, of the same Church, at Dr. Geddie's station, Anelcauhat; Mr. and Mrs. Robertson, (Presbyterian Church of Canada) at Dillon's Bay, Eramanga; and Mr. and Mrs. McDonald (Miss E. Geddie) at Havannah harbour on Efate. Mr. McDonald is the first missionary trained and commissioned by the Presbyterian Church of Victoria. Dr. Geddie died at Geelong, 14th December, aged fifty-six.

1873: January 6, *Dayspring* wrecked. Mr. Annand (Presbyterian Church of Nova Scotia) arrived at Melbourne *en route* for the islands.

---

During all these years Dr. Geddie, in conjunction with Mr. Inglis, was engaged in visiting the various islands of the group, seeking to get into friendly relations with the people, and to open new doors for teachers and missionaries. On him, too, fell the main work of translation. Besides the New Testament, the Psalter, and the books of the Old Testament, many tracts and books, suitable to his people, were not only translated but printed on Aneityum. With the view of carrying on the printing of the remaining portions of the Old Testament under his own eye in Melbourne, he removed his family to Geelong in the close of 1869. For reasons of health the removal was exceedingly desirable. It was hoped, both for him and his wife, that the change to a more bracing climate might restore some of their wasted vigour. But the rest he so much needed was denied; for each of the three following years he found himself under the necessity of returning to the islands to assist in the growing work of the mission. Perhaps he overrated this necessity. It was one of the heart—the necessity of a master builder who must see the work he has begun carried on to his mind—of a father who longs to see the children whom he has begotten in the Lord, and to minister to them some spiritual gift. So he went—went for the last time, in the voyage of the *Dayspring*, 1872. But the messenger of Death went with him; and while he was attending the annual conference of the mission, in the month of June, he received a paralytic stroke, admonishing him that he must come home to die. Mr. Neilson, his son-in-law, accompanied him to Geelong, where for a little while he seemed to gather strength, and hopes were entertained of his being spared to bless his family with his gentle presence, and the mission with the ripened fruits of his experience. But it pleased God to take him to himself. A second stroke—falling on a vital part—utterly disabled him. His consciousness remained, but his power of speech was gone. And so he lay—like a weary pilgrim at the gates of Heaven—enjoying the peace of God's beloved; answering the question of his trust in God by a smile—calm and beautiful. In the early hour of a bright summer morning, in December, he fell asleep.

"Blessed are the dead that die in the Lord. They rest from their labours, and their works do follow them."

The announcement of Dr. Geddie's death was received with much sorrow in the circle of his friends in Victoria. His warm-hearted children in Aneityum wept very bitter tears when they heard that their good father was dead; and the records of the churches of Nova Scotia testify to the reverence and love in which they held their first missionary. They are making generous provision for his widow and family; and the people of the Presbyterian Church of Victoria, to whose keeping God has consigned his mortal remains, are preparing to erect a monument in the cemetery at Geelong—a monument which will command observation, and will declare to their children the honour in which they held the unassuming piety and self-denying zeal of the Founder of the New Hebrides Mission.

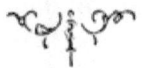

## VIII.

### PROSPECTS OF THE MISSION.

THE New Hebrides mission is singular in this respect—that it is not the mission of any society, or of any one church. Like Wisdom's seven-pillared house, it is sustained by seven separate churches: Nova Scotia has three men in the field; Canada, one; Scotland, three; Victoria, two; New Zealand (north) one; Otago, one. New South Wales had one, and is prepared, I presume, to have another. Then the churches of South and Eastern Australia and Tasmania, although not supporting missionaries, have contributed to the funds of the mission. The bond of union among these churches, beside their common faith, is that they are Presbyterians. They represent the four quarters of the Church of Scotland—the Established, the United, the Free, and the Reformed. But I can assure my readers that there is no intention on the part of the missionaries to *quarter* the Church of the New Hebrides. I don't know upon what model exactly they will form it—perhaps that of the Culdees, which was an island church. They have taken the first step toward the formation of a body ecclesiastical. They have asked leave to be allowed to constitute themselves into a Court, with synodical authority—a request which, I am sure, the parent churches will see it to be their duty to concede. The brethren on the spot are the only competent judges of what the necessities of their work require. They know, too, where their wisdom and strength lie. They may be well trusted to do what is right.

The establishment of church authority would deliver the mission from an element of weakness to which it is exposed while there is no government, or seven governments divided from each other by the whole diameter of the earth; and instead of endangering, I believe that it would preserve the harmony which, in an eminent degree, has characterised the past history of the mission. And that desideratum of self-government being supplied, there is an obvious advantage in the mixed nature of the missionary staff. Coming from so many different churches, they draw after them a vast amount of prayerful interest and affection. It would be a serious loss if any of the seven pillars were to be withdrawn.

There seems no reason, however, to fear that they will grow weary in this work of well-doing, or that the supply of men will be inadequate. It will be seen from the previous notice of the progress of this work that half of the present staff have been settled within the last three years. This indicates a growing strength, and zeal in the missionary spirit.

And it may be encouraging to our friends elsewhere to know that although we in Victoria have as yet contributed only one Recruit, there are two or three other young men with us who have expressed their wish to be employed in that service. Our proximity to the islands, the visits of the *Dayspring* with the missionaries, Mr. Paton's tour, and Dr. Geddie's residence among us, have attracted our young men to the work. Then the evangelistic duty of the church has been made a prominent part of the student's training in our Theological Hall, and the principle laid down, that ministers are not to choose their own work, but, like good soldiers of Jesus Christ, are to go where He leads them. The other Australian churches will gradually come into the position of being able to send their quota of men; so that there is good ground for believing that, as new doors open, men and means will be adequately provided.

I have spoken of the singular construction of this mission.

Its history is equally singular. During the first five years, as much work was done as has been done, *apparently*, during the succeeding twenty. There was a brilliant dawn, and a splendid flush of success at the commencement; but the day that followed has been dark and cloudy. The mission has been tossed on stormy waters, and been exposed to disaster, and death, and massacre. And these calamities have been compensated by no signal victories—at least to the eye of man. If we cannot explain this mystery, we can still say, with our Lord, "Even so, Father; for so it hath seemed good in thy sight." At the same time, there have been causes at work—such as the sweeping visitations of disease, the malign influence of traders and the cruel acts of the man-stealers—which have kept alive the power of superstition, and made the islanders dread the white man's presence. These causes are, we may hope, disappearing. We may hope that the time to favour these dark places of the earth is close at hand.

Then we must not forget that that long night of toil has not been altogether barren. Besides the church of Aniwa—the whole population of which island are receiving the kind christian care of our beloved friends, Mr. and Mrs. Paton—in Tana, Eramanga, Fotuna, and Efate, there are little bands of people whose hearts the Lord has opened to attend to the gospel message, and whose faith, in some cases, has endured sore trial and triumphed over very formidable obstacles.

And, finally, we ought surely to mark it as a matter of unqualified thankfulness to God, that Aneityum was so early and, to speak comparatively, so easily won. If Mr. Geddie had met with the repulses which have driven the missionaries from the other islands, it is difficult to see how the mission ever could have had a beginning. But Aneityum gave it a favourable start, and has ever since afforded shelter and safe retreat to the teachers and missionaries when they were hunted from their own stations; and it still forms the base of those operations which are gradually spreading through the group. Certainly, it was by the good hand of God upon him that Mr. Geddie was led to choose, out of the thousand islands of the South Seas, that little island of Aneityum, for his home and field of labour.

Of the missionary brethren on the islands, I have just this to say: Let no man think that they are throwing their lives away. The authors of the "South-Sea Bubbles"* deplore the abstraction of such men from the work of evangelising the masses at home. Let the Earl and the Doctor set themselves to that work. The Church's duty is to "go to all nations." They admit, however, that "if these races can be taught to appreciate the superior beauty of christianity for its own sake, a nobler purpose for a man to devote his life to can scarcely be conceived." No one who has read the brief sketches of Aneityumese christianity which I have given, can doubt that that result has been attained there; and our brethren need no other vindication of their self-sacrifice, than the assurance that God's word "shall not return to Him void, but shall accomplish the thing whereto He sent it"—whatever that thing may be.

But if we knew how difficult their work is—how depressingly it settles down upon them at times—and how languor, fever, and ague, invade and weaken them, and dry up the sources of joy and the powers of thought, we would feel that their devotion calls—not for our pity; they do not want that—but for our warmest sympathy, and constant affectionate remembrance in prayer. That many prayers are offered on their behalf, in the various churches which they represent, I have no doubt; but there ought to be something more definite. There ought to be

---

* A book of which the writers ought to be ashamed. Many of their "Bubbles" show that they have failed to appreciate the superior beauty of christian holiness.—They are very profane and very foul,—blown out of foulest waters. We don't expect heathen people to be pure; we don't expect even professedly Christian people, living at French ports and much-frequented harbours, to be pure; but we do expect English noblemen, and English doctors. and English books to be pure. When will men learn that it is only the pure in heart who can see God!

some arrangement and agreement, some concerted hour and day of prayer, which would unite all the people of these widely-scattered churches at the throne of grace. I venture to make the suggestion. If the next mission conference will put it in shape, and issue a proposal in terms of it, I am sure that it will meet with a general and cordial compliance.

And now, may God be merciful to us, and bless us, and cause His face to shine upon us; that His way may be known upon the earth, and His saving health among all nations.

Then shall the earth yield her increase, and God, even our own God, shall bless us; and all the ends of the earth shall fear Him.

And then shall the great Promise of the Desert receive its high fulfilment; and "THE WHOLE EARTH SHALL BE FILLED WITH THE GLORY OF THE LORD."

# THE VOYAGES

OF

# THE "DAYSPRING."

BY

D. MACDONALD, D.D.

Brigantine "Dayspring" in full sail

## HISTORY OF THE MISSION VESSEL,
### "DAYSPRING."

HOW often does God bring good out of evil! and how often does the wrath of man work out the righteousness of God! The interest which has been felt for several years by the Presbyterian Churches of Australasia in the New Hebrides mission, is directly traceable to the suffering and sorrow caused by the breaking-up of the Tana mission, early in the year 1862. On no island in the South Seas have greater efforts been made to establish the Gospel than on Tana; and on none with, till very lately, less seeming success. The Tanese are the fiercest people south of the line. Captain Cook could not land on their island in 1774, without the protection of a broadside. In 1839 John Williams escaped from the Tanese, to fall, alas! next day on Eramanga. In 1843 Messrs. Turner and Nesbit, of the London Missionary Society—now Drs. Turner and Nesbit, of Samoa—attempted to establish a mission on Tana; though, after a few months' trial, they had to flee with their lives: and in 1862 our own Mr. Paton had to abandon the field, broken in heart and health, after three years' labour. The other missionaries on the group, sympathising with Mr. Paton's afflictions, advised him to take a trip to Australia—partly for the benefit his health, and partly, also, to awaken an interest in the mission among the colonial churches.

The mission had hitherto been dependent, for its temporal support, on far-away poor churches in Scotland and Nova Scotia. Recently, however, a large population had congregated in the colonies of Australia ; strong churches were being formed there ; and wealth was fast accumulating. It was natural and right, in such circumstances, that Australian. christians should be appealed to for aid to a mission almost at their doors. And so Mr. Paton came.

The effect of his visit to the colonies was very extraordinary. Never, before or since, did our congregations enter so heartily into any one movement, as they did into Mr. Paton's.

Mr. Paton came to Australasia in the middle of 1862, and presented himself before the General Assembly of the Presbyterian Church of Victoria in November of that year. The impression which he produced marks an era in the history of our church. His visit was remarkably well timed. By that date we had got over the heavier portion of the secular work, resulting from the consummation of our union; and we were yearning for something better and higher to do. Then, Mr. Paton had a tale of sorrow to tell; and he told it well. The affecting story of the Tana mission—of the death of his wife, and of the death of his colleague, Mr. Johnston, with his own almost miraculous escape—filled many a heart at the time, and is not even yet forgotten. Then again, Mr. Paton did his work very systematically, and, we are bound to add, with immense bodily toil. He visited almost every Presbyterian congregation in New South Wales, Victoria, South Australia, and Tasmania; preaching and delivering addresses as he went, and carrying on his work, with great encouragement indeed, but with great labour. Then again, further, Mr. Paton set before us a definite project, which took wonderfully, especially with our children and Sabbath schools—that was, that the children of Australia should give to the New Hebrides mission a mission ship, to be owned and supported by the children themselves.

The mission already possessed a small schooner, the "John Knox," which had been built in Glasgow, and had been sent out to Sydney on the deck of a ship. But the "John Knox" was a very small thing, of only a few tons' capacity, and could only sail between the islands in summer weather. What was wanted now was a real ship, that could go anywhere—even to Sydney or Melbourne—and that should have a real captain and crew, like the "John Williams," and not like the "John Knox," which was sailed by a missionary and two or three blackfellows.

Mr. Paton's proposal took at once; and in a very few months upwards of £3000 were collected, and remitted to Nova Scotia, wherewith to build a suitable vessel. The success of the movement may be inferred from the fact, that within a year-and-a-half of the time when the scheme was broached in Australia, the "Dayspring" was launched in Nova Scotia.

The vessel was built under the auspices of Dr. Bayne, of Pictou, the then convener of the Nova Scotia Mission Committee; and we believe that to Dr. Bayne first occurred the happy name by which the vessel was thereafter known—"The Dayspring."

Soon after the keel was laid, the actual superintendence and care of the structure was given to Captain W. A. Fraser—our own Captain Fraser, who subsequently commanded the "Dayspring" for eight years, and whom we still remember with much affection and regret.

The "Dayspring" was built at a cost of £3432; in this, however, was included all the furnishings, and a double set of sails. A deck-house was afterwards found to be needed, and this was put up at Sydney, at a cost of £344 5s. 11d.; so that the "Dayspring," as we afterwards knew her, cost altogether close on £4000.

The new mission vessel—a brigantine, that is, rigged as a brig, with square sails on her foremast; and as a schooner, with sails fore and aft on her mainmast—left Halifax in October

1863, having on board the Rev. Mr. and Mrs. Morison, the Rev. Mr. and Mrs. McCullagh, and the Rev. J. D. Gordon, missionaries; together with Captain and Mrs. Fraser and crew. We need scarcely add, that her departure from Nova Scotia awakened much good feeling, and that she was sent away with many a blessing and many a prayer. Early in January she was abreast of the Cape of Good Hope, and it was voted desirable to call at Capetown. The vessel remained two or three days there, and the Captain was afterwards always loud in praise of the kindness which the party experienced at the Cape.

In March, 1864, the "Dayspring" put in her first appearance in Port Phillip waters, and took our young people all captive. It was but as yesterday since Mr. Paton moved them to collect for a ship to take the gospel to the heathen, and here now was the reality—beautiful and buoyant as a seagull, and having actual missionaries on board. After being exhibited to the good people of Melbourne and Geelong, she passed on to Sydney, where she shipped stores for a long cruise, and whence, along with our own missionaries, she took the Rev. Mr. and Mrs. Ella, of the London Missionary Society, to their station on Uea, one of the Loyalty group.

The arrival of the "Dayspring" at Aneityum was like life from the dead to the fathers of the mission, and arrangements were at once made for entering on the proper work of the mission ship. Her first trip was to the Loyalties, the impression being then that the "Dayspring" might serve the purposes of both missions. The authorities of the London Missionary Society, however, did not take kindly to this suggestion, and the proposal was soon given up.

Captain Fraser got into some trouble at this time with the French commandant at Lifu. The French officials were then carrying things with a very high hand on New Caledonia and the neighbouring islands, against the natives and all Protestant missionaries: and the mission vessel was ordered away. It was on this occasion that Captain Fraser performed the feat which so astonished the French on Lifu, as related by the Rev. S. Macfarlane in his interesting book called the "Story of the Lifu Mission." The "Dayspring" had got into a narrow bay, where she could neither luff nor wear; and as there was a strong breeze blowing at the time, the French officers looked on with ill-concealed delight, expecting every moment to see the vessel on the rocks, and indulging in the hope of some loot. Captain Fraser, however, had just left a school of navigation where every device of escape had to be practised—namely, running the American blockade; and, to the astonishment and chagrin of the onlookers, he trimmed his sails so as to cause his vessel to move out stern foremost—one of the rarest and most difficult resources of the master of a sailing ship.

Making for the New Hebrides, Mr. and Mrs. Morison were settled on Efate, and Mr. Gordon on Eramanga, where his brother had been massacred a few years before.

Just at this time intelligence came to the New Hebrides to the effect that the first "John Williams" had been lost on Danger Island (17th May, 1864); one of the consequences of which must be, that the missionaries on the Loyalty islands should be left without stores, and, not improbably, without communications, for a whole year. On consultation, it was resolved to send the "Dayspring" again to the Loyalties—even though at the risk of offending the French, who were the terror of the missionaries in those days; the fear being that, after desolating the Loyalties, they might take the New Hebrides too.

In January, 1865, the vessel was again in Sydney; and, after an overhaul, she visited Hobart Town, Launceston, and Adelaide. Mr. Paton was on board during this intercolonial voyage, and his presence added much to the interest felt by the children of these towns in their own ship. In June she returned to Aneityum, and then made three voyages round the

New Hebrides group, and three to the Loyalties. The feeling of the French authorities had changed much from last year. Appeals had been made from London to the French Emperor, in the interest of the Protestant missions in the South Seas; and Captain Fraser was more cordially welcomed at Lifu this year than he was the year before.

It was while the Mission Conference was in session on Aneityum, in 1865, that H.M.S. Curaçoa visited the islands, and that her commander, Sir William Wiseman, shelled one or two villages in Tana and Eramanga, on account of murders of white men recently committed there. The Tanese were awed by Sir William's display of power, and to this day they are under the wholesome fear of another visit of a ship of war. But there was an outcry at the time against the New Hebrides missionaries, on account of their supposed approval of shooting the poor blacks; and there was a difference of opinion even within the mission itself on the subject. Some missionaries go the extreme length of holding that they should not employ force, even in self-defence; while others feel that they are British subjects, and think that, on occasions, they have a right to appeal to Cæsar.

The truth is, however, that the New Hebrides missionaries were in no way responsible for Sir William Wiseman's acts, right or wrong. At Sir William's requisition, Captain Fraser undertook to pilot the "Curaçoa" to Tana, and Mr. Paton undertook to interpret *for the natives*—just as they might have been called on in Melbourne to aid the authorities in any judicial inquiry, without being responsible for the results. It would be ridiculous to fancy that a British commodore, responsible to the Imperial government, should consult missionaries as to his duty or conduct in the dispensation of justice, on account of the murder of British subjects; though, for a time, an attempt was made to injure the mission by an outcry to the effect that the New Hebrides missionaries were seeking to spread the gospel by the aid of powder and shot!

It was during this year also that Captain Fraser was sent, for the first time, to Eastern Polynesia, to give such aid as he could to the missionaries of the London Missionary Society, while they were without a vessel of their own. The "Dayspring" spent three months on this Eastern trip, calling at Samoa, Raratonga, and the Ellice group. The inhabitants of the Ellice group speak the language of Samoa, and it is said that the visit of the "Dayspring," with teachers and books from Samoa, is still noted as a great era in their history.

In 1866, Captain Fraser made a voyage to the Loyalty islands and round the New Hebrides group; and besides, made three trips to Sydney and back to Aneityum. The first of these three trips was the usual one, for stores for the mission; but there was a special history connected with the other two. Dr. Geddie, who had gone with his family to Nova Scotia on furlough, was expected back to these colonies about the middle of the year. Other missionaries were expected with him. Mr. Paton was in Australia, making permanent arrangements for the support of the "Dayspring." Mr. Copeland was also similarly engaged, chiefly in New Zealand. And so the "Dayspring was sent up in June, to bring all these brethren and their families to the Islands. In August she returned to Aneityum with Messrs. Paton, Copeland, Cosh, and McNair, and their wives, Dr. and Mrs. Geddie, with Mr. and Mrs. Neilson following in the new "John Williams."

The second "John Williams" was a splendid vessel of her size; but she was ill-fated from the first. In coming to at Aneityum harbour, she grounded on a coral reef, and hung there for three days. She was so injured that it was judged necessary to send her back to Sydney for repairs; and it was at the same time resolved that the "Dayspring" should convoy her crippled consort, in case of any emergency by the way. The "Dayspring" attended the "John Williams" to the Australian coast, and yet she was back again on her own field within five weeks. The "John Williams" was lost soon thereafter on Savage island; the fine vessel herself and every article on board going down into the deep, though, happily, there was time to save the lives of the passengers and crew.

The "Dayspring" this year settled Mr. and Mrs. Copeland on Fotuna, Mr. and Mrs. Paton on Aniwa, Mr. and Mrs. Cosh on Efatè, and Mr. and Mrs. McNair on Eramanga; and besides, acted as a very considerable check on kidnapping traders, whose evil deeds began now to be felt on the New Hebrides group.

The question of the support of the "Dayspring" was by this time becoming an anxious question to all the friends of the New Hebrides mission. Experience proved that the cost of her maintenance would be considerably higher than was anticipated. Mr. Paton had made three visits to the colonies, and had raised large sums, especially in Victoria, through his appeals; but it was felt that spasmodic efforts could not be depended on. No fewer than ten churches were looked to, to provide for the support of the mission vessel, some of them being small, and more than one of whom had already failed to furnish their expected contributions. In these circumstances, it was resolved, at a conference between representatives of the mission (Dr. Geddie and Mr. Paton) and the Mission Committee of the General Assembly of the Presbyterian Church of Victoria, that Melbourne should become the head quarters of the "Dayspring" in the colonies, on the understanding that the Victorian church, being the largest and wealthiest church supporting the mission, should guarantee the maintenance of the vessel—that church receiving from the other churches a fair proportion of the whole cost. On this arrangement the "Dayspring" came to Melbourne in January, 1867; and, from that time till the end of her history, there was henceforth abundance of means found for her support; and her popularity in the leading colony of the Australian group was always unbounded.

Before leaving this year for the Islands, she was taken up to the Melbourne wharf, to give the public an opportunity of visiting the children's mission vessel.' She was boarded by multitudes of young and old. Captain Fraser made himself and his ship immense favourites with everybody; and the "Dayspring" was sent away, on her outward voyage, with any amount of presents, and with the good wishes and best blessings of thousands of the best people of Victoria.

The year 1867 was a dark year on the Islands. The whole group was swept by more than one epidemic. First, hooping cough, and then diphtheria, cut off numbers of old people and children. The heathen, always superstititious and suspicious, attributed the loss of their children to the missionaries; and it was feared, for a time, that a general massacre might ensue. The missionaries stood, wisely, to their posts; and in due time the feeling of hostility passed away. Even this year the "Dayspring" received a remarkable proof of her popularity from the natives of Aneityum. Towards the end of the year's work, it was found that the vessel's foremast was decaying; and as it was dangerous to venture so far as Melbourne, with a weak mast, the forest of Aneityum was searched for a suitable tree. One was found at a distance of about two miles from the sea, and was taken, by sheer force of native labour, to the harbour, and at length put on board the vessel. The valley in which the tree grew was among the mountains, and it was a great undertaking to drag it by main force to such a distance. Captain Fraser had got many a valued gift on behalf of the "Dayspring" during his career in command of the vessel; but the one which he boasted chiefly of was the new foremast, presented to him by the converts of Aneityum. The spar would have cost £50 in Melbourne.

During the year 1868, the "Dayspring" did a large amount of work among the Islands, but without any noticeable events. Mr. William Sim, a Christian gentleman belonging to Ballarat, and deeply interested in the mission, went with his wife to the New Hebrides in the vessel, and was able, on his return, to tell how missionary affairs looked to a business man, from a colonial point of view. His report was to the effect that he was profoundly impressed with the degradation of the heathen, with the self-denial and abundant labours of the missionaries, and with the power of the gospel over such of the natives as had come under its influence. We find, by the report for the year, that the "Dayspring" had been once at New Caledonia, twice at the Loyalty Islands, five times at Fotuna, seven times at Tana, nine times at Aniwa, nine times at Eramanga, five times at Efatè, and once at Santo, Ambrym, Tonga, Metas, Three Hills, Makura, and Nguna. Several of these islands are hundreds of miles distant from each other, the sea-area of the group being about 400 miles in length and 200 miles in breadth.

In 1869 it was judged desirable to send the "Dayspring" to New Zealand. That colony is so far distant from the continent of Australia, and so far out of the straight course from Australia to the New Hebrides islands, that it had not been found convenient before to call at any of the ports of New Zealand. There were many reasons, however, why that important colony should be brought within the influence of a visit from the mission vessel. New Zealand is, in fact, the nearest point of British territory to the mission field. Several sailing vessels from Auckland trade amongst the islands. Both the north and south ends of New Zealand—which, by the way, has a north and south both politically and ecclesiastically—and especially the south end, are Presbyterian provinces. And so the Presbyterian mission vessel was sent to New Zealand, to awaken an interest in the Presbyterian mission, the field of which is within a week's sail of Auckland, one of the chief towns of that colony. Advantage was also taken of this visit to secure an insurance fund for the "Dayspring," and thereby to relieve the maintenance fund of a large strain on its means. The revenue in Victoria had by this time so accumulated beyond the outlay, that it was proposed to set apart £1500 for an insurance fund, provided as much more could be got in addition. This project was submitted to the friends of the mission in New Zealand, and the matter was taken up most enthusiastically. Upwards of £1460 were raised for the fund; and this amount, with £250 from Nova Scotia, and the Victorian contribution, made a fund of over £3000, from the interest of which the "Dayspring" was thereafter stately insured in Melbourne offices for £2000.

The popularity of the "Dayspring" in New Zealand was beyond all precedent. The visit to Dunedin was so timed as to be there when the Synod of Otago was in session; and the Synod adjourned over a forenoon to go on board the "Dayspring." The mission vessel became the rage. A great public meeting was held in Dr. Burns's church, at which glowing orations were delivered on Presbyterianism, missions, the "Dayspring," and—the insurance fund! Steamers with large parties boarded the vessel, as she lay at anchor in the bay; children, in multitudes, thronged to see a real mission ship; and never was Heber's hymn, "From Greenland's icy mountains," sung with greater heart than it was on the deck of the "Dayspring," by the young Scotch colonists of Dun-Edin—the Edin-Burgh of the South.

An amusing incident occurred at Dunedin. At a great open-air gathering in Vauxhall gardens, the recreation ground of the city, a few Christian blacks who had come in the "Dayspring" were put up to sing one of their hymns in their own language, but set to the dear old Scotch tune of "Auld Lang Syne." The Dunedin people, not perhaps distinguishing the language in which the hymn was sung, took up the chorus in their own mother tongue, and gave the well-known refrain in broad Scotch, with a vigour that astonished the blacks, and did not by any means shock the visitors who were present. Scottish feeling is to be found everywhere, all the world over; but in Dunedin it overflows.

The "Dayspring" likewise visited Wellington and Auckland, the chief cities of northern New Zealand; and the impression produced in these towns also was most favourable.

As showing the work which any vessel like the "Dayspring" is capable of doing, it may be mentioned that this year the "Dayspring" visited New Zealand twice, Aneityum eleven times, Fotuna nine times, Tana twelve times, Eramanga nine times, Efatè seven times, and Santo twice; besides calling at the smaller islands of the New Hebrides group, and crossing over to the Loyalty group, to serve the brethren of the London Missionary Society stationed on Marè, Uea, and Lifu. A third "John Williams" had arrived in the South Seas by this time; but it was found that she had so much arrears of work to do among the Eastern groups, that once more the services of the "Dayspring" were put in requisition for the Loyalty mission. The vessel and her good captain, however, were found equal to all this work, as appears by a special commendation given by the missionaries to Captain Fraser, in their annual report for 1869, to the following effect :—" Captain Fraser continues to perform his varied ship duties in a praiseworthy manner, takes a deep interest in our mission, and is a universal favourite among the natives; and from his obliging, kindly, and gentlemanly bearing to all connected with the mission, he proves himself qualified for the responsible and noble work to which God has called him in the New Hebrides."

On her voyage up to the colonies next year (1870) the "Dayspring" called at Sydney, where she had some repairs executed;

and she then came on to Melbourne. It had been previously arranged that on this occasion she should go into Geelong harbour, with the view of adding to the interest felt in the mission by the residents of the western district of Victoria. In no portion of the colony did Mr. Paton get greater encouragement, when collecting money for the building of the mission ship, than in the Western District—pre-eminently the garden of Victoria; but that was eight years before, and, meanwhile, a new generation of children had sprung up, to whom Mr. Paton and the "Dayspring" were only a tradition. And besides, Ballarat, which in 1862 was not much more than an encampment of tents, was in 1870 a city with many churches and multitudes of Sabbath school children. And so the "Dayspring" was sent to Geelong harbour, or, as it is called, Corio Bay, the most western point of the great land-locked sheet of water called Port Phillip.

The following notice, taken from a Melbourne periodical, gives the impressions of an eye-witness as to the effect of the visit of the "Dayspring" on Geelong and Ballarat :—

Corio Bay, or Geelong harbour, is the inmost point of Port Phillip, and is surely intended by nature for the site of a seaport. The bay is quite land-locked, and any amount of shipping could ride at anchor inside of Point Henry. The time was when Geelong thought that its natural advantages would give it the start even of Melbourne, and make it the commercial metropolis of Victoria: but it requires more than natural advantages to make a great town; and Melbourne, though standing on an open bay which is little better than a roadstead, has outstripped not only Geelong, but even Sydney, and has really no rival on the south side of the line. Geelong, however, though not equal to Melbourne, is yet a considerable town; and with its safe harbour, and with railways to Colac and farther west, will be sure to advance. Geelong has a population of, say, 20,000 souls, and the town is already getting a character of its own. Without the bustle of Melbourne or Ballarat, it is becoming a domestic town, remarkable for the number of people who are settling there for the education of their families and for the enjoyment of society. Such a place is sure to be more open to religious influences than mere money-making towns, and Geelong is, in fact, better supplied with churches than any other town in Australia.

On the morning of Friday, the 4th of February, the Presbyterian mission vessel 'Dayspring' cast anchor in Geelong harbour. The 'Dayspring' is one of the institutions of the Presbyterian church, and her name is famous throughout all our congregations and Sabbath schools. The vessel is supported by other Presbyterian churches as well as ours; but Melbourne is her head-quarters, and she is well known, by sight or by report, to all our people. Her visits to the colonies have done very much in awakening a missionary spirit throughout our borders; and it is now felt that, as time will permit, she should visit all the seaports of Australasia. Last year she visited the chief towns of New Zealand, and this year it had been resolved to run her up to Geelong. This was known before her arrival, and arrangements had been made to have meetings and services appropriate to the occasion. The local ministers entered very heartily into the arrangements, and they, together with Dr. Geddie (who had come from the mission field with the 'Dayspring,') and the convener of the New Hebrides Mission Committee, were able in a few days to address all the Presbyterian congregations in the town and neighbourhood. These services culminated in an afternoon gathering of Sabbath-school children in the hall of the Mechanics' Institute on Sabbath, the 13th. The assemblage of children was really immense, and their bright appearance augured well for the future of the church and colony of Victoria. During the same week the 'Dayspring' was taken alongside the wharf, and for several days her decks and cabin were crowded with visitors. Altogether, the missionary impression produced on the town was very strong, and will, no doubt, also be lasting.

Services like those held in Geelong on the previous week, were conducted in Ballarat and the surrounding country on the week beginning Sabbath, the 20th. It is well known that Ballarat is the metropolis of the gold-fields of Victoria, and the town itself is indeed one of the wonders of the world. It is so new a place that rats have not found their way thither yet; but still it has its 50,000 inhabitants, with no end of stores, churches, hotels, public buildings, and gold mines. It will be readily understood how missionary financiers would have an eye to operations on such a place; though, as Ballarat is an inland town, fifty miles from Geelong, the fact that the 'Dayspring' could not be taken up to the diggings, and exhibited at 'The Corner," or on Lake Wendouree, was a sad damper to our expectations of telling on the mind and pocket of the Golden Town. In a happy hour, however, it occurred to the Rev. Mr. Inglis, of St. John's Church, Ballarat, that as the 'Dayspring' could not be taken to Ballarat, Ballarat, or at least young Ballarat, might be taken to the 'Dayspring' and to Geelong. The idea at once took, and an idea which takes at Ballarat is usually soon put into execution. Meetings of Sabbath-school teachers were held, letters were written, deputations were sent, telegrams were despatched, the Railway Department was applied to, and it was very soon arranged that excursion trains should be sent to Geelong to bring the children of Ballarat and its neighbourhood to see the 'Dayspring' and the sea. Some people may think that so young a town as Ballarat cannot have as many children as other towns, in proportion to the number of its inhabitants; but just the reverse is the case. The immigrants who came to Victoria in the great rush some sixteen and eighteen years ago, were chiefly newly-married people, and one can scarcely walk a street in a town now without treading on children. I can say at any rate for Ballarat that the Sabbath-school children's meeting, which we held in the Alfred Hall, was the largest gathering of children I ever addressed, and was, in fact, the largest religious meeting I ever saw in this country.

An excursion train from Ballarat to Geelong under such auspices and arrangements was sure to be popular. Many of these children had never seen the sea; the 'Dayspring' had often been described to them, and was an object of intense interest to them; the Sabbath teachers wanted a holiday; and so when the excursion day came it was found that the railway was required to convey 3000 people, old and young, to Geelong and back. It is understood that this is by a long way the largest multitude that ever left Ballarat at the same time by rail. They needed three separate trains, but the department was equal to the occasion; and in due time Geelong was astonished to see its streets invaded by an immense procession, chiefly of well-dressed youngsters, all marshalled in excellent order, and preceded by a couple of stalwart Highlanders, magnificently arrayed in tartan, and discoursing excellent music out of the bagpipes! The 'Dayspring,' of course, was the great attraction; but the children were also taken to the Botanic Gardens, where within sight of the shipping and the bay, they had several hours of sport and rare enjoyment. Nor were their juvenile appetites forgotten; a providore had been sent down from Ballarat the day before with lots of provisions, and the rapid consumption of buns was a sight to see.

By four o'clock in the afternoon the various schools began to assemble on the railway platform for their return to Ballarat, and by five o'clock four trains were despatched, taking back as happy a lot of children as ever were out for a holiday; and it is but due to the Victorian Railway Department, as well as to the Presbyterian Sabbath-school teachers of Ballarat, to add that all these children reached home without one having gone a-missing, without, so far as I know, one painful feeling—God be thanked!

After this rush of popularity, the mission vessel sailed for the islands, taking with her several missionaries and a great cargo of stores; she reached Aneityum on the 5th May. Two missionaries were settled this year on fresh islands—namely, Mr. Milne on Nguna, and Mr. Goodwill on Santo. Santo is the largest island of the group; and being also the northernmost, it is the farthest away from civilization and protection. The deepest interest has therefore been always felt in Mr. Goodwill's Christian venture, in trusting himself and his young wife among untried savages, hundreds of miles away from even a brother missionary. But he knew in whom he believed; and the shield of God's providence had hitherto protected him and his.

It is unnecessary to follow the "Dayspring" in her voyages round the islands this year, as there must be much sameness in her visits; though it is not therefore to be inferred that she was not doing important work.

In the annual report for 1870, it is stated that the mission vessel fell in with several kidnapping vessels from the colonies, which were found prowling among the islands for victims, and that at length the victims were turning round to retaliate; accounts are given of ships'-boats seized and sailors killed.

Towards the end of 1870, the "Dayspring" called once more at Auckland, to land Mr. and Mrs. Cosh, and then went eastward to the Hervey group, for native teachers for the New Hebrides. The brethren of the several Eastern missions have always encouraged the best of their christian natives to go to the islands beyond, for evangelising purposes; and, more than once, the "Dayspring" took several married couples as far west as the New Hebrides for christian work—but it may be added, that the experiment has not been much of a success. Several influences operated against it. The languages of Eastern and Western Polynesia are utterly unlike. Although, strange to say, the language of Eastern Polynesia, from New Zealand to the Sandwich islands, is virtually one; yet from Figi, westwards, there is a new language—not only in every group, but also in every island. Then, there is a difference of race: the long-haired, yellow-coloured, tall Malay race, typified in the Maori, and inhabiting Eastern Polynesia, is altogether different from the woolly-haired, black-skinned, thick-set, almost-negro race found in the groups nearer Australia and New Guinea; And yet again, the damp climate of the western islands tells fatally on the softer constitution of the eastern race. Few of the native teachers taken from the eastern groups have survived for any number of years, and it is therefore understood that the practice is to be discontinued. The missionaries on the New Hebrides group, though yearning for the assistance of the more advanced native christians of the eastern groups, feel that they must henceforth depend wholly on native teachers reared by themselves.

Such had been the success of the visit of the "Dayspring" to Geelong in 1870, that it was resolved to send her to the outer western ports of Victoria in 1871. To the west of Cape Otway there are no harbours, strictly so called; but there are three bays—Warrnambool, Belfast, and Portland, at each of which there are considerable townships, with a back-country well peopled: and it was thought advisable that during her stay in Australia in 1871, the mission vessel should visit the places named, and by her presence appeal to the children of these districts on behalf of the mission. It is a curious fact, that the further west you go in Victoria the more Presbyterian you find the population; the explanation being, probably, that Scotchmen know where good things are to be found—particularly good land : and on this occasion the interest shown in the Presbyterian ship was just what one might have expected in the circumstances. The visit of the vessel was so timed as to occur during the holiday season of farmers and squatters; and the whole population, young and old, turned out to see the "Dayspring:" some families coming fifty miles to enjoy the sight. A romp on the deck was an immense treat, and some brisk boys never rested till they got up to the masthead. The farmers were lavish in their gifts of potatoes and other produce of all kinds; and the very boatmen of Warrnambool were glad to ferry the children to the "Dayspring" for nothing.

The "Dayspring" left Portland Bay on the 22nd April, 1871, and reached Aneityum on the 17th May. The following summary of her work among the islands for this year is given in the admirable language of the Rev. Joseph Copeland :—

During the season she made several trips among the islands. In the first she landed stores and mails at all the mission stations, and took Mr. and Mrs. Goodwill from Aneityum, where they had been during the summer, to their station on Santo. On her way south she settled in the vicinity of Efatè some of the eastern teachers, brought to the group in the end of 1870. That done, beginning at Nguna, she took up the missionaries on her way south for the annual meeting, and landed them at Aniwa on the 1st July. In the second trip, beginning July 11th, she first of all returned the missionaries to their stations, calling at Tana, Fotuna, Aneityum, Loyalty islands (to send away a mail) and Nguna. After that she visited Havannah harbour, Efatè, and Eramanga, and returned to Aniwa August 20th. The following day her third trip began, in which she took a number of Aniwans to Fotuna, and a number of Fotunese over to Aniwa, for a friendly visit. Having taken them back to their respective islands, she went to Tana, to enable the missionaries there to visit some parts of that island. That done, she took a party of Tanese and some Aneityum teachers across to Aneityum. After a few days she took them home, and returned to Aneityum September 23rd. After lying in harbour for repairs, she started on her fourth and last trip,

October 25th; called at all the islands occupied by missionaries and teachers, and took to the several islands the annual supplies for the teachers. On her way south she took up the letters and orders of the missionaries, her passengers, and the arrowroot prepared by the natives to pay for the printing of the Scriptures. Taking her departure from Port Resolution, Tana, on the 14th of December, she arrived in Melbourne, January 4th.

We must again mention here what has been often stated in these reports, viz. :—that the 'Dayspring' is indispensable to the comfortable and successful prosecution of the mission work on the group. To some of the islands she is of far more service than to others. Some of the missionaries might get along after a sort by means of the occasional visits of trading vessels; but there is no island and no department of the work that would not suffer materially were she withdrawn. On some the work would have to be abandoned. The last cannot be regarded as her busiest year, as she did not during the sailing season either visit any of the Australasian colonies, or the Eastern islands, or New Caledonia. Her services were not required at the Loyalty islands, and she settled no new missionary, and visited no new island. Still the summary shows that she was not idle, always in harbour and always in ballast. From the colonies she brought down passengers and stores of every description for fourteen months' use for nine families, say between thirty and forty persons, with letters, papers, and books, supplies of clothing, barter, and food for the native teachers; and mission-boxes, books, and other requisites for the work among the natives. When she had landed her passengers and cargo her work was not done; passengers and cargo, European and native, were going to and fro every month. She brought the missionaries together for the annual meeting, and when their deliberations were over she was ready to take them on board, and return thence to their stations. She enabled the most of the members of the mission to have a little change from the monotony of island life to visit one another for a time, and some to take a trip for the benefit of their health. She carried the inter-island letters, and took a mail to the Loyalty islands, whence it could be forwarded to Sydney. She carried cattle, pigs, goats, and fowls to islands where these were wanted, as also yams and beans to islands where native food is scarce. She took house-building materials, workmen to assist the missionary in their erection, and servants for some of the mission families. For a short time she afforded shelter to a shipwrecked crew. She settled some native teachers, took home others after a period of service, and enabled others to take a holiday and visit their relations. She carried a great many natives from their own islands to some other, and returned them with the hope that the gospel would be regarded more favourably by them. And when she left, at the close of the year, she took away the letters and orders of the missionaries, the contributions of the natives for printing the Scriptures, and passengers leaving for health or to superintend the press.

What ships from other countries are; what steamers and coasters are; what railways, canals, and roads are; what cabs and coaches are; what drays and horses are; what post-offices, postmen, and telegraphs are in Australia, New Zealand, Great Britain, and Nova Scotia—all these the 'Dayspring' is to us, the missionaries and teachers in the New Hebrides. Were all these means of communication to be withdrawn suddenly, what would you do? Your respective countries would be brought to the verge of ruin in a day; such a state of things you could not tolerate; indignation meetings would be held everywhere. I hope you will never suppose that it matters little to us should you cease to support the 'Dayspring.' Let all who contributed to the building fund, though many of them have grown to be men and women, remember their own vessel still; let them train their children to maintain what they initiated; let all the youth occupying the various Sunday-schools interested in the mission, and all who desire the evangelisation of the heathen, take the vessel into their affectionate support.

On the arrival of the "Dayspring" at Melbourne, early in 1872, the first duty of those in charge was to find a new captain. Captain Fraser had been in command eight years, and at length resigned: with an increasing family, without any settled home, and with health by no means robust, he resolved to go back to his native country. The following extract from the minutes of the Mission Conference of 1871—the last held before Captain Fraser left the Islands—shows the estimation in which he was held by the missionaries:—

22. That Messrs. Inglis, Paton, and Copeland be appointed a committee to confer with Captain Fraser with reference to a continuation of his services in the 'Dayspring' for the ensuing year.

23. The committee appointed to confer with Captain Fraser report that he has stated to them that, owing chiefly to his rising family, and the

expenses connected with their education, he cannot consent to remain in the 'Dayspring' after the expiry of his present engagement.

24. That as Captain Fraser has tendered his resignation, this meeting in the circumstances agrees to accept the same, and to record the obligations of the mission to Captain Fraser for his Christian and gentlemanly conduct, and the skill and care with which he has sailed the 'Dayspring' during the eight years he has been in command of the vessel, and their best wishes for the usefulness and happiness of himself and his family; and that a sum of two hundred and twenty pounds (£220) be allowed him as payment for their passage from Melbourne to Halifax.

In addition to the testimony of the missionaries in favour of Captain Fraser's character and seamanship, we give the following brief extracts, showing how he was appreciated in Victoria:—

*From the Melbourne "Christian Review."*

The good captain is anxious at length to retire. He has had charge of the 'Dayspring' since she was launched in Nova Scotia in 1863, and we own that it is not without a pang that we can think of the mission vessel and the mission work with Captain Fraser away. The popularity of the 'Dayspring' in the colonies is due very much to Captain Fraser, and it is even a question whether the mission vessel would now be in existence but, under God, for the seamanship and self-denial of her commander. It is no light task to sail a vessel for so many years among the shoals and reefs of Polynesia without shipwreck; to have much intercourse with many native tribes and races without a collision; to control a crew without insubordination; to convey so many mission families without a complaint; and to maintain the missionary character of the 'Dayspring' in so many of the ports of Australasia—and this Captain Fraser has done. It will be very hard indeed to get a man to fill his place.

*From the Report of the New Hebrides Mission Committee of the General Assembly of the Presbyterian Church of Victoria.*

The committee regret much to learn that the captain of the mission vessel has resigned his command. Captain Fraser is well known in the colonies as a gentleman eminently fitted by character and skill for the position which he has occupied; and the usefulness of the 'Dayspring,' both in the colonies and among the islands, is due very much, under God, to Captain Fraser's wisdom and care. The committee feel deeply that his retirement is a loss to the mission.

*From the Deliverance of the General Assembly.*

The General Assembly, learning that Captain Fraser is about to retire from the command of the vessel, instructs the committee to assure him of the high estimation in which this church has always held his character and labours.

Captain Fraser was succeeded by Captain Robert Rae, a shipmaster well known in Hobart Town and Melbourne, who had been highly recommended to the committee; under whose charge the "Dayspring" left Melbourne on the 12th April, 1872, and reached Aneityum harbour on the 1st May. On that occasion she carried, as passengers—Dr. and Miss Geddie, Mr. and Mrs. Inglis, Mr. and Mrs. Murray, Mr. and Mrs. McKenzie, Mr. and Mrs. Robertson, Mrs. Neilson and two children, Rev. D. Macdonald, and Mr. F. A. Campbell of Geelong.

In consequence of Dr. Geddie's illness, and for other reasons, it was determined, at the annual meeting of the brethren, to send the "Dayspring" a second trip to the colonies. She arrived at Melbourne in October, and left again early in November, in charge of Captain Jenkins, who had been appointed in room of Captain Rae, resigned. She was looked for back in Australia towards the end of January; but February and March passed, and still no tidings. By this time great fears for the safety of the vessel began to be entertained, and at length a communication from the Rev. Mr. Inglis confirmed the worst anticipations, and informed us of the total wreck of the "Dayspring" in Anelcauhat harbour, Aneityum. An account of the disaster will be found in the accompanying narrative by another hand.

Thus "The Dayspring,"—the Presbyterian mission-vessel in the South Pacific—which, during her time, was one of the most popular and useful of all mission vessels, has passed away, and her work is only now a matter of history. Her services to missions were not less important in Australia than on the mission field. She had, in fact, two mission fields—one in the New Hebrides, and another in the colonies; and I think I am justified in saying, that her influence for good, in Melbourne and other colonial seaports, was as important in its place as her work among the islands from Aneityum to Santo. It is too soon to say, at present, what should be done for the future; but the history of the "Dayspring" shows what can be done; and let us hope and pray that Christians in Australia may never forget what they can do, and should do, for these dark islands of the sea.

# STATEMENT

## SHOWING THE SUMS RAISED FOR THE MAINTENANCE AND REPAIRS OF THE "DAYSPRING,"

### FROM 1865 TILL 1872, INCLUSIVE.

NOTE.—*During 1863 and 1864 the Maintenance Fund and the Building Fund were not kept separate.*

| | 1865. | 1866. | 1867. | 1868. | 1869. | 1870. | 1871. | 1872. | Total for the Years 1865-72 |
|---|---|---|---|---|---|---|---|---|---|
| N. S. Wales | 416 9 9 | 247 0 0 | 159 13 4 | 324 9 0 | 319 17 5 | 219 5 9 | 290 0 0 | 247 10 0 | 2224 5 3 |
| Nova Scotia | — | — | 250 0 0 | 400 0 0 | 250 0 0 | 250 0 0 | 250 0 0 | 500 0 0 | 1900 0 0 |
| New Zealand | — | 580 0 0 | 111 16 2 | 124 15 11 | 278 17 0 | 287 0 9 | 491 4 8 | 152 0 0 | 2025 14 6 |
| R.P.C. of Scotland | — | — | 250 0 0 | 280 0 0 | 250 0 0 | 250 0 0 | 500 0 0 | — | 1530 0 0 |
| South Australia | 635 5 3 | 222 16 0 | 86 11 9 | 235 10 8 | 109 16 5 | 83 13 11 | 157 11 0 | 104 8 7 | 1635 13 7 |
| Tasmania | 228 3 1 | 76 12 9 | 193 6 9 | 221 19 6 | 90 2 10 | 125 8 4 | 96 8 4 | 109 11 8 | 1141 13 3 |
| Victoria | 305 14 0 | 1864 14 8 | 792 11 3 | 1397 18 7 | 1036 9 4 | 1343 12 0 | 851 13 10 | 500 0 0 | 8092 13 8 |
| Queensland | — | 101 2 4 | — | — | — | — | — | — | 101 2 4 |
| TOTAL | £1585 12 1 | £3092 5 9 | £1843 19 3 | £2984 13 8 | £2335 3 0 | £2259 0 9 | £2636 17 10 | £1613 10 3 | £18651 2 7 |

# A YEAR

AMONG THE

# NEW HEBRIDES,

LOYALTY ISLANDS AND NEW CALEDONIA.

BY

F. A. CAMPBELL.

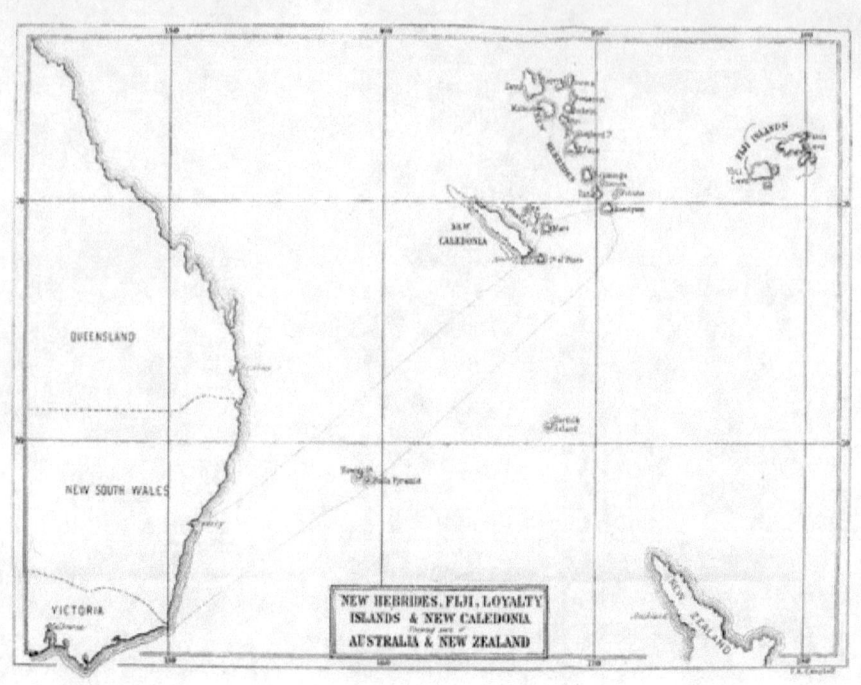

## LETTER I.

THE VOYAGE FROM MELBOURNE TO ANEITYUM, AND FIRST IMPRESSIONS OF THAT ISLAND.

*Anelcauhat Aneityum,*
*May,* 1872.

How strange and how different is the scene before me now, from that which used to meet my eye, but one short month ago. Glancing from my open window I see the tall stately palm and the luxuriant orange tree, instead of the familiar blue gum and wattle. I see the graceful savage strolling with an easy motion along the beach, instead of the well-dressed business man hurrying to town, or the eager men and women rushing towards the railway station. No discordant shrieks of impatient steam-engines are here to break the stillness of the morning. No loud rattle of cars and carriages is heard; but there floats towards me on the soft balmy airs of the tropics, the pleasant murmur of the surf on the outlying reef, and the faint shouts of the natives as they tumble about in the still waters of the bay. Everything is quietly beautiful and lazily pleasant. The sea, the wind, the trees, the natives, all seem infected by the same dreamy laziness, and I myself feel a strange desire to throw down my pen, to curl myself up in the shade of some great tree, and dream.

But it will never do for me to land you in the tropics in this way, without the preliminary voyage down. So you must be satisfied, for the present, with this glimpse from my window and return with me to the little brigantine "Dayspring," when, having passed Port Phillip Heads, she turned her bow towards the New Hebrides and her stern towards the fair west wind.

It was on the morning of Saturday, the 13th of April, that our voyage really began. There were thirteen adult passengers on board—a considerable number for a vessel of only 120 tons to carry; the "Dayspring" however having wonderful cabin accommodation for her size, we all managed to stow ourselves somewhere without much inconvenience. With a fresh fair wind, our square-sails alone being set, we ran along the coast of Victoria as far as Cape Howe. There we left the land and struck out across the watery waste, with the good wind following.

The majority of the passengers did not seem properly to appreciate the glorious breeze which was doing us such good service, but looked as if they would have infinitely preferred a dead calm and a smooth sea. I was able fortunately to take quite a different view of the matter, and used to stagger about the deck triumphantly, glorying in my newly-discovered sailing powers.

By Wednesday the 17th we had gone 900 miles—fully half way—which wasn't at all bad work. Towards evening on that day two lonely little islands appeared, and helped to break the monotony of the voyage; Howe's Island and Ball's Pyramid. The first is inhabited I believe by a few whalers, while the latter is but a bare rock, rising abruptly from the sea, to the height of about 1800 feet.

After bringing us this length in such good style the wind died away, and then we had the usual amount of calms, light winds and occasional breezes. Though some days we did not make much progress, still at the end of each twenty-four hours there was always something to be added to the number of miles accomplished ; thirty-five miles being the poorest day's work recorded.

A sea-voyage is always more or less monotonous, as there is so little to interest outside the vessel, and we saw perhaps less than usual of the sights of the sea. Both air and water were remarkably lifeless. Of the inhabitants of the mighty deep we saw none except a few flying fish, three sharks and a school of porpoises; while few birds honoured us with their notice or their company. The sharks, as is usually the case, caused great excitement on board; everyone apparently being filled with anxiety to have the ugly creatures hauled out of their native element without delay. We did, after a good deal of haggling, succeed in hooking one, and lugged it up on deck. Standing round at a safe distance we watched its ungainly flounders and its subsequent decapitation with great interest, after which we retired to dinner with feelings of placid satisfaction.

Though there was not much life apparent outside the vessel, there was no lack of it inside. There were men, women and children in great variety, there were pigs and goats, sheep and fowls, a young bull calf, a small dirty kitten, and cockroaches. We were a most harmonious company with the exception of the last-named creature. From the beginning to the end of the voyage there raged unceasing war between man and cockroach, and on the whole I think that the latter had the best of it. 'Tis true that man might annihilate a few by one stamp of his foot, but then the cockroaches, assembling at night by the hundred, would retaliate, by biting their adversary's toe-nails, flying against his face and running into his boots, until man would give up the fight in despair and the cockroach reign in triumph.

All vessels frequenting these seas seem infested with these creatures, and there appears to be no way of getting rid of them. You may deluge the vessel with water, smoke it with chemicals, strew it with poison, but still they swarm, so "what can't be cured must be endured."

Though the cockroaches did not diminish in numbers, there is no doubt but that the rest of the live stock did, as we approached the end of our journey; and the sheep-pens and the hen-coops began to present rather a deserted appearance before the welcome cry of " Land, ho ! " resounded through the vessel.

It was on Tuesday the 30th that we caught the first glimpse of Aneityum looming faintly in the distance ; and by next morning we lay safely anchored in Anelcauhat harbour, after a very fair passage of nineteen days.

The view from this harbour is truly magnificent. It would require the pen of a Ruskin and the pencil of a Turner to do justice to it, and unfortunately neither the one nor the other is in my possession. I did indeed open my sketch-book and try to transfer the fair scene to my paper, but it was useless. The outlines perhaps were caught with some degree of accuracy, but where the rich colouring of earth and sky and sea ? where the delicate shades and brilliant lights ? and where the enchanted atmosphere of the tropics through which the whole was viewed ? No! to get a true idea of the appearance of a tropical land one must see it for oneself.

You dwellers upon the flat plains of Victoria, picture to yourselves, if you can, a scene like this.

A magnificent mass of mountains rise from the sea with a graceful curve. With the exception of a belt comparatively bare of trees, these mountains are clothed from their base to their summits with a mantle of rich green foliage. Looking from the sea, this covering appears upon the distant hilltops like soft green moss ; but as the eye follows the descending sweep of the landscape towards the shore, the surface becomes more uneven and the outline of trees more distinct, until finally the eye rests upon the well-defined groves of stately palms, waving and nodding their heads over the white sand. Deep valleys and gorges, resting in shadow, throw out the spurs of the mountains into high relief, causing a beautiful variety. A bright blue sky overhead, a sparkling many-coloured sea around, and a clear balmy atmosphere everywhere, set off and complete the picture. Imagine this, my friends, if you are able, and you will have some idea of the appearance of Aneityum, one of the sunny islands of the South.

The Line of March.

## LETTER II.

THE NEW HEBRIDES — THEIR DISCOVERY — ANEITYUM — ITS CHARACTERISTICS — INHABITANTS — THE MISSION STATION AT ANELCAUHAT — RAMBLES ALONG THE SHORE AND INLAND — A MARRIAGE — NATIVE SERVICE.

*Anelcauhat, Aneityum,*
*May,* 1872.

THREE men seem to have been concerned in the discovery of the New Hebrides. First Quiros, who in the year 1606 stumbled across the most northerly island of the group, whilst sailing in search of a great southern continent; and who, thinking that he had found the land which he was looking for, gave it the somewhat grandiloquent title of Tierra Austral del Espiritu Santo, and sailed off without exploring its coasts.

Next Bougainville, who came in the year 1768; but he did nothing more than discover that the continent of Quiros was only an island, one of a large and extensive group, to which he applied the name of The Grand Cyclades.

Lastly came Cook, in the year 1774, who sailed twice along the entire length of the group, determining the positions and sizes of the various islands and assigning names to each, while the whole he re-christened by the name which it now bears—The New Hebrides. So observing and accurate was Cook in this work, that it is doubtful if even the smallest islet escaped his notice, and all were laid down on paper in position and form so exactly, that but little alteration has since been made upon his original plan. He landed upon the islands of Malicolo, Eramanga, Tana, and Santo, and has left us a good deal of information about the natives as he found them— the main facts of which, in many cases, are true of them still..

He found that the group consisted of about thirty islands, lying between 15° and 20° S. latitude, and 166° and 171° W. longitude; that they extended for about 400 miles N.N.W. and S.S.E.; and that all of the islands, except the very smallest, were thickly populated with tribes of savage men, with whom on several occasions he had quarrels and skirmishes.

The names which he gave to the various islands were in some cases English, but for the most part derived from the natives themselves. The northern island he allowed still to bear the title applied to it by its discoverer; and the southern, —the island that I wish now to speak of more particularly,—he called Annatom, a name which he got from the Tanese when he was on their island.

Annatom—or, as it is now more generally and more correctly called, Aneityum—although one of the smallest, is by no means one of the least important islands of the group. It was the first to be settled by European missionaries, and its inhabitants are now ahead of all the other islanders in point of civilization; its harbour has been the resort for many years of vessels trading in these seas ; and it is the only island whose coasts have been thoroughly surveyed. It is nearly circular in form, has few indentations or bays, and is said to be forty miles in circumference. If it were not almost entirely taken up with mountains it might support a large population ; but as it is, the only arable lands are in the valleys, and on the narrow flats which here and there occur between the base of the hills and the sea coast. These wood-covered hills, nearly 3000 feet high, do good service however in drawing from the clouds an abundant supply of fresh water, and this running down the valleys and gorges, in never-failing streams, irrigates and enriches the lower lands most effectually. The only bay in which vessels may lie safely is this one, upon the south-west side of the island, going by the name of Anelcauhat Harbour, a name it takes from the district lying round it. The bay is formed by a point of the mainland, two islets, and an outlying reef. It opens towards the west, upon which side it is rather too much exposed for the safety of vessels in harbour; for, although the anchorage is tolerably good, such a sea comes rolling in with a westerly breeze, that, more than once, vessels at anchor have broken ground and been cast ashore.

It used to be quite a lively port in the old sandal-wood-seeking days, there being then two establishments on the harbour and whaling being carried on as well ; both of which industries brought vessels frequently into the bay.

But these days are over—happily so, say the missionaries—and all that can be seen now of these places, are a few buildings upon the islet of Inyug, still occupied as a whaling station.

At the head of the bay, the most attractive object is the native church—a large building, which, with its white shining walls, stands out very prominently upon a gentle slope. To the right of it other white walls are seen glimmering through the thick green foliage — the mission store and a native's house along the beach; while on the hill above is the house of Lathella, the chief, and near it that in which the family of Captain Fraser, late of the "Dayspring," used to reside. The mission house itself is not visible, being hidden by the intervening trees and shrubs, but it is situated a little way to the right of the church. (*See Frontispiece.*)

The population of Aneityum is now estimated at 1500—just half what it was thirteen or fourteen years ago. This frightful depopulation is said to be due, mainly, to foreign diseases, such as measles, hooping-cough, diphtheria, &c., brought to the island by trading vessels.

These epidemics sweep off the natives by the hundred; in one case a third of the whole population being cut off in the space of three months. They have no strength of constitution to withstand such attacks, and they cannot take the usual means for the prevention and cure of them.

During the last few years, however, according to the census taken by the missionaries, there is a turn in the right direction; and probably, could epidemic diseases be kept out of the island, the extinction of the people, which for some time seemed imminent, would be warded off.

But I must now resume my narrative. Last letter was concluded with the announcement of our arrival in Anelcauhat harbour, and with a slight description of the character of the scenery which surrounds it. The anchor was not long down, before the boats were lowered and we were landed on the beach. What a delightful sensation it was, to tread the *terra firma* again, after those weeks of ceaseless motion and confinement; how fresh, and green, and beautiful everything appeared to our eyes, accustomed of late only to the flat and monotonous surface of the watery waste. We sniffed the balmy airs, wandering leisurely under the palm and the orange tree, and were happy. It was a pleasure to exist, a pleasure even to breathe, in a land where the winds were such as those ascribed by Milton to Paradise :—

> " Now gentle gales,
> Fanning their odoriferous wings, dispense
> Native perfumes, and whisper whence they stole
> Those balmy spoils."

The mission premises, over which we rambled, are both extensive and pretty. The dwelling-house is substantially built of stone, and roofed with sugarcane-leaf thatch—the substitute for slates down here. At the back of it, stand the kitchen, various storehouses, natives' houses, &c.; whilst a little way off, at the side, is the dispensary and a large school-house.

In front, stretching down towards the shore, is the garden. Around the dwelling grow some very fine orange and lemon trees, and in an enclosure at the back, bananas and pine-apples are cultivated. Fortunately for us, a good deal of the fruit was ripe at the time of our landing, so that we enjoyed quite a feast. The well loaded branches of the orange trees, although the fruit was just ripening, suffered severely, and the mangled remains which lay strewed on the ground beneath bore witness to the vigour of the attack. From the lofty palm-heads the natives showered down bottled lemonade upon us, of which refreshing temperance drink we partook to a considerable extent, as it is cool and very pleasant to the taste. From the bananas we got contributions of their delicious fruit—fair, fat, and yellow, larger, and finer in taste, by far, than anything I had met with before. A small piece of cooked taro, which did not however meet with general approbation, concluded our feast; after which we climbed to the top of a hill near at hand, had a fine view of the country towards the mountains, and then went off to the vessel for the night, well satisfied with our first day ashore in the tropics.

For some days the "Dayspring" lay in harbour, landing the goods of Mr. Murray, the missionary who was to occupy the station of Dr. Geddie, and this gave me a good opportunity of exploring the regions round about the harbour, while the request of Dr. Mueller, the Government botanist of Victoria, that I would collect for him some botanical specimens, supplied me with a definite end in view during these rambles, and engaged me also in a work which I found increasingly interesting as my collection grew in size.

The second morning after our arrival I went ashore to commence my peregrinations; but before doing so, picked up a native to act as guide and general servant. He was squatting under a palm-tree, busily engaged in the ordinary native occupation of doing nothing; so I made proposals to him (couched in the orthodox hashed English) to come with me. He understood me, agreed to my terms, took my coat and bag, and followed me. A native will never think of going before or alongside a European, unless specially directed to do so; naturally he will fall behind as a mark of respect.

Naublo—for that was the name of my man Friday—was not, I afterwards found out, an Aneityumese, but an Eramangan; and a very ugly Eramangan he was too. A large head and mouth, woolly hair, square jaws, rather a squat body, and a very dark skin, were the outward characteristics of my humble follower; but his disposition quite made amends for his somewhat uncomely appearance, as he was extremely good-natured, willing and trustworthy, and, in addition, possessed the usual savage virtues of being easily pleased and innocently happy.

During the first excursion, which was along the beach, I found much to interest me, in the new forms under which animal and vegetable life appeared. One curious-looking tree, about twenty feet high, growing along the beach just on the line where the herbage meets the sand, attracted my attention in particular. It was a species of the Pandanus or Screw pine. (*See Litho. of Mau and Pele.*) The tree has the appearance of being supported in mid-air upon a number of stilts: sometimes it resembles a monstrous animal rearing on its hind legs, or a giraffe with an enormously long neck. These stilts or props are in reality the ærial roots of the tree, which it sends down from the stem at regular intervals, whenever it feels in want of support; thus being enabled to take up a very strong position upon spots where the soil is loose and sandy. It throws out bare straggling branches on all sides, and their extremities are crowned with tufts of leaves, arranged spirally, and bearing a great resemblance to pine-apple plants. The fruit is round and massive, about six inches in diameter, and contains edible kernels not unlike jordan almonds in appearance and taste. It is a curious-looking tree, but a very useful one. The leaves, plaited, make good bags and mats, which last are generally used by the missionaries instead of carpets.

The Casuarina or ironbark is another tree that clings to the neighbourhood of the sea-coast. It is generally found, however, upon eminences a little way above the shore, and exposed to the full blast of the sea-breeze. There it roots itself firmly in the ground, and waves its strong arms in the wind, defying its utmost fury. It bears considerable resemblance to its relative, the she-oak of Australia; but is more massive, straggling, and attains a greater size. Its wood is excessively hard, and is used by the natives in the manufacture of anything that they wish to be durable.

From the beach we made detours occasionally, out upon the flat rocky reef, to inspect the pools left by the ebbing tide, and amply did they repay the trouble. Each was a little world teeming with busy inhabitants—a beautiful aquarium, stocked with an infinite variety of subjects. There were little polypes, in their brightly-coloured cells, or lying hidden in their beds of soft jelly, drawing from the ocean small particles of lime and building them up into their coral cities; there were starfish, moving their snaky arms restlessly to and fro, and little shellfish, opening their shells to feed on their invisible food; there were nimble crabs running over the rocks and disappearing into dark mysterious recesses; and in the still water there flashed a multitude of small fish of gorgeous colours—blue, green, or striped with many shades; while along the bottom of the pool there lay the dark, sluggish, and hideous-looking body of the holuthuria, or beche de mer.

The manners and customs of the last-named animal are so decidedly peculiar, and it is so much sought after and valued, that I will devote a few lines specially to it.

The holuthuria has the wonderful power of turning itself inside out when in an unhappy frame of mind, and this, apparently, without suffering the slightest inconvenience. Then if it be cut into halves, instead of dying, as most creatures would under such painful circumstances, it developes into two holuthurias, each half becoming a separate and complete animal. I got my man to fish out for me the one in the pool, but it was a lazy specimen; at all events it did not distinguish itself in any way whatever, but submitted to be hung over a tree without opposition.

Repulsive as these creatures are in appearance, they are much esteemed by the Chinese as an article of food, being boiled by them into a thick rich soup, which is considered a great delicacy. £150 per ton is a considerable price to pay for fish; but all that John will give, if he only can get his holuthuria broth. When taken from the sea, they are boiled and dried on the spot, which process reduces them from say a foot in length to three or four inches, but renders them quite solid and hard.

There are, I believe, a good many about these islands, but

the principal fishing ground is the north coast of Australia, where the fishing is mainly carried on by Malays.

After gathering a few specimens of grasses and various small plants, which grew close to the shore, we turned back. The tide was out, and the fine flat beach before us presented rather a curious appearance. It was covered with shells of various shapes and sizes, but these, instead of lying motionless as shells usually do, were skimming over the sand in a most extraordinary manner. Catching one, I found on examination that the shell was occupied by a hermit crab, and that it was the nimble legs of these creatures which gave the shells their wonderful powers of locomotion. These crabs, not being able to build their own houses, take possession of all the empty shells lying about the beach—a habit of theirs which has sometimes disgusted me exceedingly; for after returning from a stroll along the beach with a pocket full of shells, I would find that I had also—what I didn't bargain for, a pocket full of those vicious little hermits, in a state of lively irritation. I need hardly say that my pocket was generally emptied much faster than it was filled.

I had not time, however, to make lengthened observations of crabs or anything else, as I wished to reach the vessel while my specimens were in good order for pressing; so hurrying on, I reached the boat, and, making an appointment with my man for the following morning, went off to the vessel.

Next day we turned our steps inland. Winding along a narrow pathway, one of the highways of the island, we came, before we had gone far, upon several of the natives' little plantations, and I saw also several of their huts nestling amidst the trees. In the plantations, which average about half-an-acre in size, taro, bananas, and sugarcane are grown; and the work which is involved in the cultivation of these plants is by no means inconsiderable. First the ground has to be cleared of trees and scrub, fenced with reeds, the soil to be loosened with hoes or sharp sticks, and pulverised with the fingers; the plants are then put in, and require to be attended to with diligence and care during their growth.

These clean, neatly-fenced little spots have a very pretty appearance amongst the surrounding disorder, and give one some idea of what the place would look like were it extensively cultivated and settled upon. The soil, wherever it was turned up, appeared very rich and black, and the vegetables and fruits planted in it seemed thriving very luxuriantly.

The huts of the natives are very poor affairs. In the way of architecture at least, the Aneityumese seem to have made little or no improvement since the days of heathenism. They still live, with a few exceptions, in miserable huts consisting of a framework of wood overlaid with plaited cocoanut or sugarcane leaf, and having the appearance of narrow thatched roofs planted on the ground, for they have no walls; they are about six feet high in the centre, and are entered by a hole at one end. I believe that they find these places healthier than a house with walls; at all events they seem to prefer them on the whole, for although the chief at Anelcauhat has put up a very good specimen of a plastered house, but very few of the people seem inclined to follow his example.

Sometimes the path wound through open spaces, covered thickly with long reeds six or eight feet high; and then it would lead us under the shade of great trees, and into woods so dense that we could not see more than a few yards in any direction. These reeds, which grow so plentifully here in the open spots, are exceedingly useful; all the fences are made of them, the natives use them for arrows, and they can be woven into a wickerwork which makes excellent seats and couches.

Amongst the trees of the South-Sea Island forest, the breadfruit stands pre-eminent. It is both useful and ornamental; its fruit is a staple article of food with these natives, and probably a great encouragement to laziness on their part, as the tree does not require cultivation. From the stem the natives generally make their canoes, as the wood is good and easily cut. There is a great difference between the forests here and those of cold climates: for here you can get food from almost every second tree—bread-fruit, chesnuts, almonds, and the like; so that the natives can not, I should think, ever suffer absolute starvation.

Thus we marched and observed, until at last we emerged upon the banks of a beautiful little stream, that came rippling down in miniature cascades until it opened out into a quiet deep pool at our feet. It looked exceedingly refreshing to hot perspiring mortals, and proved so to me, when I plunged into it. After I had bathed, we sat on the banks munching sugarcane and admiring the scenery—the thick, bright foliage near the stream, and the magnificent ferns along the earthy banks. Then we marched back, and Naublo brought the remains of the sugarcane, with which spoils, together with some specimens of ferns, I reached again the deck of my floating home.

Next day the inhabitants of the district of Anelcauhat were in a state of great excitement, and well they might, for a great event was about to happen. Exactly such an event as this,—viz., the marriage of two white individuals upon a South-Sea island—has been, I am sure, of very rare occurrence; so that it is worthy of notice. At a certain hour all the rank and fashion of the place assembled at the church to witness the approaching ceremony, and we went ashore from the ship suitably rigged up. The Rev. J. D. Murray officiated; and before him stood Miss Geddie (daughter of Dr. Geddie) and the Rev. D. McDonald—the bride and bridegroom, who shortly afterwards left the building man and wife. When the marriage ceremony was over—and it was simple and short—a select company sat down to an elegant *dejeuner* spread in the mission house, to which, as the papers would say, they did ample justice. When the feast was over, the company dispersed, and Anelcauhat once again resumed its wonted appearance of tranquil repose.

The marriage took place on a Saturday, so that next day was the first day of the week, and I had then an opportunity of observing the natives on their Sunday behaviour. There was morning service in the big church at about half-past nine o'clock, and to this we went. The service, of course, was conducted in the Aneityumese language, and was not very interesting to me; so I studied the church and the people.

The church is a massive building, with low stone walls and an immense thatched roof; it is large enough to hold about 800 people, I should think. Great beams extend across from wall to wall, and upon these rest the principal supports of the roof; the fastenings seem to be all cord, no nails apparently having been used. It is quite a wonder of missionary architecture and native workmanship, and stands a monument of the ingenuity and industry of Dr. Geddie, the builder of it. As for the congregation, there might be 150 altogether. They were seated mostly on mats spread on the floor—the men on one side, and the women and children on the other. On fulldress occasions like this, the men generally wear crimean shirts and pants, or shirts and lava lava, that being a sort of calico kilt hung round the loins; some of them have waistcoats, and a few come out in full suits. The fair (?) sex appear in their most tastefully decorated grass skirts, a calico shawl or cloak, a plaited coal-scuttle bonnet—waving a fan gracefully with one hand and clasping a hymn-book with the other. None of them ever wear anything on their feet, and but few of the men anything on their heads but their own natural covering of woolly hair.

They seemed attentive as Dr. Geddie spoke to them in their own language; but their efforts in the way of music were not of a very successful character, an instrument being much wanted.

As we expected to sail next morning, we bade adieu to our friends before going on board. Seeking out Naublo, I told him that I should want him again when we returned, and dismissed him with a present that made his ugly face beam with satisfaction.

Accordingly, early next morning we hauled up anchor, set sail, and stood out of the harbour.

## LETTER III.

THE MISSION STATION AT ANAME—FOTUNA—A DAY ASHORE—
ANIWA—THE COCOA-NUT PALM—TANA—APPEARANCE OF
THE VOLCANO — PORT RESOLUTION — DEPOPULATION —
BLACK BEACH.

*Anelcauhat, Aneityum,*
*June,* 1872.

WE were now started on a trip which promised to be interesting and very delightful. The vessel was to sail out and in amongst many islands, touching at some and sighting others, nearly all of which are famed for their beautiful scenery. The fair steady trade winds were blowing, and would carry us onward to the north upon a sea wonderfully and pleasantly calm, and nearly the whole group of islands, one by one, would pass before us like a lovely panorama. This was what I was led to expect, this was what I looked forward to, as we sailed out of Anelcauhat harbour on the 6th of May; whether or not I was disappointed may be gathered from the notes of the voyage which follow.

After leaving the harbour, the first place we called at was Anamé, the station of the Rev. John Inglis, situated upon the opposite side of the island from Anelcauhat. Four hours' sailing brought the white houses and the thin smoky spirals of the mission premises into sight, and opposite them, in lee of a coral reef, we dropped anchor. On landing we were met by a crowd of natives—neatly-dressed women, and healthy happy-looking men, who favoured us with a most demonstrative welcome.

This station, although it occupies a low and unhealthy situation, has a very pleasing and romantic appearance. The palms and the bananas, the white shining houses with their brown thatched roofs, the fanciful reed fences, the orange trees loaded with green and yellow fruit, the large mimosas hanging over the sea, and the dusky forms of the natives—all combine to make a scene of peacefulness and soft contrast, upon which the eye rests with much enjoyment.

During the few hours spent here we were kindly entertained by Mr. and Mrs. Inglis, and were shown over the grounds and premises. The magnificent orange trees in front of the house were amongst the most noticeable objects. They are more than twenty years old, are I should think about twenty feet high, and each bears several thousand oranges per annum. I saw here also the largest shell I had ever met with; it was an immense bivalve, each side of which was almost large enough for a bath, being about three feet in diameter. The shell, minus the fish, was found up in the bed of a stream which flows past the mission station. They are found alive, I believe, on the east coast of Australia, and are immensely powerful, being able to snap in two a good stout cable, by closing suddenly upon it. I cannot vouch for the truth of this statement, and I confess to a slight scepticism regarding this creature's vaunted powers.

Towards evening the flag of recall was hoisted, and we returned to the vessel, which by dark was well off from Aneityum, on her way towards the island of Fotuna.

The distance between Aneityum and Fotuna is about forty miles, and, as we had a steady breeze with us, before daylight we were close to the shore of the latter. I had a fine view of

this extraordinary island as we approached and rounded it, and had an opportunity also of making a sketch, which will give a better idea of its appearance than twenty pages of mere description would.

It is a huge table-topped mountain, fifteen miles in circumference, rising abruptly from the sea to a height of 2000 feet. Upon its sides, apparently bare and precipitous, a population of 900 natives exist—a fact that appears to be almost an impossibility upon first seeing the place from a distance. On approaching the island, however, and observing it closely, small fertile ravines open out, little flats covered with rich vegetation appear; while along the beach and in every nook and corner the lofty head of the palm-tree may be seen. These fertile spots the natives cultivate with great assiduity, and though sometimes rather hard put to for food, generally manage to have plenty.

Upon this island the Rev. Mr. Copeland and family have resided for upwards of six years; and a very lonely, buried-alive sort of life it must be, for their only reliable means of communication with the civilized world is the 'Dayspring,' which visits them but once or twice in the year.

When we rounded the island and hove-to opposite Mr. C.'s house, we could observe a great commotion on the beach, natives rushing about and canoes being launched. Several of these came towards us, paddled swiftly by strong and dexterous arms, and in one of the foremost was seated the worthy missionary himself. While Mr. Copeland was receiving news of the principal events of the last few months, I went ashore in the first boat going, and on landing found myself confronted by a crowd of Fotunese—the first real savages I had ever met with. They did not impress me very favourably; for a real savage, when standing within a few feet of the observer, is not a pretty object, however picturesque he may appear when "distance lends enchantment to the view." I had heard that the Fotunese were a fine race of men, much superior naturally to the natives of Aneityum; but my untutored eye only caught the impression of naked bodies, painted heads, cannibalistic grins, sullen scowls, mixed up with spears, bows, clubs and muskets. To me they seemed the most hideous set of wretches imaginable, beside whom the Aneityumese were positively beautiful. I might be mistaken, probably was; but these were my first impressions of the South-Sea Island cannibal. When I have seen more, and know more of them, I will be better able to enter into details as to their appearance and customs.

Passing through this crowd of Fotunese, I reached the mission house, introduced myself to Mrs. Copeland, and entertained her with a budget of news until the rest of the party arrived. During the day we went for a ramble up the hillside, which was very steep, crossed a small stream rushing furiously down towards the sea, and reached a point from which we had a very fine view. I should have liked very much to have gone to the top of the hill and explored the table, but our time was too short for such an extensive ramble.

After our return, I went out again alone, botanizing; and after wandering about the bush for some time, found myself in the midst of a number of natives—men and women—who were returning from the beach. They crowded round me, holding small pigs, fowls, vegetables, shells, bags, and other commodities, which I had no difficulty in understanding they wished me to purchase. Whether they could not or would not understand my sandalwood English, I do not know; but anyway I had considerable difficulty in persuading them that they had come to the wrong market, and that they had better move on. After a little time most of them did, and then I bought a few shells and native bags, giving, in exchange, tobacco. This soon became known, the horde returned, and I was again blockaded by a crowd that seemed determined to get my tobacco, at any price; one would shove towards me a little bony pig and point to my bag, another direct my attention to a fowl, another to a bunch of yams. It began to get tiresome. I set my back against a tree, and told them that I would give them no more tobacco, simply because I had none, and explained to them how foolish it was for them to waste their valuable time in such a manner. I don't know that they understood my address, but they did understand what my bag turned upside down meant, and so tailed off with disappointed faces. One poor woman, who had been eagerly pressing on me a meagre dilapidated chicken, rather excited my compassion; so I gave her a piece of turkey red, wherewith to "tie up her bonny brown hair." It never reached its destination, however; for no sooner did she get it than a man (her husband, probably) stepped forward, snatched it away, and tied it round his own ugly head. I then went on my way, feeling as much disgusted with the manners of these people as with their appearance; and I wondered if it were possible for any educated man or woman to live among such beings, without any other society whatever, and be happy. This question I hoped to be able to answer, after I had seen more of mission life down here.

After a pleasant and somewhat novel day spent ashore, we rejoined the vessel, and set sail the same evening for Aniwa, a small island lying about fifty miles to the north-west of Fotuna.

When the sun rose next morning we were within a mile or two of our destination. Aniwa is a coral island—the only real coral island in the group—and it presents a decided contrast to the great massive block we had left the evening before. The highest part of it is not more than 100 feet above the sea level; its length is about six miles, and breadth from two to three miles.

There is no sandy beach round this island, no outlying reef to break the force of the waves; so that when the wind blows strongly, the sea comes rushing upon it as if to overwhelm the land, and bursts into white foam upon its hard and well-worn sides. The flat platform of coral rock which does duty as a beach, rises very abruptly from the sea and stands a few feet above its surface; there grow cocoanut-palms in splendid groves, casuarinas, and a few other trees. Some distance inland another rising takes place in the form of a steep cliff, forty or fifty feet high, beyond which the land lies in gentle undulations, covered with vegetation, wondrously luxuriant, considering the scantiness and poverty of the soil.

The cocoanut palm (cocos nucifera) is a wonderful and noble tree, and deserves greater attention at my hands than I have as yet given it. It appears to be endued with a power almost creative, it produces such magnificent results from such scanty material. Upon spots so bare and dry that all the other trees shrink from them in disdain, this palm rears its woody column, and its crested head often waves eighty or a ninety feet above the ground. From the sand, the air, the light, it draws those materials that its instinct prompts it to select, and these it labours with and converts, by mysterious processes, into the hard woody stem, the graceful leaves, the useful nuts—into oil, into sweetened water, into a fibrous matting to protect the nut and coarse strong cloth to strengthen the leaves.

The manner of its growth is wonderful. Botanists tell us that the palm is really an annual,—that looking at the tree we do not see one live whole, but the results of the lifework of many plants piled one above the other. The new plant shoots forth, waves in the sun awhile, then droops and dies, and leaves its hardened body for the next to mount upon. So these palm-tree builders work, always upward, till they reach their limit—for, like all things earthly, they have a limit to their growth.

The palm-tree has not great far-extending roots like those of the exogenous tree, nor has it props like the pandanus; but its roots are weak and thin, and were the palm-tree plants to be too ambitious—to build on too long—they would make their edifice top-heavy, and bring it to the ground. But they do not. They know how much the roots will bear—so much they build, and then the germ of life ceases to exist: since they cannot grow upward, they will not grow at all; for they cannot live and not grow, they cannot grow and not ascend.

The cocoanut-palm is remarkable for the crookedness of its stem; it often leans over bodily at a considerable angle, and exhibits, besides, a great variety of curves, and even tolerably sharp angles.

In addition to this crookedness of the stem—supposed to be the result of the wind and the nature of the tree acting in opposition; the former throwing it out of the perpendicular, the latter striving to attain uprightness—I have observed that this palm always emerges from the ground with a curve. This is particularly noticeable in the young trees, although the old ones never lose the peculiar appearance that this youthful fancy of theirs gives to them. I have never heard any reason assigned why the cocoanut-palm should rise with this invariable curve, but no doubt the shape of the nut has something to do with it, for the nut when it falls from the tree lies naturally lengthwise on the ground; and so the young shoots, which come out of one of the holes at the end, grow first in a horizontal direction; the one then curves upward and forms the tree, the other downward and forms the roots. This upward curve that the first one takes is then, probably, what gives to this species of palm that peculiar form of stem which I have been speaking of.

The drawings of this palm are often very incorrect. They are frequently portrayed with stems as straight and upright as a factory chimney, or bent in one smooth curve like a Turkish scimitar, and with leaves arranged round the top like those of a Norfolk Island pine. One of the best likenesses of the cocoanut-palm that I recollect having seen, was in a book of Kingsley's on the West Indies. There the crooked stems and the graceful lines of the intercrossing leaves are excellently brought out.

As almost everyone who writes about this tree gives a list of the uses to which its various parts may be put, I will dismiss this part of the subject in a few words.

Its wonderful power of producing, and supplying on demand a cool and pleasant drink, rank it at once as perhaps the most useful tree in a tropical climate, although as a food supplier it must give way to the bread-fruit. This drink is found in the green nuts, and, as I once said before when alluding to it as "bottled lemonade," is exceedingly pleasant and refreshing. On Aniwa I do not know how the natives would exist without it, for there are no springs of fresh water on the island, and it is the only liquid they drink. The meat of the nut is used as food for the pigs and fowls, as a flavouring for native puddings, as a means of keeping naughty little black boys and girls in good humour, as an article affording to all gentle exercise of the jaws when not otherwise employed, and lastly, as a stand-by when other food fails.

The leaves are not the least important part of the tree, for the natives plait them together and use the result as thatch for their huts, as mats to lie upon, and as bags for carrying what they may wish to carry.

But I must now leave the cocoanut-palm tree, and return to the vessel, which was just coming up to the island when I last spoke of her.

Our visit to this little island, and to the hospitable missionary and his wife who reside on it, was very similar to that spoken of in the beginning of this letter. Not very long after we reached the mission house, the goods and mails were all landed, and the captain's flag waved impatiently at the masthead for our return; and so we went. Before quitting the subject of Aniwa, however, I must say a few words about its inhabitants.

Mr. Paton, the missionary, has been on it for about six years, and has a comfortable house about half-a-mile from the boat landing, from which he has prepared a road with much labour. I give a sketch of the house, taken from the front, which will give some idea of the appearance of one of the most comfortable mission houses in the New Hebrides.

The Mission House on Aniwa.

Judging by the appearance of the natives, Mr. Paton has lived among them to some purpose. They have the same quiet, friendly, civilized look that the Aneityumese have. The population is estimated at 240. They speak almost the same language and are naturally much like the Fotunese. Had I not been told this, I certainly do not think I would have found it out for myself; for Christianity makes such a wonderful difference in the appearance of a savage, not only in clothing him, and washing the paint off him, but in giving to him an intelligent and pleasing expression of countenance.

I feel that it would be unjust were I to give anyone the impression, as I am afraid I may have done from what I have hitherto said, that the Fotunese are in no way improved by the teachings of Mr. Copeland their missionary; for even amongst them I recollect noticing many who evidently were more advanced than their neighbours; although the heathen were in such preponderance, and appeared to me so outrageous, as to draw my attention principally to them. This by the way.

From Aniwa we sailed for Tana, only sixteen or seventeen miles distant. While on our way over, we could see from the deck at one time the five southern islands of the group:— Aniwa behind us, Tana stretching out in front, Eramanga on one side, and Fotuna and Aneityum on the other. We had even a more attractive object, however, in the active volcano of Tana as we approached it. By daytime it certainly was worthy of notice, but at night it was magnificent. That day we touched at the mission station of Mr. Watt, landed his goods, and sailed for Port Resolution, the principal harbour of Tana, just as the darkness was coming on. It was then, as we sailed slowly along the coast, in the dark still night, that the burning mountain appeared to greatest advantage. Every five minutes, sometimes oftener, an eruption would take place. First, a great cloud of crimson flakes would shoot high into the air, then massy volumes of smoke would roll up after it, tinged with red; and then the roar, like that of artillery or loud thunder, would reach our ears. Ere this noise had ceased, the red flakes would pause in the air, as if undecided whether to go back or fly away altogether; then, having agreed amongst themselves to return to the earth, would sink slowly downward, like a fiery snow-storm, getting less and less brilliant as they fell.

This volcano is a splendid lighthouse; there is no mistaking it: the noise of its eruptions is heard distinctly upon Aneityum, and in some weather the concussion produced will shake the windows there, though it is fully forty miles away.

Next morning we anchored in Port Resolution. It is a circular bay, opening out towards the north-east by rather a narrow passage, and possesses good anchorage at ten fathoms and less. The scenery round it is perfectly lovely. I feel that were I to commence to rave about it I might never stop, so that it will be wisest not to commence. I will merely refer all who wish to know the nature of the scenery to the lithograph of this place, taken from the vessel when just off the mouth of the harbour. *(See Litho. opposite Page 32.)* Tana is the largest and richest island we had up to that time visited. It is about thirty miles long and ten miles broad. There are mountains in the southern and northern parts of the island, those in the south rising up in lofty wood-covered peaks to a height of say 3500 feet, while those in the north are not so high, are rounded on the top, and are comparatively bare of vegetation.

The population of this island is said to be now 8000. The natives have the character of being ferocious and warlike, much broken up into small tribes, which are continually fighting and eating one another.

On this island also, I am told, the natives are dying out. Depopulation seems to be the rule amongst these islands; indeed, I believe it is true, not only of the New Hebrides, but, more or less, of nearly every group in the South Pacific.

The causes of this are various. Foreign diseases, as already spoken of in the case of Aneityum, have done much deadly work, and latterly, the labour traffic has been assisting greatly to depopulate the New Hebrides. But even before the natives came in contact with and were affected by Europeans, they were, according to their own account, decreasing gradually. Their naturally vicious habits, frequent wars, and the practice of infanticide, seem to have been lessening their numbers, as it was doing upon the islands of Eastern Polynesia, where Ellis says that the people spoke of themselves as being merely a remnant of the population that formerly existed.

One thing only can apparently stay this destruction, and that is Christianity. It has done so in the case of some the Eastern islands, and it is doing so here. On the island of Aneityum a census is carefully taken every year, and this is its verdict. It stands to reason that whatever can put a stop to that which is causing the extinction of a people, will also stay the extinction. This Christianity has done on Aneityum and Aniwa; for there the vilest of their old customs are done away with, wars are never heard of, and infanticide is no longer practised.

In this direction, then, Christianity can and does tend towards saving these tribes from extinction; but what can the missionary do to prevent plagues being introduced into the island by trading vessels? It may be absolutely necessary for a vessel having disease on board, to touch at some island; but then every means should be taken to prevent its spreading on shore; and when men who, from carelessness or mere brutal inhumanity, indirectly destroy the lives of hundreds of human beings, and cause infinite suffering to many more, they ought surely to be made aware that the lives of even the most degraded of men are not to be sacrificed with impunity.

There are two missionaries upon the island of Tana— Mr. Watt at Kwamera, and Mr. Neilson at Port Resolution. We spent a very pleasant day ashore with the latter, wandering about the bay and seeing the lions of the place. The great roarer, the volcano, was kept for a better occasion, when more time could be given to the trip. Next day the vessel left the harbour *en route* for Eramanga, *viâ* Black Beach, a roadstead upon the north side of Tana. This was a very enjoyable sail; the weather was fine, and the scenery sometimes exquisite, as we glided round in the smooth water within a couple of miles from the beach.

When about half-way round, a sail was observed in the distance, and through the glass we made out a topsail schooner bearing down on us. She quickly came up, heaved-to, and lowered a boat, which, manned by a strong native crew, came dashing alongside. The captain and two other white men came on board. She proved to be the "Lyttona," having sixty or seventy New Hebrideans on board for Queensland; and the captain had come to tell us something about the boat of the late Mr. Gordon, of whose murder we had heard on arriving at Aneityum. Having received from us the latest news from civilization, he departed; the vessels filled their yards, (a nautical term) and soon were out of sight of one another.

On reaching Black Beach—a beach composed of black stones, instead of white sand—a boat went ashore for the purpose of ascertaining whether or not the natives would like to have a European missionary settled amongst them. A favourable report was brought back, several having expressed their willingness to receive a missionary, one man in particular showing considerable anxiety about it. It is a good place for a mission station, being at the opposite end of the island from the other two mission settlements, and there being good anchorage just in front of it.

That matter being concluded, we stood out from the shore and steered for the well-known island of Eramanga.

## LETTER IV.

ERAMANGA—ITS APPEARANCE AND CHARACTERISTICS—DILLON'S BAY—WHALING ESTABLISHMENT—EFATE—ITS NATURAL FEATURES—PANGO BAY—THE ISLETS OF FILI AND MELE AND THEIR INHABITANTS—VISITS PAID TO THEM.

*Anelcauhat, Aneityum,*
*June,* 1872.

MORE than a hundred years ago, a British ship hove-to off one of the islands of Western Polynesia, and sent a boat ashore for wood and water. The natives, filled with astonishment at this strange and unwonted sight—for it was the first time that they had seen any vessel larger than their own miserable canoes—crowded down to the beach, and met the boat's crew on their landing. They mixed with the strange white beings at first with fear and caution; but that soon wore off, and then they began to provoke the whites by pulling up the boat and trying to run off with the oars. A quarrel arose, and the arrows and spears of the natives began to fly through the air, till the loud report of the white men's muskets rang in their ears, and the fall of one or two of their number drove them into the bush. The boat then went off to the vessel, which sailed away after firing a heavy gun to frighten the natives still further.

The vessel was that of Captain Cook, and this was the manner in which the natives of Eramanga were first introduced to civilization and its powers.

The next white visitors to the island were the sandalwood traders, who, finding Eramanga to be rich in that precious wood, opened trading stations upon it.

I need say nothing about the general character of this trade, and of those concerned in it; for enough has been already said about the matter to show it in its true light. Next to a slave trade, perhaps no traffic on earth has been so polluted with human blood, or connected with such fearful atrocities, as this traffic in the sandalwood.

The crimes and evil actions of the demoralized vagabonds engaged in collecting the sandalwood, cannot be too strongly condemned or too greatly abhorred; for they not only ruthlessly sacrificed the lives of many of the natives, but indirectly they have destroyed many noble and pure-hearted men who have fallen by the avenging hands of the incensed savages.

The number of white men who have been murdered upon Eramanga affords, I think, a very good proof that the trade there has not been conducted on a more just footing than in other places; for I firmly believe that if the natives had been fairly and kindly treated from the beginning, we should have had little or nothing to complain of them now.

The first victims on Eramanga were John Williams and his companion Harris, who were murdered soon after their landing at Dillon's Bay on a visit, in the year 1852. Next Mr. and Mrs. G. Gordon, a missionary and his wife who had been residing at Dillon's Bay for four years, were murdered in the year 1861. Lastly, Mr. J. D. Gordon—a brother of Mr. G. N. Gordon—a missionary residing at Portinia Bay, was murdered there in February last. It is a fearful story; but one can hardly blame the natives, when one knows of the treatment that they have received at white men's hands, although, even making every allowance for them, I cannot help fancying that a good broadside or two occasionally would help to convince them that white men's lives are not to be sacrificed with impunity.

Before taking up the tale again, I must say a few words about the general characteristics of the island, and its appearance.

In point of size it is about equal to Tana, but is more massed together in the form of a square. It is not so mountainous as that island, nor so beautiful in appearance. The southern and eastern were the only sides of it that I saw, and they had rather a rugged and barren appearance. In the north, mountains rise to a considerable height, while the centre of the island is apparently a sort of table-land, intersected by valleys and ravines. Dillon's Bay is the principal anchorage that the island possesses; it cannot be called a harbour, for it is merely a wide open bay, protected from the prevailing S.E. winds. Cook's Bay and Portinia Bay are upon the other side; but as they are quite exposed to the trade winds, they are useless as places of shelter for vessels.

The exact number of inhabitants upon this island is not known, but from one to two thousand is the usual estimate—a small population for an island of its size. What I have already said will be sufficient to show that they are not of a very peaceful or trustworthy disposition. They have certainly a very bad name, for they bear the character of being equal to the Tanese, if not worse, in all that is bad, and of lacking any redeeming qualities that the latter may possess, such as straightforwardness and boldness.

On the morning of Sunday, the 12th of May, the vessel

came to anchor in Dillon's Bay, just opposite to a deep valley, down which a stream find its way to the sea. Although the scenery on the coasts on each side is not beautiful, the appearance of this valley is certainly very pretty. The hills on each side are high and steep, and in some parts well wooded. Upon the right, near the top of the hill, is the spot where Mr. and Mrs. G. N. Gordon lived, and were killed; down on the beach, to the right of the river, just where it joins the sea, John Williams was killed. The house that was occupied by the last missionary, Mr. McNair, who died there in 1870, is a few hundred yards up the stream, on the left-hand side, but not visible from the anchorage. A few white houses stand down on the beach, facing out to sea, and these are occupied as a whaling station. A litho. of my sketch of this scene is given in one of the letters which follow: the sketch was taken when the sun was shining down the valley, lighting up one side with its rays and throwing the other into deep shadow, which again was transferred as a dark reflection to the surface of the still water.

On going ashore we found seventy or eighty natives gathered together in a native building, and one of their number addressing them. This was the entire Christian party of the island, assembled for public worship—those who had been taught by Mr. G. Gordon and Mr. McNair at Dillon's Bay, and those who had been taught by Mr. J. D. Gordon at Portinia Bay. They had all come to this side of the island for safety, as the heathen, when they murdered Mr. Gordon a few months ago, had threatened to kill them also.

Several of the heathen natives of the Dillon's Bay district were lounging about the river side as we went up, and more degraded specimens of humanity I could not imagine to exist. They were so frightfully repulsive that the Tanese and the Fotunese, by comparison, went up fifty per cent. in my estimation. But here again I noticed that wonderful difference between the native in his natural condition and the native as influenced by Christianity; for those in the church had a brightness of expression on their faces which seemed to make them totally different beings, quite irrespective of the clothes they wore and the paint that they didn't wear.

The building which has been occupied as a mission house was somewhat out of repair and the garden had all run wild, for no one has occupied the place since the death of Mr. McNair two years ago. Round this building we found barricades erected, in case of an attack on the place, which was threatened by the heathen natives a few months ago. Mr. Smith, head of the whaling establishment on the other side of the river, was for some time prepared for an invasion; but the Christian party mustering strong at Dillon's Bay, the enemy were afraid, and kept out of the way.

The Christian natives were naturally very much enraged against those who had had anything to do with the murder of Mr. Gordon; and a young chief, with three others, went right across the country, through the land of the heathen, for the purpose of avenging his death; but being unable to get hold of the murderer, they shot several of the tribe to which he belonged, and returned in safety to their own land. It is a native way of doing justice, certainly; but one cannot help admiring the courage of the young fellows, as well as the spirit which prompted them to do this.

In the afternoon several of us went for a stroll along the banks of the river. We passed the graves of Mr. and Mrs. Gordon and Mr. McNair, which were marked by simple mounds of stone plastered over with white coral lime. They are fenced in with reed fences, are situated under some lofty palms, and altogether have a peaceful and pleasing appearance.

A mile or so up the river we came to a series of short falls or rapids, to the foot of which the salt water comes at high tide. The river is navigable for boats up this length, and here vessels send for water, filling the casks readily from the running stream. We crossed at this place upon stones, and came down the other side, enjoying the pretty scenery that this valley affords.

Next morning we were off again, and on Tuesday cast anchor in Pango Bay, island of Efaté, eighty miles north-west of Eramanga.

Less is known of Efaté and its people than of any of the islands to the south of it. In size it is about the same as Eramanga and Tana. In appearance it will hold its own with any of them. It has drawn high praise from many travellers: One says of it—"The rainbow tints caused by the setting sun gave a peculiar beauty to the landscape, and many of the officers considered that none of the islands we had yet visited offered so beautiful a scene as that which lay before us." Another—no less than Captain Cook, its discoverer, says— "The surface whereof appeared very delightful, being agreeably diversified with woods and lawns." Efaté is no doubt a beautiful island, and its beauty is different from that of the islands we had met with before. There is more flat country on it than on some of the others, and the mountains do not, as in Aneityum and Tana, rise up from the sea in one continuous curve, but appear in lofty ranges in the centre of the island; while between them and the sea are undulations, covered with luxuriant tropical vegetation.

Efaté is rich in harbours and bays—more so than any other island of the group. There is Pango Bay, the one we anchored in, having a secure inner harbour at the head of it; Havannah Harbour, a fine sheet of water completely land-locked, which lies twenty miles round the coast; then, four or five miles in the other direction, is a lagoon which runs a long way into the land and opens it up for boat communication; while on the north, also, there is both good anchorage and shelter for vessels.

The vessel took up a position at the head of the bay just off the little island of Fili, which protects the inner harbour of that name. Shortly after the anchor was down, a flotilla of canoes put off from the islet, and in ten minutes we were surrounded by an armada, manned by crews of large and loquacious females. They had not the slightest reverence for the character of the vessel, but banged its venerable sides with their canoes, so as almost to cause the old "Dayspring" to reel with astonishment and offended dignity. They had not the slightest respect for our nerves, but shrieked and yelled at the top of their voices, as they scrambled about and tried to get into good places round the vessel. They were not at all bashful, these Fili women, but quite the reverse, and were altogether a most decided contrast to the downcast dejected-looking creatures I had seen at the southern islands. Some of them were of an immense size, and all were bright and active. Many had rather good features, and I saw one girl in a canoe by herself that was really pretty.

They had come to barter, bringing shells principally, and wanting in return a great variety of articles. I opened business with the dusky charmer in the small canoe, and produced several objects which ought to have taken her savage fancy; but no, she would only shake her head and shriek "shooshah," at the top of her voice. Though puzzled, I still continued my endeavours to tempt her with various objects, but without success; and I was just about to give it up as a bad job, when, holding up by chance a jews-harp, the problem was solved. The mysterious "shooshah" was nothing but the well-known jews-harp. She immediately grabbed the Israelitish instrument with a smile of satisfaction, bundled the shells over to me, and paddled off in triumph. Some women wanted beads, and only one kind of beads would their majesties deign to look at; for these dames have fashions as well as any others: the small blue beads "were in" at the time of our visit, and there was a great run on them. Others again wanted knives; while some, I am very much afraid, went off with sundry figs of black tobacco about their persons, which we will say were for their brothers.

This little island of Fili, and another called Melé, about three miles from it, are inhabited by two very powerful tribes. Fili, the larger of the two, is not over a few acres in size, and both of them are used by the natives merely as places of residence, their plantations all being on the main island.

It is a curious fact, that although these two islets are within a hundred yards of the main island of Efaté, and the natives of them must come into frequent contact with the Efatése, that they are inhabited by quite a different people. They speak a totally different language from that of the Efatése—nearly pure Malay; and in form they resemble the Eastern Polynesians more than any of the New Hebrideans. There seems little doubt but that these people have come in canoes, probably at no very distant date, from some of the eastern islands, have settled on these islets, and that since there has been no intermarriage between them and their neighbours on Efaté.

I went on a solitary exploring expedition to the island of Fili, going ashore in a canoe which two men had brought off, and engaging these men as guides. Villages are thickly scattered over the place, and appeared very clean and neat. I sketched one or two of the huts from the inside of the fence which surrounded them, and was rather amused at the crowd of women and children that gathered round me, and watched the mysterious doings of the stranger with open mouths. When it was finished however, I was flattered by the shout of recognition which they raised, as they pointed to the drawing and then to the huts, showing that they understood what it was meant for. As may be seen in the sketch given below, the huts are somewhat different from those of the Aneityumese, in that the entrance is by a long hole at the side instead of at the end. They are larger, too, than those of the latter people, and altogether have a better appearance.

Huts on Fili Island.

As I wandered on again, accompanied by the two natives, I was struck with the appearance of groups of hollowed-out trunks of trees or posts, fixed in the ground in a circle, a a space being cleared all round them. They had something druidical in their appearance, and quite mystified me. So I pointed inquiringly towards them, and in reply my guides stepped forward and commenced beating them with their fists, and so producing a loudy melancholy sound which varied according to the diameter of the post operated on. I noticed also that upon the largest one of the circle some rude kind of figure was generally traced, the nature of which I could not make out.

These drums, I afterwards found out, were used for the purpose of assembling the natives for feasts or public meetings, and also did duty as a band at the native dances, the open square around them being the ball-room.

A sketch of these drums will be found at the head of the following letter.

We had a *contretemps* while returning to the vessel in the canoe, which might have been more serious than it actually was. The wind had risen somewhat since we had gone ashore, and soon after putting off I saw that the canoe was overweighted. The water began quietly to ripple over the sides, and the further we got out the worse it was, for the wind was off shore; so I set one of the natives to bale, while I took his paddle. But it was of no use, for faster and faster the water came over; so the man at the pumps struck work in disgust, and he and I jumped overboard just as the vessel was preparing to go down. Fortunately for us, one of the armada was returning from the vessel, and the lady canoists seeing the mishap, paddled vigorously to the rescue. They picked us up, and, accompanied by the canoe which the other native had managed to empty, we reached the vessel; whereupon I rewarded my boatmen, and also my gallant rescuers, with some of that pernicious article generally called trade tobacco.

The other island of Melé I also visited, going with the captain, who went down in the ship's boat for yams. It is smaller than Fili, and more populous, so that it is covered with huts, which form quite a town.

I saw more of the men here than on Fili, for it was later in the day and they were returning from their plantations. They are fine strong men, but have the name of being great rascals. A good many both of the Fili and Melé men have been away in Fiji or Queensland, and they are none the better for that.

We managed to get a good supply of yams at Melé, and very fine ones too, giving in exchange knives, calico, tobacco, &c., and returned to the vessel with our load.

After visiting the mission stations lately occupied by Messrs. Cosh and Morrison—the first being on a point which forms one side of Pango Bay, and the latter at Erakor, about three miles round the coast—the vessel weighed anchor and sailed for Havannah Harbour.

Native Drums, on Fili Island, Efate.

## LETTER V.

HAVANNAH HARBOUR — TRADING ESTABLISHMENTS — VESSEL GRAZES A REEF — NGUNA — TWO HILLS — ARRIVE AT SANTO.

*Anelcauhat, Aneityum,*
*June*, 1872.

HAVANNAH Harbour is the principal port of Efaté, indeed I may say of the New Hebrides. It is named after the vessel of Captain Erskine, who visited it in the year 1843. It is a long tortuous sheet of water, the distance from the entrance to the head being about seven miles. On one side is the main island of Efaté; on the other two small islands, named Deception and Protection islands which completely enclose it, with the exception of three channels—one a boat passage, and the other two large enough for vessels of any size. The greatest disadvantage in connection with this harbour is its depth; for no anchorage can be found anywhere except quite close to the shores, and the only good spot is at the head of the bay, where a cable's length off from the beach there is fifteen or sixteen fathoms of water.

As this harbour is not more than twenty miles from Pango Bay, the anchor did not hang long after being lifted in the latter before it was down in the former.

As we entered the harbour there was quite a fleet of canoes under sail, crossing from Protection Island to the main island; they looked very pretty, and caused some astonishment to the passengers in the " Dayspring," as no such sight had been seen during any part of the voyage previously. Here, as on Fili and Melé, many of the natives live on the islets, in preference to the main land, considering them to be more healthy: but as they have their plantations on the latter, constant communication is kept up between the two sides of the harbour; and further, as these natives appreciate anything which will save them labour, they have got calico from the traders and made it into sails. Hence the fleet which greeted our eyes.

There are several traders' establishments at this place; the principal one is just opposite the anchorage, and is under the management of Mr. S. Hebblewhite. On going ashore, Mr. H. kindly took me over the premises, which are extensive and bear an appearance of prosperity. The principal buildings are the store, dwelling-house, ginning and engine-house, store for cobra, &c., overseers' and natives' quarters; while a large building is in the course of erection, which is to be used as a machine-house for the manufacture of coir matting, brushes, &c. from the cocoanut fibre.

Then there is a plantation of twenty acres of Sea Island cotton, which seems thriving well, and a large piece of ground is being prepared for planting next season. The manager is speaking of trying coffee also, of the success of which he has little doubt.

The business done by this establishment—without doubt the most important in the group—consists of importing and selling goods of every description, including grog, to vessels and traders, growing cotton, and also buying it from other growers; ginning and exporting it to Sydney; making and buying cobra and arrowroot, and also dealing occasionally in beche de mer and candlenut berries. Of all these industries carried on in the New Hebrides, I shall speak in another letter.

For the purpose of carrying on this business, there is the manager, two overseers, engineer, and twenty or thirty natives, as well as the "Defiance,"—a schooner of 200 tons, which runs between Sydney and Efaté,— and a ketch for inter-island work.

We only stayed a day in this harbour; sufficiently long, however, for the missionaries to decide that it afforded a good opening for a mission station, and to fix upon a suitable spot whereon to place it.

Next we sailed to Nguna, a small island with rather an unpronounceable name, only ten miles to the north of Efaté. While going there we had rather a narrow escape from being lodged on the top of a reef. Not long after we left the harbour it began to get dark, and the captain resolved that instead of knocking about off Nguna all night, he would come to anchor somewhere, so ran for a sandy beach in the lee of Deception Island. That island is well named; for we ran on until the vessel was almost on shore before the man with the lead could find any bottom. Suddenly he shouted 'fourteen fathoms,' then next heave 'four fathoms,' next came shrilly the cry, 'two-and-a-half fathoms.' We began to get uncomfortable, as the vessel draws two fathoms. The sails having been backed, however, she began to move slowly astern, and we thought that we were all right, when a quiver like an earthquake shock ran through the vesssl, as her keel grazed some rock—only grazed, fortunately, so that she swung off without damage; and drifting out into ten fathoms water, the anchor was let go, and we lay comfortably all night.

Next day we reached Nguna, and anchored opposite the mission house of Mr. Milne. This island is about six miles long and three or four broad, and is mountainous, the principal hill being evidently an extinct volcano. It is prettily wooded in the valleys, and up the sides of the hills, while the summits are mostly bare. The population is estimated at about 800, and they are much like the Efatese in appearance and manners, and speak a dialect of the same language.

The Rev. P. Milne and his wife have been on the island for three years, and appear to have gained the respect and goodwill of the natives. He has built a neat little house a short way up from the beach, which occupies a pleasant and, I believe, a healthy situation.

As usual, a number of natives met us on our landing, amongst whom was an albino woman. She was a very repulsive-looking object, being of a spotted dirty-white colour. The brown skins of the other natives had a far more pleasing appearance.

After a few hours at Nguna, we set sail again, for Metas or Two Hills, fourteen miles north of Nguna, for the purpose of landing supplies for a native teacher stationed upon that island. We quickly ran down to it, and hove-to while a boat went ashore. As its name implies, this island is composed of two hills, and these are connected by a narrow flat neck of land, over which the sea breaks during a storm. The principal hill is pyramidal in form, and is about 1500 feet high; it mounts up very abruptly from the sea, and has a very fine appearance. From the vessel we could observe signs of cultivation on its steep sides, in the shape of green terraces. The natives of this island must have feet like flies or spiders, for it seems to be impossible for ordinarily-constructed men to travel about on an island that lies at an angle of about 45° off the horizontal. There are ninety of these crawlers, and they resemble the Efatese and Ngunese in customs and language.

About a mile from this island is a curious rock, rising perpendicularly from the sea to a height of 400 feet. It is very aptly named Monument Island, and is densely populated by numerous tribes of feathered bipeds.

Leaving Two Hills, we spread our sails to the trade winds, and steered for Santo, the most northerly and the largest island of the group. As we sailed on we found ourselves surrounded with islands of every shape and size, eleven being visible at one time. The whole scene suggested to me the idea of a sunken continent, now wholly submerged, save the lofty tops of mountain ranges.

We sighted Api in the distance, an island upon which Dr. Murray, of "Carl" brig notoriety, resided for some time. It seemed well wooded, and conical hills of some height were visible. We next passed the great island of Malicolo, said to be sixty miles long, and inhabited by fierce and treacherous people. We could observe fine ranges of mountains running principally north and south, and covered thickly with timber.

Little is known of this island or of its inhabitants. Cook visited it, when he came first to the New Hebrides, and he discovered a harbour on its eastern side—Port Sandwich, said to be the finest harbour in the group.

Santo was descried about three o'clock in the afternoon of the day after leaving Two Hills, and entering Lisburn Bay by moonlight, we anchored at eight o'clock, opposite the mission station of Mr. Goodwill.

## LETTER VI.

HISTORY OF THE DISCOVERY OF SANTO—ITS APPEARANCE—BARTERING WITH THE NATIVES—THE QUEEN'S BIRTHDAY—MAU AND ITS PEOPLE—VISIT ASHORE—RETURN TO ANEITYUM.

*Anelcauhat, Aneityum,*
*June,* 1872.

IT is no doubt true of the South-Sea Islanders and the South-Sea Islands, that they have no history; but I must claim for the island of Santo the place of an exception to this rule, for it has a history—a brief one, 'tis true, but still an interesting one; and I am sure that I cannot do better now than briefly run over the incidents which led to its discovery nearly three hundred years ago.

Early in the seventeenth century a Spaniard, Pedro Quiros by name, coming to the conclusion, after much thought and investigation, that there lay in the South Pacific a great continent still unknown, petitioned the Spanish government most assiduously to fit out for him an expedition, that he might go and settle this question. After considerable delay his request was granted, and he was despatched, in December 1605, with three vessels, six priests, and a large complement of men, on a voyage of discovery. In April 1606, after touching at several islands before discovered, he sighted land in a position where nothing of the kind had been known to exist, and from its apparent size and beauty, was led to rejoice in the idea that the great southern continent lay before him. He named it Tierra Austral del Espiritu Santo, entered a large bay upon the north of it, and there anchored. For thirty-six days he lay in that bay, sending boats ashore and exploring the neighbouring country. The more he saw of the place, the more he fell in love with it; his excited imagination enhanced the great natural beauties of the land to such an extent, that he looked upon it as a second paradise—a land which far exceeded even what his most extravagant expectations pictured the southern continent to be.

A river at the head of the bay he called the Jordan, and upon its banks he founded a city named the New Jerusalem. Then, in the words of Torquemada, the historian, "they set sail, desirous of discovering lands to windward, to found the other cities in honour of his majesty, as had been done in this bay, where they founded one named the New Jerusalem, to which were named alcaldes, regidores, royal officers and other ministers of justice."

However, when they got out of the bay they met strong winds, the S.E. trades, I presume; at all events, winds which prevented their sailing southward: so, after being carried far to leeward, they gave up in despair all attempts to see more of this wonderful land, and made for Spain. On arriving there, Quiros gave most glowing accounts of his new continent. He says, "Its length is as much as that of all Europe, Asia Minor, and to the Caspian Sea and Persia, with all the islands of the Mediterranean and ocean which are within its limits embraced, including England and Ireland.—The people of these countries are many, their colours white, negroes, mulattoes, Indians, and mixed of one and the other.—They use earthen pots, have looms and other nets, they work stones, marble, flutes, drums, and spoons of wood varnished.—The islanders have their embarkations well wrought, and sufficient to navigate from one country to another.—The flesh are many hogs, tame like ours; and fowls, capons, country partridges, geese, turtle, ringdoves, and goats.—The riches are silver and pearls, which I saw, and gold, which the other captain saw."

He speaks further of marble quarries, of lovely scenery, of splendid groves, filled with "thousands of different birds, some to appearance nightingales, blackbirds, larks, and goldfinches;" and winds up thus: "It appears that all together will make the country so rich that it will be alone able to support itself, and also America, and will aggrandise and enrich Spain in such a manner as I will show, if I am assisted by others in the execution."

This is what the Americans would call loud writing or tall talk. Those old navigators disdained to stick at plain prosaic facts when speaking of anything that they had done, or any place that they had discovered; and in this case Quiros has decidedly let his imagination have free play. To us who know the size of the island, and also to a certain extent its capabilities, there is something extremely ludicrous in the deliberate way in which Quiros, who had only seen one side of it, asserts that it is as large as Europe, Asia Minor, the Mediterranean and all the islands thereabouts put together, and that it can not only support itself, but also America, besides enriching Spain.

Poor old Quiros—he evidently wished to be a second Hernando Cortez, and no doubt he pictured to himself his going out to the newly-discovered continent at the head of a numerous company—his subjugating the many peoples—his getting possession of all their riches—his living in the New Jerusalem on the banks of the Jordan, in palaces built from the marble quarries—and his ruling over that country, living on its many productions, and enjoying its numerous pleasures. But that was not to be. He never again saw Santo: he could not persuade the king of Spain to send him out again as he desired, and he died at last in obscurity, without the great wish of his heart being accomplished.

There is, no doubt, some truth at the bottom of this rhodomontade of Quiros, when he speaks of the things that he actually saw; for most of his wild writing is about those things which he didn't see.

Very likely at the time of his visit the people were more mixed than they are now, and also their canoes and arts in a better condition. This would not only be possible, but reasonable; for there is little doubt but that the natives of Polynesia have been and are sinking in the scale of civilization. Also the live animals, such as pigs, fowls, goats, of which he speaks, very likely were on the island; for the two former still exist, and although I have never heard of goats being originally on any of the New Hebrides, still this may have been the case on Santo. The gold and silver I am afraid he has coined from his own imagination, or, in the case of the former, has been misled by the appearance of mica, a mineral which does, I believe, exist on Santo. As for the singing-birds, I fancy they are mythical altogether; for the New Hebrides are lamentably deficient in this respect.

Bougainville, who arrived at the New Hebrides in 1768, dispelled the idea of Santo being a continent; and Cook sailed completely round it, went into the bay in which Quiros had anchored, and there found a stream which he supposed to be the Jordan of Quiros; but he found no traces of the New Jerusalem, which, with its alcaldes, regidores, &c., evidently never got further than the fertile brain of its projector.

Leaving romance, and coming to fact, we find that Santo is about eighty miles long by forty miles broad, and is without doubt a fine island. What of it could be seen from the vessel was well calculated to excite anyone's imagination, and inclined one to look rather leniently even upon the exaggerated panegyrics of Quiros. The mountain ranges are magnificent; some of them cannot be far short of 5000 feet high. This island possesses the beauties of the other islands, only upon a larger scale. It is exceedingly fertile, so much so that not a bare spot could be seen anywhere, the very precipices being covered with masses of thick green creepers, and everywhere the trees and shrubs appeared packed so closely together as to make one wonder how they could find room to grow.

No accurate estimate can be arrived at as to the population, but it is known to be thickly inhabited. The natives are superior in some respects to their southern neighbours, for they still have the art of making a rude kind of pottery, which Quiros speaks of; their native weapons, too, are of a superior kind, and their chiefs have considerable power. Some of their spears are very curiously made, the shaft being of bamboo or some hardwood, and the points of human bone, neatly adjusted at the end. On the other islands, the natives make use of a man's flesh as food; but here they use up his bones as well, for pointing their spears and arrows. Not because they consider that there is any peculiar virtue in a spear tipped with human bone, but merely because a man is the largest animal on the island, and so his bones are best suited for their purpose.

A number of them—men, not bones—came off to the vessel, bringing spears, clubs, &c., to barter; and the canoes which they came in were certainly not what I would have called "embarkations well wrought," for they were in no way superior to those of the other islanders, and not quite fit, I imagine, to "navigate from one country to another," unless the countries were remarkably close to each other.

The natives who came off were fat friendly fellows, medium

height, naked, and very dark-skinned. They clambered on to the deck, and offered their native commodities for sale. Bartering with natives is an art which requires some practice, before one can be proficient enough to avoid being taken in. They have all sorts of dodges by which to palm off on the unwary worthless articles. They will bring up shells, shining and beautiful and wet, barter them and go off, and shortly the purchaser finds that the shells are miserable weatherbeaten things, that the savage has picked off the beach and dipped in the water, so as to make them appear glossy and fresh.

The great matter in trading of this kind is to offer the natives what they are most particularly in want of at the time. A man may be in want of fish-hooks, and then one may get from him, for a pennyworth of hooks, what a shilling's-worth of calico wouldn't purchase. The exchangeable value, not the intrinsic value of an article, is the thing to be ascertained in this case. On different islands, too, a different class of articles is required. On Tana, calico is worth next to nothing; but it is good trade on Aneityum, Efaté, Aniwa, &c. Tobacco is good trade on most islands; but it is useless on Ambrim, for there they hav'nt learnt to use it. Generally those articles are best which can be made up into small parcels, such as beads, fish-hooks, and tobacco; for it is very often difficult to get anything from them of the value of a good tomahawk. I had with me calico, turkey red, hatchets, fish-hooks and lines, knives, and also some tobacco for private consumption; but I found that all over the group the tobacco was the most useful as well as the cheapest article of barter. Gradually I had been accumulating a collection of varieties, and by this time it was mounting up to a respectable size. It consisted mainly of native weapons, bags, baskets, and shells.

The vessel stayed in Lisburne Bay for two days, during which time the stores of Mr. Goodwill were landed. This missionary, and his wife and family, have suffered severely from fever and ague, which prevails much on this quarter of the island; and as they have none of those comforts that we in a civilized community enjoy—such as medical attendance, servants' assistance, and friends' society, they are much to be sympathised with.

Before the vessel left, I took a day in the woods, when I added twenty botanical specimens to my collection, and would probably have got many more, only the damp moist heat was so overpowering that I was obliged to return before I otherwise would have done.

Sailing from Santo we commenced the return voyage. Now we began to feel the force of the trade wind, and some of the disadvantages of a wind blowing steadily from one direction. It was very pleasant as long as it went with us, going north, and it would have been very pleasant to have had it turn round again and blow us back; but as it did not seem inclined to do that, we made up our minds to some days of weary beating and tossing about; and it was well we did, for we got it. We took four days to reach Nguna again. Touching at that island, we took Mr. Milne on board, and sailed for Mau, a small island twelve miles to the eastward. It was the 24th of May, and so the mate and I resolved that her gracious Majesty should not be forgotten, even amongst the cannibal islands. Rummaging out our revolvers and supplying ourselves with a large quantity of ammunition, we adjourned to the forecastle, and there fired a salute in honour of the day, with such vigour that the rest of the party rushed up in alarm, imagining that we were attacked by savages. Then in the evening the National Anthem was performed with great good will by hearty voices, accompanied and assisted by a shaky accordion. Thus we showed our loyalty, and, as we did our best under the circumstances, we separated with the conviction that no man could do more.

On reaching Mau, we had some difficulty in getting an anchorage, as there are plenty of reefs about, and the charts give no information regarding this island. After dodging about a little, the anchor was at last let go in twenty fathoms water on a rocky bottom.

Mau is simply a range of mountains about eight miles long, rising from the plain of the ocean. There are several hundred inhabitants on it, who speak a dialect of the Efatese language. They are a fierce and treacherous people. Not long ago, a party of them were in a vessel as crew, and rising together they murdered the white crew, obliged the mate to navigate the vessel to Mau, and there murdered him also, and broke up the vessel.

A party of us went ashore and visited a village of these lively cannibals, to confer with a friendly chief about the sale of some land for mission purposes, which piece of business was eventually performed to the satisfaction of both parties. I noticed that many of them looked at us very suspiciously, and one of them, —a chief, a great strong fellow, sat apart with his musket, looking as surly as a bear, and would have nothing to say to us. He would probably have been much delighted to have got the opportunity of making "long pig" of a few of the fattest of the party; but the opportunity did not occur, for everything went on smoothly. The boat, after going off to the vessel, returned again and brought barter for yams. It was very exciting work, for, as soon as the boat touched the shore, crowds of men and women came round it with their vegetables, and yelled and splashed about till they got what they wanted. The crowd gradually increased, and far along the beach strings of men and women could be seen coming with yams enough to load the vessel; but having got half-a-boat-load, and having had some calico stolen in the scrimmage, the second mate, who was in charge, thought it high time to be off. So away we went, leaving scores of disap-

Mau and Pele
From Nguna

pointed and angry natives standing on the beach with their unsold yams.

When we reached the vessel, she was again got under weigh and proceeded southward. Calling at all the mission stations, and taking on board the missionaries for the annual conference to be held on Aneityum, she reached that island on Sunday, the 2nd of June, having accomplished the voyage round the group in a little under four weeks.

## LETTER VII.

THE MISSION CONFERENCE—SETTLEMENT OF MR. ROBERTSON AT DILLON'S BAY, ERAMANGA—SETTLEMENT OF MR. M<sup>C</sup>DONALD AT HAVANNAH HARBOUR, EFATE—VISIT TO AMBRIM.

*Aniwa,*
*August, 1872.*

SOON after the vessel arrived in Anelcauhat Harbour, the missionaries held their annual conference, there being present Dr. Geddie, Messrs. Inglis, Paton, Neilson, Watt, Milne, Murray, McDonald, McKenzie, and Robertson. Two—viz., Messrs. Copeland and Goodwill—were absent. The sitting lasted for about a week, during which time the reverend gentlemen seemed to be very busily employed.

The questions, as to where the new missionaries should be settled, and as to a change of head quarters for the "Dayspring," were perhaps the most important matters discussed. Finally it was decided that Sydney should be the vessel's port henceforward, instead of Melbourne, while the new missionaries were allocated thus :—

        Mr. Murray,    Anelcauhat, Aneityum.
        Mr. McDonald, Havannah Harbour, Efaté.
        Mr. McKenzie, Erakor and Pango, Efaté.
        Mr. Robertson, Dillon's Bay, Eramanga.

Mr. McDonald was the only one sent to open a new station, all the others going to those which had been occupied before.

Dr. Geddie was unable to attend the closing meetings of the session, through a sudden and very severe stroke of paralysis, which quite disabled him. He recovered a little before the vessel left on her second tour, but still was very much shaken and weak.

During this session, too, a communion service was held in the native church, which was attended by about 300 natives. I was much struck with their neat appearance and quiet respectful behaviour during this service; and as I compared them with many of the natives on neighbouring islands, was more than ever convinced that the work which the missionaries are doing is a real and a permanent one. I had now been round the group, and had seen something of missionary life and doings—not, perhaps, of the real hard work of it, but still enough to enable me to entertain very decided opinions upon this subject. What I have just stated is my conviction as regards the work that they are doing; and as to themselves, I am also as strongly convinced that the missionaries make a very great sacrifice when they come to these islands; that the work is to them one of toil and great discomfort, not to speak of danger; that those who speak sneeringly of missionaries and their work, ascribing to them motives of personal gain, are very much in the wrong; and that those persons are influenced, not by a desire to find out and express the truth, but by a bitter prejudice against everything Christian and philanthropic.

This is the result of my experience so far, as regards the missions carried on in the New Hebrides.

Another event occurred whilst the Synod was holding its meetings, and that was the arrival in the harbour of a vessel having mails on board from the colonies. Those who are in the habit of getting daily deliveries of letters and papers can have no idea of the excitement that the arrival of letters causes, after the lapse of three or four months without news of any kind. The most miserable newspaper has an interest hardly credible, and is read eagerly from beginning to end, advertisements and all; and if this be the case with the papers, I need hardly say how letters are received and welcomed. It is only by being deprived of certain things for a time that one can properly appreciate them; and on going to places where mails are not delivered oftener than once in four months, one will have a very much greater idea of the benefits which the postal arrangements confer than one ever had before.

After the Synodical meetings were concluded, the "Dayspring" started on a second trip round the group, the work portioned out for her being the return of the missionaries to their islands, the settlement of Messrs. Robertson and McDonald, visits to Ambrim, Santo, and Maré in the Loyalty group, and finally, visits to each mission station, for mails before taking her departure to Melbourne.

As this voyage was a good deal the same as the last, I will merely notice the exceptional events that occurred in it, which were the settlement of the new missionaries and the visits to Ambrim and Maré.

On Tuesday, the 25th June, we reached Dillon's Bay, and lay there four days, during which time the old mission house was made as comfortable as circumstances would permit, and the Robertsons, with their stores and furniture, landed.

We had an uncomfortable time of it, on board, while lying here; for soon after we anchored, the wind veered round to the west, and a nasty sea came rolling into the bay, so that we lay bobbing up and down on the waves, with the stern of the vessel a hundred yards or so from the shore, upon which the waves burst with an angry hiss. We

had also the consolation of knowing that if the vessel did begin to drag her anchors, she would be almost certain to go ashore, as there was no room to get under weigh.

Smith, the whaler, came into the bay while we were there, in a small steamer which he had built on Eramanga. He was well satisfied with her performance, asserting that she could steam eight knots per hour, and he expected to make her useful in the next whaling season for towing out the boats and towing in the whales.

A ketch appeared also, and a boat from her went ashore, in which was a titled gentleman, well known in these seas,—Ross Lewin. He has a cotton plantation on Tana of a considerable extent, and has been down amongst these islands for a very long time now. He does not bear a particularly good character, his title consisting of the word "notorious" prefixed to his name. To appearance he is a short, elderly, strongly-built, quiet-looking man, who has plenty to say and is not at all troubled with bashfulness.

After getting the Robertsons installed, the vessel made sail for Efaté, called at Pango Bay, and then went ashore at Havannah Harbour—literally went ashore, for she lay all night with her bow on the beach half way up the harbour. It happened thus. While going up the harbour, the captain tried to get an anchorage near the spot destined for the mission station, which is about half way up from the entrance, and tacking in, the vessel ran so close that there was not time to go about or wear, so she consequently ran aground. Early next morning, with the high tide, she was got off and went up to her usual anchorage, none the worse for her mishap.

We stayed in the harbour a fortnight, while Mr. McDonald's house was being erected and his goods landed. First the land was bought from the chief; then a party went from the vessel, with the carpenter at their head, and the ground was cleared of the heavy timber and scrub with which it was covered. The frame and boards were brought from Aneityum, and quickly were rattled up, no one wielding the hammer and axe to more purpose than Mr. McDonald himself. Two weeks after we had arrived in the harbour, Mr. and Mrs. McDonald took possession of their house. It consisted of two rooms, with a verandah at front and back, and two native houses behind—one for a kitchen, the other for a store. The house has a nice situation on a point, and commands a view both up and down the harbour, and out to sea through the centre channel. Whether it will prove a healthy locality or not remains to be seen.

Going from Havannah Harbour, we called at Nguna and Two Hills, reaching the island of Ambrim on the 18th of July. Our object in calling at this island was to land upon it six Ambrim natives who had been working on Tana for a trader, and who had been left there by him unpaid and unprovided for. They had been cared for by Mr. Watt, the missionary, for some time, and were now being returned to their own island by the mission vessel.

Ambrim is one of the richest and most beautiful islands in the South Pacific. One gentleman, Mr. Murray, speaking of it, says that he has "seen many beautiful islands, both in Eastern and Western Polynesia, but one more lovely than the island just named he never beheld."

I had looked forward to seeing the gem of the New Hebrides, as it is sometimes called; but, unfortunately, the gem would not condescend to show itself. In the middle of the island there is a lofty hill, over 3000 feet high; and this hill is a volcano, in full activity, pouring forth a continuous stream of smoke and darkening the air all around. It was engaged in this pursuit when we arrived off the shores of the island, so that we found the latter enveloped in a thick smoky curtain, and almost completely screened from public view. It was extremely inconsiderate in it to do this; but as such was the case, we had only to take it for granted that much fine scenery lay behind the curtain, and to make out as best we could some parts not quite hidden.

While speaking of volcanoes, I might mention the fact of our sighting another active one, while on our way to Ambrim, and not more than forty or fifty miles from it. It is on a small island called Lopevi, said to be 5000 feet high. We passed a long way off, but still we could distinctly observe the smoky appearance to leeward of the island. It is like a sugar-loaf rising out of the sea, and at its summit, often above the clouds, it puffs out a stream of black smoke. It must greatly resemble, I fancy, Volcano Island in the Santo Cruz group, to the north of the New Hebrides, which is thus described by a visitor:—
"A magnificent cone in full eruption, rising almost perpendicularly out of the sea, at the height of between 2000 and 3000 feet.—It was a glorious sight to see the great stones leaping and bounding down the side of the cone, clearing 300 or 400 feet at a jump, and springing up many yards into the air, finally plunging into the sea with a roar, and the splash of the foam and the hiss of the sea combined." Of course we were not near enough to Lopevi to see anything of this kind; but it appeared quite steep enough to cause stones to roll from the top to the bottom of it. It would be rather a fine sight if they do so, to watch the great stones roll down 5000 feet and then plunge into the sea. I shouldn't think there were any inhabitants on Lopevi.

This volcano, with the one on Ambrim and the one on Tana, comprises all the active volcanoes on the group. But to return to Ambrim.

Mr. Watt and I went ashore in the boat. Close to the beach there was a flat reef, through which there appeared no opening; so we had just to bump over it as best we might, assisted by the waves, which were large enough to wash us over, but not so large as to render such a feat dangerous. The Ambrim people have had but little communication as yet with whites; so when we landed they gathered round us with much curiosity, feeling our arms and shouting with surprise. When they discovered that their friends had at last returned, their joy knew no bounds, especially as said friends had some pigs and other trade with them—none of which, however, I may remark, had they got from the trader for whom they had worked. Before we had been long on shore, one of those who had been on Tana came up to Mr. Watt, and told him, in a low voice, to get into the boat and go off as quickly as possible. He gave no reason, but appeared very much in earnest. We did so, and, bumping over the reef again, rejoined the vessel. One of the Ambrim men had been killed on Tana, and probably his friends had come up and were inclined to make a row; so the friendly man had been afraid of our getting into trouble, and thought it best to advise us to retreat; and as it takes very little to excite these savages, and as they are never very particular whom they may kill by way of revenge, perhaps it was as well for us that we did leave thus abruptly.

The Ambrim natives appeared to me a well-grown, healthy people, and dark-skinned. They wear their hair cut short, and have a curious custom of powdering it white, and I cannot say that it has an unpleasant appearance.

Leaving Ambrim, we sailed for Santo, and thence to the island of Maré. As this island belongs to a different group, and is under a different mission, I will give some little information about it and the other two islands which comprise the group, in another letter.

## LETTER VIII.

THE LOYALTY ISLANDS—THEIR NATURE, CHARACTERISTICS, AND PEOPLE—MARE—THE MISSION STATION OF MR. JONES—A RIDE ACROSS THE ISLAND—A FEW REMARKS ABOUT THE NATIVES AND THEIR HOUSES—THE VESSEL SAILS AGAIN FOR THE NEW HEBRIDES.

*Aniwa,*
*August,* 1872.

THE Loyalty Islands lie directly between the New Hebrides and New Caledonia, being within ninety or a hundred miles of the former and sixty miles of the latter. The group is composed of the three principal islands, named Maré, Lifou, and Uea, and a few smaller ones, scattered round them. Lifou, the central island, is said to be ninety miles in circumference, Maré seventy miles, and Uea fifty.

They are all upheaved coral islands, similar in formation to Aniwa in the New Hebrides. Nowhere does any part of them rise more than 300 feet above the level of the sea. The two southern islands, Maré and Lifou, have no harbours; vessels being obliged to anchor in open bays, which they can do only when the wind is blowing off shore. Uea, the northernmost island possesses good shelter for vessels in an extensive lagoon which is well protected by a surrounding reef.

As Maré was the only island which I visited, I shall speak of it alone, although, from the great similarity which exists between the islands of this group, nearly all that is said of one will apply equally well to the other.

On approaching this island I was struck with the curious resemblance which the outlines of the land exhibit to long ranges of fortifications, and also with the peculiar appearance which the pines give to the landscape, as they stand clustered in sombre groups, like giant sentinels guarding the coral forts. These pines are not found on the New Hebrides, being confined to the Loyalty Islands and New Caledonia. They bear, however, a considerable resemblance to the Norfolk Island pine. Some of the islets near Maré are thickly covered with them, and from a distance their appearance is highly suggestive of marine hedgehogs with bristles erect.

The islands of this group were at one time thickly populated, but the natives are now greatly diminished in numbers. They are a strongly-made people, active but not good-looking, the women especially being the reverse of beautiful. Thirty years ago they were amongst the worst of heathen tribes; now they are the most advanced of any natives in Western Polynesia. This remark applies especially to the inhabitants of Maré.

For the change that has taken place, there must be a cause. Shall we ascribe it, as some may be disposed to do, to their contact with the traders and ship captains? or with others, shall we put it down to the influence of missionary operations?

Here is a specimen of what happens too frequently in the attempt to establish a trade with these natives.

A boat's crew goes ashore from a vessel, for yams: a quarrel arises,—all the whites are killed and eaten. Another ship arrives off the island, and the boat's crew from this vessel meet the same fate. In another case, a chief goes off to a vessel to trade, quarrels with the captain, is rope's-ended; and in return, the whole ship's company are killed and the vessel burnt. Three natives swim off to a sandalwood vessel, to trade, are murdered on the deck; and a cutter arriving off the island not long after, is taken by the natives, and all hands killed by way of revenge.

I do not wish to justify the conduct of the natives, but if this is the manner in which intercourse has been carried on between them and the traders, I would ask if the natives were at all likely to be improved or civilized by it.

Of the other influence which has been at work, the following is a brief account.

Many years ago, teachers—natives of Eastern Polynesia—landed on Maré, and worked quietly but assiduously amongst its inhabitants. About seven years after their landing, many of the natives began to abandon their heathen practices and make endeavours to follow the instructions of these teachers. A missionary of the Church of England lands on the island and found that there was already a congregation of 1000 natives, anxious for further instruction. After a short but not a fruitless residence, this missionary died, and his place was supplied by two sent by the London Missionary Society; and from that time the natives have made both steady and rapid progress, until, as I said before, they are now entitled to be ranked as the foremost tribes of Western Polynesia.

On Lifou, teachers were landed at a later date, and they were longer in making any impression on the natives, who are now, consequently, behind Maré in Christian civilization; while the people of Uea are still further back. There are now two missionaries on Maré, one on Lifou, and one on Uea—all supported by the London Missionary Society.

The Marémen have a pretty good idea of the value of money, and in many cases prefer it to any other article of exchange. They like to hoard it up, one chief being reputed to have over £100 stowed away. They are beginning to trade on their own account, too, on a more extensive scale than the Western Polynesians usually indulge in, growing cotton and selling it to white traders. They do more steady hard work than their neighbours on the New Hebrides, although, in justice to the latter, it must be said that the climate of the Loyalties is very much superior to that of the New Hebrides. It is both cooler and more healthy, owing to the want of luxuriant vegetation, and so more conducive to hard work. Yams, sugarcane, banana, bread-fruit, and cocoanuts grow on the Loyalties; but as the soil is not rich, they do not attain very great perfection.

We anchored in Jones's Bay, on the north side of Maré, on the 25th of July; and several of us went ashore to visit Mr. Jones, the missionary stationed there.

When speaking of Aniwa, it may be recollected that I mentioned that the island rose up in two stages or steps—first a shore flat rising from the sea, and then, a little way inland, a cliff rising from that. On this island the same thing is observable; there is the ground flat, and the upper flat which extends as a low table-land across the island. The lower flat on Maré, at least on the north side, is open and grassy, here and there dotted with palm-trees and tall handsome pines, and presents quite a relief to the eye, sated with the unbroken luxuriance of the New Hebridean vegetation. Mr. Jones's establishment is on what I have termed the ground-flat, and lies close to the foot of the steep white cliff. It is a busy and prosperous-looking station. Dwellings, and school-houses, and stores, and sheds, are scattered about in great profusion; while natives, pigs, fowls, cattle, horses, and even donkeys, give life to the scene. Donkeys in the South-Seas are rather rarities, I should fancy; but Mr. Jones has two, and very good-looking donkeys they are, appearing quite satisfied with their lot on a mission station in the Loyalties. They will probably have easier times of it than many a poor donkey in the old country.

The great object of attraction in connection with this station is the church, or the cathedral, as it is sometimes called.

Native Church on Maré, Loyalty Islands.

It is composed of stone, plastered both on the inside and outside, the roof being of thatch. It is built in the form of a T, and a square tower rises up at one end, from the top of which a fine view can be obtained.

At the time of our visit the church was not quite completed, the pews, platform, and gallery still remaining unfinished. When finished, it will hold, perhaps, 800 people, and is certainly a credit to the missionary and his people who have designed and built it. It seems, however, almost a mistake to build such elaborate places in these parts. For nine years the natives have had it in hand, and as yet have got no good of it, using in the meantime a miserable little open shed. A less pretentious building would have been finished long ago, and probably the natives would have been just as happy and comfortable in it, sitting on the ground on mats, as they will be in pews of the still-unfinished church.

As the vessel was to call at a mission station on the opposite side of the island, Mr. Jones proposed that I should ride over there and meet her — a proposal which was gladly accepted.

A boy on horseback accompanied me as guide, while another ran alongside to ride my horse back again. We had a most enjoyable excursion—now gliding quietly under the overhanging trees, now bursting into full galop over small open plains, now winding slowly round a difficult point, or rising up to a slight elevation and gazing back over the gently-undulating country, timbered in belts and dotted with tapering pines; while all this time the little foot-boy scudded along like a hare, never lagging behind or seeming a bit the worse. The surface of the island shows that it has been very roughly used. Some great power has been at work below, forcing it up from beneath the sea; and this power has left its marks, in the shape of great rents and deep chasms. These chasms are, in many cases, like wells, narrow and often very deep—most dangerous-looking places; and sometimes, when the pathway ran between two of them, I was not sorry when the sure-footed little horse had passed safely by.

The distance between the two stations is twelve miles, which we performed in about two hours.

Mr. and Mrs. Murray, who occupy the station we arrived at,

intend shortly to leave for Cape York, on the north of Australia, for the purpose of superintending a mission to be established in New Guinea.

The advancing civilization amongst these natives shows itself in the superior style of dwellings which they put up—generally being walled houses, plastered with coral lime, and thatched. The chief's house on this side of the island is quite a palace compared with the usual run of Western Polynesian native abodes. It is a stone house of two stories, with French windows which open out to a verandah and balcony in front. The interior fittings, such as the staircase, are not quite complete, and several of the rooms are still unfurnished. The furniture is of plain deal; and upstairs, or rather, up the ladder, is a great four-posted bed. Whether the chief actually sleeps in this concern or not, I cannot say; but I should imagine that he would find more congenial quarters underneath it than upon it. The old gentleman himself was from home when we called; but his son, an intelligent-looking young fellow, did the honours.

The teachers for whom the vessel had called having been obtained, we went down toward the boat to go off to the vessel. While waiting on the beach until these men could tear themselves away from their friends, I noticed a sight that I had never seen before, though I had heard of it, namely, natives swimming in the surf. They would go away outside of a sunken reef, upon which the waves were rolling and breaking in fine style; and then mounting upon the crest of the advancing wave, would career along on top of it, until hurled over into the boiling water which covered the reef. It looked rather dangerous work, but they seemed to enjoy the exciting sport amazingly, and never to hurt themselves at it. The Marémen are famous swimmers. A story is told of one, that he used to swim out to sea for the purpose of fishing. Lying on his back, he would bait the line, let it down, and when he caught a fish sling it round his neck by a string, returning to the shore when tired. Another man is said to have swum over to a small island four miles from Maré, with a club in his hand. They are fonder of the water than the New Hebrideans, and their canoes are of a superior kind. I saw a very large one lying on the beach. It was a double canoe, having a platform thrown across, and upon it a small house. It was quite a ship compared with the generality of canoes I had hitherto seen.

The teachers at last appeared, and, accompanied by an immense crowd of friends and relatives, made for the boat. No sooner had they entered it than the whole company raised and sustained a howl that almost made my hair stand on end; while a band of men and women—near relatives, I presume—rushed upon the boat, hung on the necks of the departing teachers and their wives, emitting howls, and this with extraordinary effect. At last we got the boat torn from their grasp, and shoved out of their reach; whereupon the weepers retired and dried their eyes, and those in the boat, who had been doing as much as any of them in the business, also dried their faces, and became lively and contented in a wonderfully short time.

Leaving Maré we again made Santo, and landed the teachers there; then called at Nguna, and landed Mr. and Mrs. Milne, who had accompanied the vessel during this trip. Next we called at Havannah Harbour, found the McDonalds well, and took on board their mails. Next at Eramanga; found the Robertsons also well, and took on board their mails. Next called at Aniwa, where the "Dayspring" left me with Mr. and Mrs. Paton, who had kindly invited me to visit them while the mission ship was making her next voyage to Melbourne.

## LETTER IX.

THE NATIVES OF THE NEW HEBRIDES—THEIR PERSONAL APPEARANCE—DIVERSITY OF LANGUAGE—REMARKS AS TO THEIR PROBABLE ORIGIN.

*Aniwa,*
*September, 1872.*

I HAVE said little, as yet, about the inhabitants of the New Hebrides, my remarks hitherto having had reference mainly to the principal events which occurred during the voyages of the "Dayspring," and the nature and scenery of the islands.

Being now settled for the time on Aniwa, after having seen and compared the different islanders, I shall endeavour to give what information I have been able to gather concerning these natives, — information necessarily somewhat superficial in character, but still perhaps useful in showing the light in which these people appear to a casual visitor from the homes of civilization.

The New Hebrideans are classified in two different ways. Along with the natives of New Guinea, and of those groups lying between New Guinea and the New Hebrides, they are termed Papuan negroes; while along with all the South Pacific islanders westward of Fiji (the New Zealanders excepted) they are termed Melanesians. The first is the ethnographic classification; the second is merely an arbitrary one, fixed in order that these natives may be distinguished from the Polynesians, who inhabit the islands eastward of Fiji.

Taking the New Hebrideans as a whole, they are a low and degraded people, inferior to almost every barbaric race that I have heard of, the aborigines of Australia, perhaps, excepted. On account of the limited size of their homes, they cannot, like the latter, be of a nomadic character; indeed, on account of their continual inter-tribal wars, it is frequently the case that a man cannot travel over a mile or two in any direction from his own village.

They are a cultivating people, raising, without very much hard work, sufficient yams, taro, and bananas, to supply themselves with food during that portion of the year when the bread-fruit is not in season. During those months that they have the bread-fruit (which requires no cultivation) they become a lazy people—the warlike amongst them betaking themselves to lazy fighting, and the rest to lazy doing nothing.

They are a mixed people, composed probably of two ingredients—the negro and the Malay; and on different islands these ingredients are mixed in such different proportions as to produce tribes varying exceedingly in form, features, colour, language and customs. The Melé and Fili natives seem to be nearest to the Malay, and the Eramangans to the negro. The nearer the approach to the Malay, the more do they seem to improve in outward appearance and in intelligence; from which it will be inferred that the Melé and Fili natives are the finest in the group, and the Eramangans the poorest, which is my opinion.

While speaking of good looks, it is worthy of notice, that the men on almost all the islands are much superior to the women in this respect. If the fact is plain, the cause is equally so. When you see the different modes of life which they respectively lead, you cease to wonder at the miserable appearance of the women as compared with the men. The latter, naturally the stronger, have little hard work and plenty to eat; while the former, naturally the weaker, have much hard work, comparatively little to eat, and, besides, receive much ill-treatment and and indignity. The result is, as a matter of course, that the men are strong, well formed, and consequential; while the women are bent in form, meagre in person, worn and dejected-looking.

All the men are polygamists, generally having three or four wives apiece; slaves I should rather call them, for they are treated quite as such, having to do all manner of work for their lord and husband, who, when out of temper, beats them unmercifully, and even kills them, when it suits him to do so.

In nothing, perhaps, is there a greater difference between a Christian and a heathen people than in the treatment of women; and when the inhabitants of one of these islands abandon heathenism in favour of Christianity, there is no one feels the immense benefit the change produces, more than these poor, down-trodden, much-abused women.

As a natural consequence arising from this intermingling of a dark with a light-coloured race, the New Hebrideans exhibit a great many shades, ranging from the copper-coloured tint of the Fili natives to the dusky hue of the Eramangans; while their hair varies from light brown to jet black, and is generally of a woolly nature. *Apropos* of hair, it is worthy of notice that the men and women here reverse our fashion, for the women wear it short and the men let it grow long. The latter grow little hair upon their faces, and what they have got, they are (in imitation of their betters) commencing to cut off, operating principally on the upper lip. Since this practice was introduced among them, broken bottles have been in considerable demand, for it is with these original razors that the operation is generally performed.

As a set-off against this process of self-denuding, they exert themselves to improve their appearance by the use of artificial ornaments.

It is curious how deeply the love of ornamenting the person seems to be rooted in the human mind. The most polished and civilized nations, and the rudest and most barbarous tribes, are alike affected by it. Both exercise all the intelligence and skill which they possess, to make or procure those things which they consider will improve their representation of the human form. The first class lavish enormous riches and employ no end of workmen, in satisfying this craving for ornamentation; while the latter, not having such resources at their command, make up for it by a bold and unsparing use of what they have.

The savage has his ear-rings, bracelets, necklaces—if not equal in quality to ours, at all events superior in point of quantity. For he will hang tortoise-shell rings in his ears until the lobe is lengthened some inches; and he will string shells, beads, and whale's-teeth round his neck and arms, until the weight must be quite burdensome. But especially does he delight in paint. Nothing, in his eyes, beautifies like paint; and he uses it with a prodigal hand. With what contempt would he look upon the lady of civilization, lightly tinting her cheeks and darkening her eyebrows, as he plastered on thick coats of red, black, and blue. Sometimes he lays it on in alternate stripes, or, if he be of an artistic turn, he may put in circles or in a variety of curves; but for every-day wear, he generally covers his face with a coat—one side all black, and the other red.

It will be observed that I have spoken of the male savage

in these comparisons. The reason is simply this, that here it is the men—not the women—who give themselves up especially to personal adornment and savage foppery.

From their ornaments let us turn to their weapons. On some of the islands their native weapons have been laid aside for arms of a superior kind, just as we have laid aside the smooth-bore musket. They have learnt that our fire-arms are far more deadly than even their poisoned spears and arrows; and as they are not conservative in any matter in which they think any alteration will give them an advantage over their fellow-savages, they have eagerly grasped at the gun and the ammunition offered to them by the traders. On most of the islands, however, the native weapons are still in use. They are—spears, bows and poisoned arrows, clubs, slings, kawas (a long heavy stone, which is thrown by the natives with much precision) and hatchets.

Their canoes are, as I think was remarked before, of the rudest description. Recipe for construction:—Cut down a tree having a trunk sufficiently large, say two feet or more in diameter; cut off a log the required length; hollow it out; fix to one side an outrigger, extended by poles six feet or so from the canoe; shape out some paddles five feet long, and make a wooden baler, the shape of a grocer's scoop; and the canoe is ready for use. When a tree cannot be obtained of sufficient diameter to make a large canoe, the natives add a plank on each side, fastening it by cords. The largest canoe I have seen in the New Hebrides was thirty feet long; but there are few of that size, the commonest length being from fifteen to twenty feet, which are capable of carrying three or four people. In these crafts the natives used to pass from one island to another, sometimes a distance of forty miles; but these voyages were always attended with great danger, and nowadays, when they wish to visit another island, they generally wait until an opportunity presents itself of getting over by a vessel.

The live stock belonging to these natives consists of pigs and fowls. With regard to these two kinds of animals, found very generally over the Pacific islands, it seems to be the current impression that they were originally left upon them by Cook and other early navigators. This, as far as the New Hebrides are concerned, is incorrect; for instead of giving these animals to the New Hebrideans, Cook, when he discovered the islands, found them there, and got presents of them from the natives. Quiros, too, it may be recollected, states that he discovered them on Santo nearly 300 years ago. They must, then, be indigenous to the islands, or have been brought by the natives when they originally landed upon them. To one not versed in such matters, the pigs appear much like our own, only they are, on the whole, longer in the legs and noses, and are generally black in colour : while the fowls exhibit the long bare legs, the sloping body, and reddish colour, which are the undoubted characteristics of the Malay breed. Both of these animals afford good food to the inhabitants, and both of them are fed on cocoanuts.

One of the most extraordinary things connected with this people is the number of different languages spoken by them. There are known to be at least twenty, and these languages are as distinct from one another as Greek from English—perhaps more so.

I don't suppose that anywhere on the globe there are so many languages spoken within such a small radius. On the island of Tana alone there are no less than six ; and these cannot properly be called dialects, for the speaker of one is unintelligible to the speaker of another. The cause of this extraordinary diversity lies, probably, in the facts—first, that they have no written language ; and secondly, that their continual wars keep the various tribes very much isolated, and encourage, if they do not necessitate, the use of different tongues.

It is a well-known fact, that if there be no fixed standard, a language will quickly alter; and that if, under these circumstances, peoples originally speaking the same language be separated and kept apart, and opposed to each other in war and stratagem, their language will, in course of time, be found to have developed into different dialects; and will diverge more and more, until, in the course of a generation, these become so different as to entitle them to be called different languages.

I now come to the last point in connection with the inhabitants of these islands—their probable origin. This question is rather a difficult one to settle. There seems, however, little doubt but that they are a people mixed of the Papuan negro and the Malay of Eastern Polynesia; for we find in all of them certain traces of negro blood, and, at the same time, among many of them we find undoubted signs of Malay extraction—the most convincing of which is their speaking a dialect of the Malay tongue.

The Malay fowls, too, might help to settle the ethnological problem, if any further evidence were wanted.

From what I have observed among them, I am inclined to adopt the opinion expressed by Williams, which was to this effect—that the negro races were the original inhabitants of most of those Pacific islands, but that the Malay, superior in strength and cunning, came upon them from the shores of Asia, and have exterminated them from all the islands, except the large ones like Australia and New Guinea, or those groups such as the New Hebrides and Fiji, where they were comparatively numerous and strong. In these the Malay have amalgamated with the negro.

## LETTER X.

VARIETIES OF LIFE ON ANIWA—CORALS—REMARKS ON THE FORMATION OF THESE ISLANDS.

*Aniwa,*
September, 1872.

YOU ask me how the missionary and his wife in the New Hebrides employ their time? what is their daily routine of duties? what do they eat? &c., &c. You say that you can never get any information on these homely subjects—that you read the mission reports, but are none the wiser. Now, in trying to answer you, I find myself placed in a somewhat difficult position; for although all the missionaries come here with the same end in view, each has his own way of carrying it out. Therefore, unless I were to confine myself to one, I must, to a certain extent, deal in generalities.

As there are no shops here, and no skilled workmen, the missionary has necessarily a great deal of manual labour; and instead of walking about in a dignified manner, with a black suit on and a white tie, continually preaching, (as some seem to believe) he is generally working like a slave, in his shirt sleeves, at some mechanical work the whole of the forenoon. Perhaps his dear wife will come to him with an intimation that the safe wants mending, or the kitchen chimney looking to, or a hole in the roof needs to be patched. So these things have to be attended to. Then there are houses to be built, fences to be erected, garden to be cultivated, and other multifarious duties which keep him hard at work for part of each day. In the afternoon he dispenses medicines, walks out to visit some sick native, or it may be to settle some quarrel between unruly ones, and take a look, perhaps, at his yam plantations, to see that no roving pig has broken the fence and got in. Then, in the evening, there is plenty of writing to be done, there is preparation of the Sunday's address, and the work of translation.

All this is independent of the time devoted to religious services, classes, and printing—which of itself, if much translation is being done, will keep him hard at work at all spare times.

Then the missionary's wife. What does she not do? I might ask. She has all the duties of the wife in general, such as the nursery, the kitchen, and other household work; and then, over and above these, she has all the duties of a missionary's wife in particular— such as manufacturing servants out of inert native material, taking general charge of the native women, and forming them into classes and teaching them— duties as important in their own way as those of the missionary himself.

In the culinary department, for instance, these ladies show wonderful skill in the use of the somewhat limited resources at hand, producing a *menu*, which seldom fails to tempt the appetite, often feeble in this hot and enervating climate. I would apply to them the same language that I did to the cocoanut-palm, inasmuch as they seem to be endued with a power almost creative; for they produce such magnificent results out of such scanty materials.

Here is what they have to work upon. Pork and fowls, eggs, fish, yams, taro, sweet potatoe, beans, oranges, lemons, bananas and pine-apples; also, tinned meats, flour, jams, &c., from the colonies. Of course, all these things are not to be obtained at every station; and although the list looks tolerably large, there is a great want of variety, especially in fresh meat, and it must task the lady of the house considerably to vary the bill of fare.

Here is what they produce. BREAKFAST :—Ham and eggs, yams, bread, biscuits, and coffee. DINNER :—Soup, fowls, yams, bananas, tea, custard and snow-pudding. TEA :— Bread, biscuits, jam, cake, honey, cheese, and tea. This is high style of living, however, and cannot be always maintained; for frequently the flour or biscuits go bad, or the supply of native produce runs short. Through these mishaps, one of the mission families was, some time ago, almost reduced to cocoanuts, before the vessel arrived with new stores from the colonies.

So much for the outer form of mission life; and as what I have said in a general way will apply, with considerable exactness, to this island of Aniwa, from which this letter is dated, I shall go on to speak of the other kinds of life which are to be found on it—that, namely, of the natives, the lower animals, the insects, and the visitor.

The first and the last seem to pass the time very much in the same way; and if either party kept a diary, I am afraid it would run very much like that of Mark Twain's,—"Got up, washed, and went to bed."

The natives appear to be quiet and good-natured members of society, but some of them do not seem quite so far removed from heathenism as to have thrown aside all the badges of it. I saw several with paint on their faces, and some, when out of sight of the mission house, seemed to prefer carrying their lava-lava over their shoulder to wearing it round their waist.

I never saw, however, a more interested and attentive audience, than these people when gathered to the Sunday service. Mr. Paton has certainly caught the way of securing their attention. On one occasion I was rather astonished and mystified when he produced a new water-tap, and held it up to view, pointing to it, and evidently speaking about it. I found out afterwards that it was used to show them what brass was, the word having occurred in the passage which he was explaining. Illustration seems to be the most effective way of instructing them. It is the way which they themselves adopt. They can best understand what is exhibited to the eye as well as explained to the ear.*

Birds are not numerous on Aniwa. There are two kinds of pigeons, some shore birds, a kind of thrush, and a small black bird with red head and hooked bill, which sucks the honey from the cocoanut flowers. Flying foxes, however, abound. These strange creatures come over from the neighbouring islands, in flocks, about sundown, for the purpose of feeding on some favorite plant which grows on this island. They are not left in peace, however; for the natives are fond of them as food, and it is a favorite sport of theirs, on a moonlight night, to go out shooting flying foxes. They are covered with a soft brown fur, and measure, from wing to wing, about two feet.

As for the insects, the most noticeable are the flies and mosquitoes. They are so troublesome that it is quite impossible at some seasons to sleep, unless you are enveloped in a mosquito-curtain: but then I think you sleep all the better to have the mosquitos, if you have the curtains—it is so soothing

---

* The readers of James Hamilton's life will remember that he tried this style of teaching—exhibiting the branch of a fig-tree at an evening lecture. But Abernyte is not Aniwa. A poor woman expostulated with him—" Oh Maister Hamilton, hoo do you give them fig-leaves when they're hungerin' for the Bread o' Life."

and delightful to hear the angry hum of the insects outside, as they go tearing round, like ravenous wolves seeking entrance into a sheep-fold. But if they do get in—well, the sooner you get up and hunt them to death, the better for your own peace and comfort.

Besides the insects on shore, Aniwa has its circle of sea insects—busy little creatures, which have all work and no play—the coral polypes.

Queer little creatures are these coral polypes. They have neither head nor legs, but seem to get on very well without them. In the scientific language of Milne Edwards, they are "animals organised for a sedentary mode of life, having no locomotive organs, and being provided with a circle of retractile tentaculæ around the mouth, and a central gastric cavity." In fact, they are all stomach, with the exception of the "retractile tentaculæ," which the little gourmands use for seizing anything eatable which comes within their reach, and stowing it away in their "central gastric cavity."

According to the way in which the polypes multiply themselves, depends the shape and appearance of those lime-like structures which we call corals. Some propagate by lateral buds, *i. e.*, the parent produces several young ones from its sides, and then the flat solid masses of coral are produced; while others propagate by vertical buds, and then the upright branching kinds are produced. Just as the properties which lie hidden in the seed influence the form of the whole tree—every shoot obeying the same fixed laws,—so do these with which the founding polype is invested, determine the form of the coral edifice. I say founding polype because each coral tree or mass is the work of one family, all sprung from a single polype, the originator of the building.

Let us take the branching coral, and look for a moment at the habits of the little builders and inhabitants of it.

A polype floats alone on the current of the sea—an offshoot from some long-established city—until it rests on some rocky ledge, which is suitable for the work of coral building. The spot, to be so qualified, must be within twenty fathoms of the surface, and must be free from shifting mud or sand. When settled, the coat of the polype begins to harden. By some mysterious power, the calcareous particles diffused in the sea-water are attracted towards it, and quickly enclose the animal in a coat of lime. Then it produces young polypes, perhaps two or three, and dies. Its body then decays, but its tomb remains—a centre and foundation-stone for the work of its rapidly increasing descendants. It is noticeable that these creatures not only make their own dwellings, but each sends in a contribution of horny substance to strengthen the supporting stem, so that as the family tree grows upward, the stem grows thicker and is enabled to bear the increasing weight. Taking a piece of branching coral, the cells are easily seen, and it will be observed that when one branch is apt to interfere with the growth of another, the weaker one ceases to advance, and allows the stronger one to grow onward without interruption, even as some branches of a tree give way to others, never coming to a maturity which would interfere with the growth of more prosperous neighbouring branches.

These coral cities are model commonwealths, governed by God's own laws of political economy. Each individual builds its own house—supports itself—sends in a contribution for the good of the community at large, and propagates new individuals for the carrying on of the work. There are no quarrels here, no strifes, nor oppressions. No rich lazy polypes, getting but not giving; no poor ones, begging from their neighbours while they will not work. All do their part, and do it well, and no doubt die as contentedly as they lived.

When I look at these insignificant little morsels, and then at the great solid structures of coral rock of which this island is composed, I find it very difficult to believe that these masses have all been drawn, grain by grain, from the ocean by such a minute agency. But even this island is a poor specimen of the magnitude of their works. Tongatabu—an island in Eastern Polynesia, 100 miles in circumference—is of coral formation, and owes its existence to the energy of these little creatures. Of course, countless ages must have been consumed in the formation of such an island as that, and countless myriads of builders must have been employed. But allowing time enough and workers enough, there is really no limit to what might be produced in this way.

Mr. Darwin tells us that where coral reefs or islands exist, there has been or is still a gradual subsidence of the ground on which they stand. For the coral insects build on a bottom always within twenty fathoms of the surface; and as this bottom gradually subsides, they keep building upwards, keeping on a level with the surface of the ocean, where they seem best to thrive. In this way may be explained the great depth of coral reefs and the high cliffs of coral islands—merely reefs upheaved, which might seem to contradict the law that no coral insect can work at a greater depth than twenty fathoms.

As I have said before, Aniwa is an upheaved coral island. It has been formed, apparently, by two natural processes—first, by the foundation on which it stands gradually subsiding, until the coral insects built up a mass as high as the cliff is above the depth to which the coral now extends under the water; and then, secondly, it has been upheaved. Traces of this great lifting force are distinctly visible on the island.

This rough section will help me to explain what has been

said about the formation of these upheaved coral islands:—
A being the water level, C the cliff rising from the shore flat,
B the crevices or wells occurring more conspicuously on the
island of Maré. The shore flat is all waterworn and honey-
combed in a remarkable way, and has evidently been exposed
for a very long time to the action of the waves; for it is
as hard as granite, and would take no small force to wear it
into the form it now presents.

All the New Hebrides islands are rising gradually,—at least
so say men of science—a consoling thought for the inhabitants;
and, from the casual observations which I was able to make,
I should certainly concur in the statement. Some small islands
near Efaté, and also part of the north-western side of that
island itself, exhibit a certain peculiarity of form, which, I
think, bears out this statement.

This section (on an exaggerated scale) will show what I
mean. It seems to me that, in these cases, the coral insects
have been at work while the land was rising instead of falling;
for supposing that the dotted line in the section represents the
original form of the island C, with its top just on a level with the
surface of the water, then round it the insects work and bring their
reefs to the level of the land-summit: then, however, a rising takes
place, and that part now a flat top is elevated above the water,
and another part of the sea-bottom brought into the working
sphere of the polypes. Again they make their reef round it,
until another upheaval takes place. The edges of these steps
marked B on the section, have much the same appearance
as the white cliffs of Aniwa. In this way their peculiar
form may naturally be accounted for, and the fact of the

rising of the group confirmed as far as these islands are concerned.

We come now to the third class of formations exhibited by the islands of the group,—the volcanic. Nearly all the islands belong to this class, and are evidently of the same formation, Aniwa being the only purely coral island in the group.

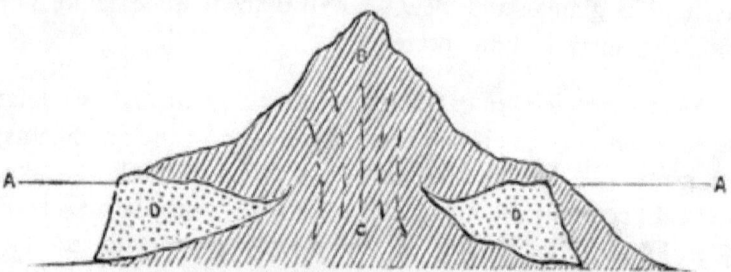

These volcanic islands are surrounded by coral reefs. The reefs, however, are seldom any distance from the shore—in most cases they merely run out from the beach fifty or a hundred yards, as a flat rocky platform. Sometimes they are not visible at all. It is very evident to any observer that the coral reefs have been formed first, and that the volcanic matter has broken violently up and flowed over it to a great extent—in some cases burying it altogether. In the above section, A represents the water-line, C the original foundation upon which the coral reef D has been built. Then through C a violent eruption, or many eruptions, have taken place; the matter B being thrown up, and flowing down, has approached closely to the edge of the reef on one side, and has buried it altogether on the other. On various parts of Aneityum and Tana, there may be seen quite distinctly, volcanic matter lying on the top of the coral bed, twisted and liquid-like, appearing as if it had just run down the mountain side a day or two ago.

The presence of three active volcanoes on the group, and the traces of many extinct ones, show that there has been some mighty agency at work here ; and perhaps the date at which many of these beautiful islands sprang from the depths of their mother earth, to adorn the surface and give homes to man, is not so far distant as we are apt to imagine.

## LETTER XI.

CROSS OVER TO TANA—DEATH OF A BULL—THE BREAKERS—
THE FOREST — THE TANAMEN AND THEIR WARS — YAM
CULTIVATION—AMUSEMENTS—KAVA DRINKING—RELIGION.

*Kwamera, Tana,*
*October,* 1872.

FROM Aniwa I crossed over to Tana, getting a chance by a trading cutter, and have now been staying for some time at Kwamera, the mission station of Mr. Watt. In observing the manners and customs of the natives—walking through the thick tropical forests and stealing from them specimens for my collection—sketching, bathing, and in other such-like ways the time has quickly passed. Soon after coming here I was called upon to slay a bull, the property of Mr. Watt. Unfortunately, both for its own sake and for that of its owner, this creature had a predilection for breaking down the frail fences of the natives; and as this caused some ill-feeling among them, it was resolved that the offending animal should be slain. Crowds of Tanese assembled to witness the execution, although, native like, most of them kept at a very respectable distance from the scene of operations. After three shots from my rifle, the bull succumbed, amid the plaudits of the surrounding crowd. For this exploit I was honoured with the title of Missi that killed the courimatow, and got the reputation of being a very good shot ! Some of them, however, after it was over, were rather jealous ; and fancying that

I had been summoned to the island for the express purpose of playing the butcher, asked, with rather an aggrieved air, why they could not have killed the bull.

The mission station is situated very close to the beach, and is on the windward side of the island. Being thus open to the cool trade winds, it is very healthy; but the situation has these disadvantages—that no flowers can be grown round the house, and that the front windows can never be kept clean, on account of the spray showers which are continually flying up from the breakers.

Mission Station at Kwamera, Tana.

There is no place like this, I think, for seeing breakers, as there is nothing to stop them until they roll in upon the rocky beach. The time at which they appear to greatest advantage is not during a gale, as might be imagined, but immediately after it. During a gale the waves come rushing on, and dash themselves blindly upon the rocks, in too confused a way to rise into breakers, but when the fierceness of the storm and the angry lashing of the waves are over—when there is left nothing but the great rolling swell—then you will see the breakers in perfection. They approach the shore with slow and stately majesty, and rising like a great wall of glass, they gently bow their crests, and then fall with a mighty hiss and a roar as of thunder; while the shattered foam, white as snow, flies up into the air like the ashes of a volcano. If the breaker strikes the shore obliquely the effect is very grand, for then it commences to break at one end, and rolls along the line with regular motion and a steady continuous roar, like the running fire of a well-trained regiment. Often on a warm afternoon I have sat down in the shade and watched the grandeur of "the green breakers and the wind-tossed foam," till the slanting rays of the sun warned me to escape from the miasma of the night air.

From the sea-beach here, the land rises gently to the top of a lofty mountain, the whole of which is clothed with a thick unbroken forest of tropical luxuriance. Down from the mountain there flow many little streams of clear cool water, two of which enter the sea close to the mission house. Many a ramble I have had into these forests, often accompanied by the good missionary and his wife, occasionally by a native boy as guide. Sometimes we would go to visit a native village nestling under the branches of great trees. Sometimes we followed a winding path up the valley of a stream, with the fern trees forty feet high overhanging it, and the ground ferns in endless variety clothing its banks. What lovely little bits of scenery we saw; what subjects for an artist—what shady nooks for picnics—what noble trees and curious creepers were there! These forests were a source of never-failing interest and enjoyment. Amongst the other trees, a species of banyan grows—an immense tree, with handsome foliage. Under it the natives make their public square for feasts and dances, and also erect their kava house; and near it you always find their villages. Naturally this tree sends roots down from its branches for their support; but the natives cut these off, so that they may not interfere with the open square beneath. There is another magnificent tree I have noticed, which supports itself by sending out great buttresses from the side of the stem, of hard stringy wood.

It is curious how many trees in a tropical country do not seem satisfied with the support which their legitimate roots give them, but must have, in addition, all sorts of outside props and buttresses. I can see no reason for it, unless it be that the gales here are more violent than in other climates, and so the trees require extra support.

There are fig-trees here too, which are, I believe, peculiar to this island; their fruit is smaller than that which we have in Victoria, is round in shape and insipid in taste. The Sago palm, and a small one called the Stone palm, I have also frequently observed; but perhaps the handsomest of all the trees and shrubs are the variegated dracænas and crotons. Some of these plants have dark glossy green leaves, spotted with bright yellow; others have them streaked with red, while sometimes they exhibit both these colours.

But enough about the trees; I suppose you would prefer hearing something about the people.

The longer that I live amongst them, the more, of course, I know of their character and ways; and I am now beginning to see how unjust it is to class all the natives of one island under the same category, or to brand all of them with a bad name for the evil actions of a few. This is very often the case however, with casual visitors to savage peoples. If they are badly received, they, making no allowance for circumstances, form a hasty judgment, and frequently come to wrong conclusions regarding them. Cook, when he visited this island, showed great liberality of sentiment towards the people in his remarks, which are so sensible and so much to the point, that I will quote them.

"Thus we found these people hospitable, civil and good-natured, when not prompted to a contrary spirit by jealousy—a conduct I cannot tell how to blame them for, especially when I consider the light in which they must view us. It was impossible for them to know our real design; we enter their ports without their daring to oppose; we endeavour to land in their country as friends, and it is well if this succeeds—we land nevertheless, and maintain the footing we have got by the superiority of our firearms. Under such circumstances what opinion can they form of us? Is it not as reasonable for them to think that we have come to invade their country, as to pay them a friendly visit? These and some acquaintance with us can only convince them of the latter."

If the intercourse which the natives have had with strangers had been only with men of the spirit of Captain Cook, I am very sure that we would have had but little to complain of with regard to them now.

They are very much like children, and require to be treated often as you treat children. They are easily offended, but are easily reconciled, and, if they get attached to anyone, show much affection.

They are as different in character among themselves as we are. Many, no doubt, are naturally treacherous and cruel; but some again are naturally frank and good-natured. Some are naturally vicious savages, while others are naturally gentlemanly savages.

The Tanamen have a great name as warriors—sometimes it is said that they are the most warlike people in the South

Pacific. This may be quite true, for it is a fact that they are much broken up into small tribes, which are continually at war with each other; but this in no way implies that there is a very great amount of hard fighting or of bloodshed. There is a great security against this in the fact that though a Tanaman has very little regard for the life of another, he has a very strong affection for his own, and will not put it in jeopardy unless he cannot help it. One day the shore tribe here went off to fight a hostile tribe three or four miles away. In the evening they appeared again, looking very well pleased with themselves—so much so as to lead one to believe that they had entirely exterminated their foes. On enquiry, however, I found that not a man had been killed—in fact, no one had been seen even. These noble warriors had gone as close to the village as they judged expedient, and there had banged away all day with the the most determined bravery, and returned at night covered with glory and perspiration.

Another favourite mode of warfare is to get behind some well-sheltered rocky point, in range of an enemy's village, and there to open fire upon any living thing that appears.

This plan has been adopted several times against a village about two miles along the beach, by a tribe living beyond it. A native teacher lives in the village, and finding that it was rather uncomfortable to sit in his house when the bullets were tearing through it, he has put up a stone wall, and when the firing commences, he creeps into cover, and lies there in safety till the ammunition of the attacking party is exhausted.

It is not thus that blood is usually shed. When a man does fall, it is by an ambuscade. A party will way-lay the unfortunate native, and shoot him *a tergo* as he walks unsuspectingly along the path. And when a victim is thus secured, the cannibal feast takes place, all the tribes in friendly alliance getting a share of the horrid meal.

Let us turn now and look at the Tanaman as a man of peace—let us see how he spends those months of the year when, quitting the field of battle, he becomes an agriculturalist.

> "The gentle island and the genial soil,
> The friendly hearts, the feasts without a toil;
> The courteous manners but from nature caught,
> The wealth unhoarded and the love unbought."

So sings Byron, and so many speak of these fair islands and their people; but it is only to a limited extent true of the New Hebrides; and so far as feasts without toil are concerned, in Tana at least, it is quite incorrect. There the natives do work, and, during the season for raising yams, work tolerably hard too.

The yam is their principal article of food, and requires careful cultivation. In the first place, the natives clear the ground with axe and fire; then fence it in, dig the soil and raise it in mounds four or five feet high; then the yams are planted—a large one generally on the top, and a circle of smaller ones round the sides of the mound. Having raised and planted a number of these mounds, they build a very small edifice in the centre of the plantation, in which they place some food. This is for the special benefit of Teapolo, the great evil spirit. The intention is, that he should go quietly into his little house, eat his dinner, and go off appeased and satisfied; instead of ramping about at large—spoiling the yams for other and better people, which they fancy he might do, were no special provision made for him. And this expedient, I am assured, is eminently successful.

Not long after the yams are planted, the green tender shoots appear, and then the natives set busily to work making trellis supports for the yam vine. Sometimes these supports run out from the mound for twenty yards or so; and along these the plant pushes its branches with great rapidity, and twines its tendrils round the reeds very firmly. A yam plantation at this season, when neatly kept, is a very pretty sight indeed. Men, women, and children join in the work, and generally they go on the principle of working in a body—all going to one man's plantation and doing it, then he joins them and they go to the next, and so on.

Fishing with nets along the reef, or with hook and line from canoes, hut-building and canoe-building, are some of their other peaceful occupations.

Their peaceful amusements are not very numerous. They are fond of shooting birds with their muskets; they seldom think of killing a domestic fowl otherwise, but rarely succeed without reducing it to a condition which we would hardly think suitable for the table. Sometimes they resort to their old weapons for amusement—particularly the boys, who have not got the length of guns. Putting up a mark on the beach, they practise very vigorously at it with their spears, and bows and arrows. They must, however, have lost much of their former cunning in the use of these weapons, or they never had any; for I found that, with a little practice, I was about as good a marksman as any of them.

Hairdressing is another favourite occupation of the Tanamen, and one to which they devote a good deal of time. In common with the natives of some of the neighbouring islands, they dress their hair in a very peculiar style—in a very troublesome style, I would say; but they are as proud of it as the wearer of the most fashionable chignon is of her upper story. Dividing the hair into several hundred locks, they wrap each of them round with a native twine, as tightly as you wrap the handle of a cricket bat, leaving the ends free and curling. They generally devote Sunday to this hair-culture, tying up what has become loosened, and following up the hair as it grows with the wrapping-twine. As " uneasy lies the head which wears a crown," so uneasy lies the Tanaman's head thus dressed; for he does not go to sleep upon a pillow, but places his neck over a round piece of wood which raises it a little bit from the ground—not very comfortable, one would think. But what is comfort to the lovers of fashion! The general appearance of the Tanaman's head so dressed has a striking resemblance to the representations of the ancient Egyptians; and though I cannot say that it improves their appearance, it certainly has the advantage of affording a better protection to the head from the sun's rays than hair in its ordinary state would do.

Their chief public amusements are the feast and the dance. I have not been able to witness either of those ceremonies, for it is only at certain seasons that they are held, and the season is now past. For a long time before they take place, preparations are going on—the women being busily occupied in making curious dresses and gorgeous ornaments. After the feast is over, which consists merely of a profusion of their ordinary food, partaken of by the men alone: the women appear, and the dance commences, to the music of wooden drums and monotonous chants. These balls are kept up generally all night long: some of them are obscene in character, and all of them are attended, more or less, with bad results to the health of the natives, in consequence of their getting overheated and then chilled.

These dances are held in the open squares under the banyan trees, and at the side of each of these squares there may be seen a long-shaped hut standing by itself. This is the Kava-house, the meeting place for the men of the tribe.

The kava (piper methisticum) is a plant of the pepper family, and grows extensively upon the southern islands of the group, but nowhere better than in this district. It is five or six feet high, has articulated stem and branches, and soft large leaves.

From the root and the lower part of the stem, the natives make that drink, which is so universally consumed in these seas. Every evening, about sundown, the men assemble at the kava

Public Square on Tana, with Banyan and Kava-house.

houses of their respective villages, each bringing with him a bit of the precious plant. These bits are sliced up, and chewed by boys who have not reached the stage of kava drinking. After it is thoroughly chewed, and all the juice contained in the wood expressed by and from the boys' mouths, the whole is put into a wooden dish, water added, and finally the liquid is strained. Each man then dips in his dish, takes his draught, and either goes away home to sleep off the effects, or lies about outside the kava-house. This liquor has a soothing stupyfying effect upon the natives, but does not excite them as ardent spirits excite us. On the islands of Eastern Polynesia, the same drink is used; but in connection with its manufacture there is this difference, that there girls are employed in the mastication of the plant; while here they not only employ boys, but they do not allow a woman to come near—no, not even in sight of the kava-house while they are drinking—evidently considering the presence of women a profanation of the whole ceremony.

After witnessing the process of manufacture, I did not feel at all inclined to try the result, even although in doing so I would only have been following the example of recent travellers, who would be highly indignant, I dare say, if I were to accuse them of doing anything which may be truly called disgusting. Being curious, however, to know how it tasted, I got some of the plant and chewed it for myself, and, after doing so once, was never tempted to repeat the experiment. It has a pungent and very disagreeable taste, and it took me about an hour's hard work, with cocoanuts and bananas, to get the unpleasant savour out of my mouth.

The religion of the Tanese seems to consist merely in a host of superstitious fears. Their gods are all evil, and their religion consists mainly in endeavours to propitiate them. They have gods of the sea and of the land, geological and botanical gods; but the most dreaded beings of all, perhaps, are their human gods, viz., the disease-makers. Our medical men devote themselves to the cure of suffering humanity, but they have practitioners who imagine that they can breed disease as well, and both, curiously, are paid with equal readiness by their patients—the one set that they may cure, and the other that they may not kill.

These disease-makers go prowling about, picking up *nahak*, *i.e.*, the refuse of what anyone has been eating; and if the disease-maker takes this home and burns it, it is firmly believed that the person whose *nahak* it is will immediately fall ill, remaining so as long as the burning continues, and dying if the whole be consumed.

To avert this, then, whenever a native falls ill, he sends out friends, blowing conches and offering presents to the disease-makers, who, if these are satisfactory, accept them, cease burning, and the sufferer thereupon recovers.

It is curious what a strong hold this belief has upon the minds of the natives, and probably it is this very belief which causes results which happen apparently through the burning of the nahak; for if a Tanaman hears that someone is burning his nahak, the probability is that he will fall ill through sheer fright; and again, if he hears that the disease-maker has stopped burning, he will often speedily recover—especially if there is nothing wrong with him. When a death does occur, even although presents have been accepted by the disease-makers, it does not shake them in their belief, for they think then that the presents were not sufficient.

Their ideas of a future state are very vague. They have some belief in a happy sort of world to come—its happiness consisting of plenty to eat and drink, and nothing to do. All go there, but the stingy. The stingy man is their especial aversion. On Tana, one man has only to ask anything from his neighbours, and he gets it. Not understanding this custom of theirs, I was once rather non-plussed. While sitting in the verandah one day, smoking, a young man came up with an old musket in his hand, and commenced to praise the appearance of my pipe. After waiting a short time—probably to see whether I would not take the hint—he said, "What for you no give me pipe?" So, by way of turning the tables on him, I said, "And what for you no give me your musket?" Whereupon, to my dismay, he handed it to me with a cheerful grin; and I was obliged to explain that I was only in joke, that I didn't want his old blunderbuss, and that I did want my pipe. He left me in high dudgeon, much offended at my breach of etiquette.

I remember it used to be a favourite subject of discussion at debating societies, whether the state of savagism or of civilization was the happier—a favourite subject, probably, because it was one which could not be settled. Diocletian, who both ruled men and planted cabbages, says that of the two occupations he preferred the latter; so I dare say the life of a South-Sea islander, with its freedom from care and responsibility, is happier than that of many an envied and busy member of a highly-civilized community. I have little doubt, too, that it is happier than the life of those who lurk in the background of our great cities, enduring want and cold, and entirely forgotten by the majority of their more favoured fellow-countrymen. I have often thought what a fine thing it would be to pull some thousands of those poor, miserable, starving wretches out of the back slums of London, and transfer them to some of these fair islands with their warm airs and abundant fruits. The thought came to me very vividly the other day in a dream, with which, for the sake of variety, I shall close this letter.

I may, possibly, have been thinking of such things before. I do not recollect; but at all events I went out one day in a meditative mood, and sat down to watch the breakers. Lulled by their pleasant murmurs, I fell asleep.

Then I thought I stood on the shore of a fair island, where the trees were rich with fruits and the airs with fragrance. Looking over the wide expanse of water before me, I saw three great ships, which came sailing towards the island with all their canvas spread. I saw a crowd of men, women, and children—a ghastly multitude, with thin pale faces, wasted frames, and tattered garments. But as they gazed on the land before them every face was lighted up with hope and eager expectation.

Then the busy sailors plied the oars, and the beach was quickly covered with this strange mass of human beings, who seeing the fruits hang over them in all their luscious ripeness, and feeling the airs of the tropics warm them to the very marrow of their bones, smiled, shouted, and wept, as the humour seized them. "No more grim, gaunt famine ; for does not the earth hang out her fruits before us, and there is none to snatch them from our grasp. No more nights of shivering misery ; for does not the warm air clothe us better than the softest furs? No more desolating loneliness in the midst of thousands of our fellow-creatures; for have we not the open sea, the earth, its fruits and flowers, God's own sweet heaven above us, and God himself to care for us?" So spake an aged man, as he stepped forth from the rest, and leading them up a hill showed them where and how to build, and how the land was to be cultivated, and how disease was to be warded off.

Then I woke. The sun was glinting over the hill behind me, and the dews were beginning to fall ; and the Tanaman was winding along to the evening kava ; so I rose and returned to the mission house.

## LETTER XII.

RESIDENCE AT PORT RESOLUTION—ASCENT OF THE VOLCANO—WHAT WE SAW FROM THE EDGE OF THE CRATER—THE DESCENT—SOMETHING ABOUT THE MANNERS AND CUSTOMS OF THIS VOLCANO.

*Port Resolution, Tana,*
*December,* 1872.

AFTER a stay of two months at Kwamera, I went round by boat to visit Mr. and Mrs. Neilson at Port Resolution. The station here occupies a fine position on the banks overhanging the bay, and commands a very fine view towards the lofty Mount Mirren. The general aspect of the country is much the same as that around Kwamera, only the land is more flat and the forests are more free of underwood. There are two traders' establishments here, the occupants of them being engaged principally in the manufacture of cobra from cocoanuts and the collection of sulphur. Until lately one of these establishments was in charge of a yonng man named Dana. He was one of that unfortunate expedition that left Melbourne some years ago to settle upon this island. Two of them—Messrs. Ross and Bell—were killed by the natives; and now Dana, poor fellow, has met his death here too. Going out one Sunday alone, with his gun, it went off accidentally, inflicting a very bad wound in the leg. He was conveyed home by natives, and Mr. Neilson went down to attend to him. For some days he seemed to be in a fair way of recovery, but then, quite unexpectedly, he took lockjaw, and shortly afterwards died. It was sad to see a young man like that dying alone, on a heathen island, far from his friends and relatives, with no one to care for him except the kind-hearted missionary, near whose station the accident happened to occur.

It is a lonely miserable life that which many of these traders lead. They are continually shooting one another, or shooting themselves. Within a few days of the death of young Dana, I heard of two other mishaps on this island: in one case, a man—said to be one of the " Carl " brig crew—was accidentally shot by another with a revolver; and in the other, a man blew himself and another up, with gunpowder. They are very careless in the use of firearms, and I am afraid that, in many cases, gin has mainly to do with the accidents which occur.

The principal event which occurred during my stay here, was the visit to the volcano.

The day fixed for the trip arrived, and proved suitable in every respect. Breakfast that morning had little attraction for me, and I looked with some disdain on the provisions which were getting packed up in a basket for our consumption on the way. In fact, I was somewhat excited. Was I not going to gaze down the gullet of a live volcano? Was I not going to stand under a shower of red hot lava, with the chance of being entombed? Under such circumstances, who could think of such a sublunary matter as grub. Fortunately, however, for all parties, the commissariat was not in my charge, and it was duly looked to.

Mr. Neilson and myself, with several natives, composed the party; and we made a start about nine o'clock in the morning. After walking along a tolerably even path for an hour and a half, we arrived at a native village, and found the villagers in a state of excitement. On enquiry we found that a feast was in the course of preparation, and that the cause of it and the material for it had not long ago arrived from the sea-coast. It was a turtle—a great fat fellow—which was lying on his back in the middle of the crowd, the very picture of stupid helplessness. The oven was all ready for him, the stones arranged, and the banana-leaves laid out ; and just as we came up they were going to kill him. Tying him to two stakes, an ugly savage let light into him by means of a sharp bamboo-knife ; but by that time we were moving off again, and I saw no more of the turtle or the expectant savages.

A turtle is a great prize amongst the Tanamen—not only his flesh being much esteemed by them, but the shell is highly valued ; for from it they make many ornaments for their necks and ears.

After leaving the village, we walked on for an hour through thick woods. Although the volcano was concealed by the foliage overhead, the thundering noise of its eruptions were growing louder, and made it apparent that we were not very far from its base. At last, after climbing a considerable ascent, we burst through the trees and bushes, and found ourselves on open ground, with the brown bare cone rising above us.

As we ploughed our way up through the soft and shifting soil, mostly composed of ashes, the outbursts grew more furious and deafening than ever. The vegetation was now all left behind, save a small plant of the lily kind, with a pretty pink flower, and the indomitable pandanus, the hardiest of the hardy, braving alike the salt sprays of the ocean and the scorching showers of the volcano.

On getting to the top, we found that we had not reached the crater yet, but merely the remains of an extinct one in the shape of an oval basin. About a hundred yards further on was the true crater, and to this we proceeded, walking along the rough surface of the hardened scoria.

Here our native guides saw fit to leave us, not caring to have a closer acquaintance with the volcano. So Mr. Neilson and I approached it alone, and reaching the edge, gazed down into its open mouth.

In shape, this crater is much like the extinct one which we had just passed; but though no eruption took place for a few minutes after our arrival, there were abundant traces of activity visible. At the bottom of the large basin, there are three or four deep chasms, down which we could not see. From these there issued jets of steam, and gasping gurgling sighs and stifled snorts, as if legions of demons were fighting and choking one another in the mysterious depths below. Up the sides of the crater numerous white jets of sulphurous steam kept rising, while the ground on which we stood was almost too hot to be touched with the hand.

About five minutes after we arrived at the edge, an eruption took place. It was the grandest and most appalling sight I ever witnessed.

First, from one of the chasms there came a preliminary growl; and then, with a roar as if the very earth were being rent in twain, there burst into the air a stream of molten lava, large red hot stones, and smoke that looked quite solid in its blackness. Hundreds of feet above our heads the fearful deluge flew, while I stood trembling in my insignificance, watching with eager eye the course of the fiery ærolites. I never felt so small in all my life before, and never so relieved as when, with many a patter and many a bang, the stones and lava reached the earth again. Mostly the burning stuff fell back into the crater again, and all of it was inclined by the wind away from us, as of course we were on the windward side of the crater.

After several displays of this kind, I became sufficiently composed to seat myself beside my companion, who had been taking it all very coolly, having often visited the place before—and attempted a sketch. The drawing, though it may give some idea as to the shape and appearance of the crater, gives but a very poor impression of an eruption. These outbursts cannot be depicted, nor indeed can they be properly described—at least by a pen so inexperienced as mine.

The fearful noise—one of the most striking characteristics in connection with these eruptions—how can it be described on paper, so as to make you hear it? From a picture or a description you might, by an effort of the imagination, be able to realise to some extent the appearance of the volcano and the nature of its action; but neither of these methods would have any effect in making you realise the quantity of noise which it emits. But inasmuch as I can't draw a noise, and can't describe a noise, I must be content with stating the fact that we stood within sixty yards or so of a roar that is distinctly heard on Aneityum, forty miles away, and then leave you to make the best of it for yourselves.

These eruptions give the onlooker a very vivid idea of what force is, when exerted in a violent way, and, if he be in a contemplative mood, will lead him to think what is the cause of them.

One theory is, that the interior of this earth is a liquid mass of molten matter, and that the volcanoes are outlets for the gases generated by this heat. It is a very uncomfortable theory indeed, and one which should not be encouraged. It is highly unpleasant to be told that we are living merely upon a thin and shaky crust, beneath which rages a vast sea of fiery fluid, which here and there breaks out in the volcanic eruption, or sways the trembling crust in the earthquake. What guarantee have we that our part of the crust won't get melted and cave in

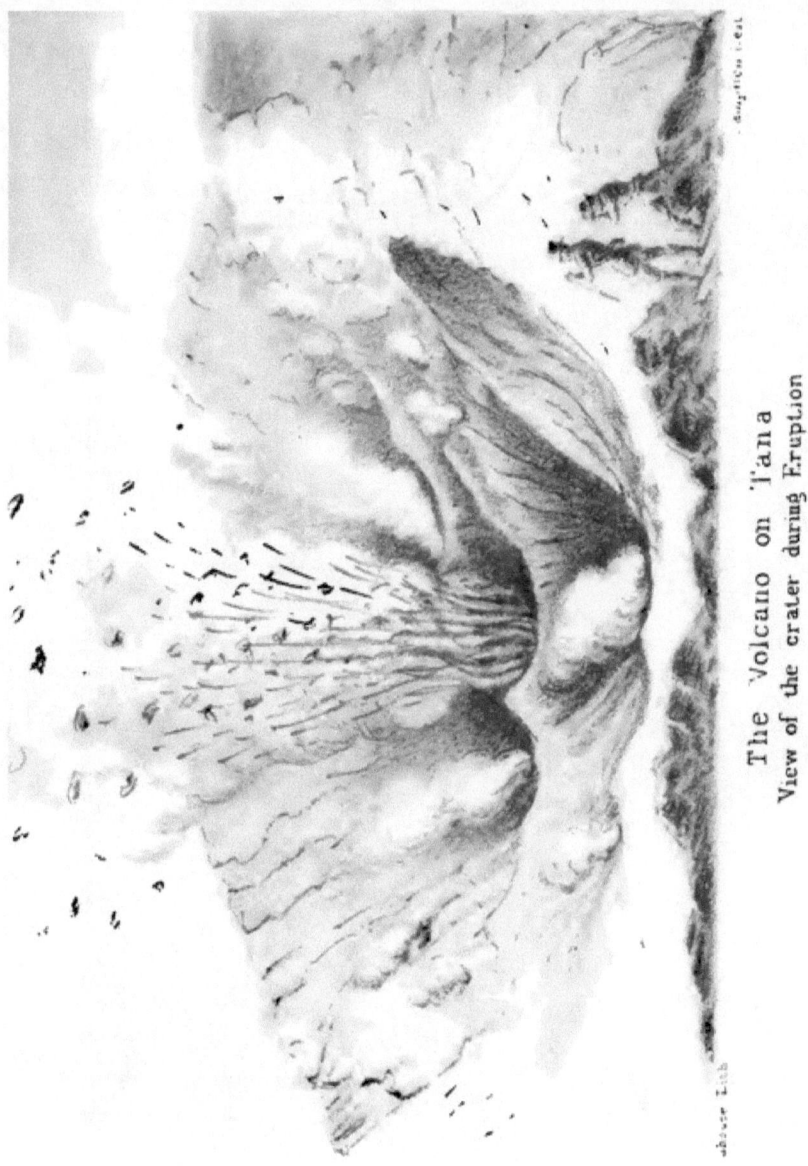

The Volcano on Tana
View of the crater during Eruption

some day, to the great inconvenience of ourselves and others living beside us? The idea is appalling. It is with a feeling of relief then that we turn to another theory, which, although it deals with a force whose deadly powers we frequently see, still gives us a good, sound, solid earth to stand upon. Both earthquakes and volcanoes are in this case ascribed to electricity. Regular currents of this fluid, says Dr. Thomson, the promulgator of the electrical theory, are continually running round this earth, along its stony ribs, which lie below the surface and which act as telegraphic wires. When the vein of conducting rocks is not sufficient to carry off the electricity which has gathered, an earthquake takes place; when two or three veins meet, and there is no way for the electricity to escape, it forces itself upwards in a volcanic eruption. What the thunderstorm is in the air, the earthquake is in the earth. That is the way, at least, in which I understand it. It sounds well, and I hope it may be right. Anything is better than the shaky-crust theory.

I must, however, return to the two lone beings on the top of Mount Yasúr, as the natives call it.

Tired at last of gazing on the volcanic exhibition, we turned, and there met our view, what I thought was the loveliest scene I had ever looked upon. Usually on these islands it is of no use going up hills to get a view, for when you get there you find yourself quite shut in by lofty trees. But here the volcano had effectually checked the approach of all vegetation, and we had a clear and uninterrupted view over sea and land. Between the volcano and the central mountains of the island, there lay a wide plain. It was green and flat—an unusual feature in the landscapes here, and was dotted with groves of palms and other trees, while embosomed in their midst lay a most lovely blue lake. At the back magnificent timbered ranges rose from the plain, riven with many a deep and gloomy gorge, down which streams ran to the lake. Spiral columns of blue smoke curled up here and there across the plain, each indicating the position of a native village. Then turning slightly round, we looked over the sea, and there the southern islands of the group lay—some appearing faintly, others with clear bold outlines, against the sky. Over each, like a white and snowy crown, there floated a pile of cloud; but otherwise the sky was clear.

What a contrast, the scene before us and that beside us! The one so fair and peaceful—the other so black and terrible.

Turning reluctantly from these scenes—so different, yet each so worthy of notice—we began to retrace our steps. The ground everywhere in the vicinity of the volcano was covered with shining substances like spun glass, very beautiful but very brittle. Some way down the active cone, there is a great mass of lava piled up in a curious twisted fashion, apparently having been forced out at some time from the side of the cone, when it has been unusually active.

Taking a shorter and rougher route backward, we came first to a round open plain, surrounded partly by a steep cliff and having a smooth floor of brown scoria. Then we marched along a ridge which gradually descended from the volcano to Port Resolution, passing here and there beds of soft hot clay and jets of sulphurous steam, and lastly, hot springs which issue from the ground just on the shores of the bay. Crossing over in a canoe, we reached the mission house, very tired and as black as sweeps, from the volcanic dust, but thoroughly satisfied with what had been accomplished.

I will conclude this letter with a few remarks about the peculiarities of this volcano. The first is the extraordinary regularity of its eruptions. A hundred years ago, Cook tells us it was acting exactly as it does now—an eruption taking place every five or six minutes.

Another curious thing about it is, that it is always more active after heavy rains. The lake which I spoke of our seeing from the top, extends to the foot of the volcano, and I am told that at its edge there are some wide crevices, down which water is continually pouring, but more especially after rains. How this should stir the volcano up to greater activity than usual, I do not pretend to be able to say, unless it is by the conversion of the water into steam. I only relate the fact.

This volcano, though a nuisance in some ways, such as covering everything with volcanic dust that happens to be to leeward of it, is still a great benefit in others. From it are obtained quantities of very fine sulphur, which is collected by the natives and brought to the traders for sale. It also produces the hot springs before alluded to, some of which are just warm enough for a pleasant bath, whilst others are hot enough to boil potatoes or scald pigs; and then it affords to inquisitive visitors an opportunity not often granted by these fiery craters of viewing, from their very edge, the magnificent spectacle of an eruption.

## LETTER XIII.

THE INDUSTRIES CARRIED ON IN THE NEW HEBRIDES—
COTTON GROWING — COBRA — ARROWROOT — WHALING —
WHAT MIGHT BE DONE HERE—MODE OF REACHING THE
ISLANDS, AND OUTFIT—THE DISADVANTAGES CONNECTED
WITH RESIDENCE HERE.

*Port Resolution, Tana,*
*December, 1872.*

ALTHOUGH at present the exports from the New Hebrides are extremely limited, I have not the slightest hesitation in asserting that some day these islands will occupy a very important commercial position in the southern hemisphere; their immense natural resources, and their proximity to Australia with its rapidly increasing population, put the matter almost beyond a doubt.

Cotton growing is now the principal industry, and is the chief export; although as yet the plantations are new, and mostly small in size.

It is found that the Sea Island cotton—the very best and most valuable kind — grows admirably upon many of the islands, the climate and soil both being suitable. A light sandy soil is the best, and the sea air seems indispensable. The closer to the beach the plantation is, the better will be the crop.

The following is the mode in which cotton is grown down here. When the ground is cleared, the soil is loosened with sharp heavy hoes or adzes. In January or February the seed is sown; and it is so distributed that when the plants have grown up they will be in rows, having sufficient space between them to allow the gatherer to pass up and down. The seeds quickly germinate, and the plant grows rapidly. When it is about two feet high it is topped, to prevent it growing out of reach of the cotton picker, and also to render the plant more sturdy and the lower branches more vigorous.

In four or five months after sowing the seed, the first crop is ready for gathering; and the plant bears regularly until November or thereabouts, during which time the picking goes on. When the plant has ceased to bear for the season, it is cut down to the roots, next year's crop coming from the fresh shoots which spring up. Every three or four years the plants are renewed. After the cotton has been gathered by natives in baskets, it is spread out in the sun to dry, and is then taken to the gin house, where this useful little machine separates the floss from the seed; after which the former is put up in bales and exported, while the latter is culled to get seed for sowing, or is exported as a material furnishing oil of some value.

A cotton plantation, when the pods are ripe and opening, has a very pretty appearance. There is something pleasing about the whole mode of growing and preparing cotton—it is so clean and so easily managed. There is no washing necessary, as there is in wool; no greasy matter stains the spotless whiteness of the glossy cotton balls. There is no shearing, neither clipping nor cutting the producer in the endeavour to get the produce, as so often happens to the poor sheep in the hands of an ignorant shearer; but quietly the plant opens its pod and displays its soft treasures, which are easily plucked out by the nimble fingers of the native pickers.

Now for a few statistics with regard to cotton-growing here, for the benefit of the commercial man and the curious generally.

I am indebted to Mr Hebblewhite, of Havannah Harbour, for much of my information upon this point; and I beg here to acknowledge that gentleman's kindness in this respect.

One acre of land should yield one ton of rough cotton, which, when ginned, will give 500 lbs. net.

If 2/. per ℔ be obtained for it—and this is not a high price for Sea Island—£50 per acre will equal the gross proceeds.

The expenses consist of wages, supply of food, machinery, freight, &c. Natives are paid at the rate of £2 to £3 per annum, besides the sum per head paid to the vessel engaged in fetching them. Their food consists of native vegetables, pork, rice, &c., and costs about £2 per man a year. One man, or one and a-half, is allowed to each acre.

The machinery may be a very expensive item or may not,—that of course depends entirely upon the style of business that is adopted; some planters have none at all, sending their cotton to be ginned elsewhere, or selling it in the rough; whereas others, such as Mr. Hebblewhite on Efaté, have several gins, and a steam engine to drive them. A small hand gin that would turn out 100 ℔s. per day costs about £15 to £20. The freight to the colonies is 1d. per ℔.

A second industry and export is cobra. Some time ago the traders down here used to manufacture cocoanut oil from the kernel of the cocoanut, and export it; but they have since found it pay better to send the kernels home as cobra, and let the British manufacturers express the oil with their more perfect machinery.

The process of making cobra is very simple. The nut is first broken into halves, and laid in the sun until the kernel is so loose that it can easily be cut out. This is next done, and the dried kernel having been cut into several pieces, is bagged and exported. The price paid the natives for the nuts varies exceedingly, but 1/8 per hundred will be about the average. Ten men will turn out about one ton per week; and the price obtained is from £8 to £10 per ton.

The trade has been for some time on the decline, as the price obtainable has sunk so low as to render it almost a matter of impossibility to make any profit out of it, after paying expenses.

Arrowroot is another export. The manufacture of this article is however principally confined to the mission stations, where it is made by the natives for the benefit of the Bible Society or other kindred institutions. This process is also simple, and the results are highly satisfactory, inasmuch as this arrowroot fetches the highest prices ruling.

When the root is obtained, it is grated down, generally upon common nutmeg graters, and put in a tub of clear water. After standing some time, the water is poured off and a fresh quantity poured in. This is repeated until all the poisonous juices of the plant are carried off, when it is spread out in the sun to dry. When thoroughly dried, it is ready for use.

Whaling and beche de mer close the list. The latter is carried on to a very limited extent, but the former with more vigour. There are three whaling stations on the group—one at Eramanga and two at Aneityum. I don't think that any of these fishers are making their fortunes; for although whales are not scarce, they seldom get more than two or three apiece in one season, and these are not worth more than £250 or £300.

I shall now say a word or two as to what might be done upon these islands.

Everything which grows in the West Indies, does grow, or I believe would grow, on the New Hebrides. The latter group is nearly in the same latitude south as the former is north of the equator. Coffee, ginger, tobacco, sugarcane, and nutmegs, exist at present on various of the islands—some indigenously, others having been imported; but none of them are as yet cultivated with a view to export.

I have seen several coffee plants, some very large, and bearing an immense quantity of berries. There is no doubt but that the plant grows well, although I am not aware whether its produce is equal in point of quality to that grown in Ceylon and elsewhere. I see no reason, however, why it should not be, and believe that, from the great variety of soil and situation which these islands afford, this valuable article might be grown on many of them with much success.

Ginger and nutmegs are indigenous plants, and, although not themselves the articles of commerce, show that their more valued relatives might be cultivated here.

The tobacco plant is found on several of the islands, and seems to thrive tolerably. It grows rather rank for making really a good leaf, but attention might amend this. The natives dry and smoke it when they can get none of the imported article; but they decidedly prefer the latter.

The sugarcane does very well, and is cultivated to a considerable extent by the natives as an article of food. The canes are thick, strong, and very sweet, and bye-and-bye, when men of capital turn their attention to them, will yield a rich harvest.

Utilising the fibre of the cocoanut-husk and banana-stem is another industry in which much might be done. I think I said before that Mr. Hebblewhite, of Havannah Harbour, is erecting a building and procuring machinery for making coir matting, brushes, &c., from the cocoanut fibre. It is to be hoped that he may be successful in the enterprise, and thus develop this new industry in the group. With regard to the banana fibre, I am surprised that nothing has been done with it. The process is simple, and the result is valuable.

The banana stems—or rather shoots, for they have no true aerial stems—are cut down after the fruit has been gathered. They are split open, and the centre removed, when both centre and outside are passed between rollers, which express all the viscid matter. After being dried, the fibre is ready for exportation. From one kind of banana the well-known manilla hemp is made, and also a fine kind of muslin. There is no scarcity of bananas here; they grow splendidly on all the islands, are very easily cultivated, and then their fruit is valuable, independently of the fibre.

In addition to these plants already mentioned, I believe that tea, rice, pepper, cloves, and other spices might be grown here readily; so that, almost in the words of Quiros, it might be said without exaggeration, that these islands will some day become so productive as not only to support themselves, but to enrich the Australian colonies which lie so close to them, and which will naturally become the chief consumers of their produce.

In case any of you may feel interested in the account of the capabilities of the islands, and in my opinions as to their future prospects, and wish to launch out on the experiment of planting in the New Hebrides, I must give you some idea of the other side of the picture, *i.e.*, some of the disadvantages and discomforts of residence here.

If you are fond of ease and the comforts of a quiet home, you had better stay at home. If you are delicate, or nervous, or unused to roughing it, you had better stay at home. If you have no capital, and no experience, or no partner who has either, you had better not come here. If you are fond of society, you had better not come here. For if you do come down, you will have to work hard, in a hot and enervating climate where much caution is required to keep off fever and ague; you require capital to start any business with, and you will be very much the better of some practical experience. You have no society, save that of the savages—unless you happen to be near some missionary station, or some planter or trader's establishment; but these are few and far between, while many of the owners are not at all preferable to the blackfellows.

Supposing, however, that you have decided to come, in spite of every disadvantage—that you have plenty of pluck and some capital—then proceed to Sydney. There get what machinery and provisions you want, not forgetting the frame and boards of a house—for you will find no hotels when you arrive here. Next, get a passage, either direct or *viâ* New Caledonia by the monthly mail steamer, and arrive here in time to commence cotton planting. The first thing you have to do on landing is to buy your land—an easy matter generally, unless you take a fancy to some of the natives' reserves. A shilling per acre will generally procure you as much as you want, and leave the natives none the worse. But then, what about labour? You cannot of course work the plantation without assistance, and you cannot get the natives of the island upon which you are living to work steadily. You must therefore get natives from other islands. I don't say anything at present upon the rights or wrongs of the labour traffic. I merely state here what would be necessary under the circumstances. Having then got your men, erected your house, and cleared your ground, you can proceed as your wisdom sees fit with the duties of such industry as you have ventured on.

The Loyalties rather took my fancy as a place of settlement, the climate being healthy and pleasant and the ground good for cotton growing. But then they are under French rule; and they will not sell, having, apparently, expectations of such large additions to their criminal population, that the Loyalties may be required for penal establishments, in addition to New Caledonia. There are one or two white men engaged in trading with the natives of the Loyalties, buying up the cotton which they grow. But I am afraid that it will be a long time before anything of this kind is done in the New Hebrides, as the natives seem greatly deficient in anything which savours of energy or enterprise.

## LETTER XIV.

THE NEW HEBRIDES MISSIONS — ATTACKS ON MISSIONS GENERALLY — MISSION WORK ON THE GROUP — BENEFITS TO SCIENCE AND COMMERCE RENDERED BY MISSIONARIES — THE NATIVE TEACHERS.

*Port Resolution, Tana,*
*December,* 1872.

IN this letter I am going to give you a few of my ideas as to the missions in the New Hebrides. What follows is not to be a report of the work done at each station, or a history of what has been done; but merely a few observations, in my usual rambling way, as to the position which these missionaries hold, the work they do as a body, and the way in which they do it.

I know that some persons will be apt to look at my statements as prejudiced in favour of the missionaries, from the circumstances in which I am placed; but I do not admit that there is any ground for such a supposition, and I am sure that what I assert would be confirmed by anyone who has observed for himself and candidly judged of what is seen.

How is it that the anti-missionary party in this world of ours is so strong and so bitter? How is it so difficult to make them credit anything favourable to missions, however good the authority? They will readily believe any story, however absurd, if it be unfavourable to missions; and missionaries themselves are loaded by them with offensive epithets, and the whole affair is denounced as a concocted business for the benefit of the churches at home and the lazy fortune-seekers abroad.

Now these attacks are for the most part so utterly wanting in sense and manliness, and so transparently false to anyone who calmly and candidly observes the real working of a mission body, that they merit nothing but silent contempt. No doubt some who have visited the actual field of mission labours have written unfavourably regarding them: but generally they were but casual visitors, unacquainted with the people or the missions, and sometimes, in the words of the well-known traveller and author, Charles Darwin, "disappointed in not finding the field of licentiousness quite so open as formerly, they will not give credit to a morality which they do not wish to practise, or to a religion which they undervalue, if not despise." These words were written of visitors to some island in Eastern Polynesia—Tahiti I believe.

But to come to the New Hebrides. There are eleven missionaries at present on the group, supported by various Presbyterian churches and governed by a Synod composed of the various missionaries, which meets annually. A mission vessel is also supported by the churches, for the benefit of this mission, and also a certain number of native teachers. The whole cost of the mission is say, in round numbers, £5000 per annum.

Twenty-five years ago there was no missionary on the group. All the natives were alike—heathen cannibals of the worst stamp, having lost all that civility and hospitality that Cook ascribes to them, through the *kind* and *humane* treatment of the sandalwood traders and others. First, on Aneityum a missionary and his wife landed in 1848, and they, with another, have been labouring on that island ever since. And if we compare the Aneityumese as they are now with the natives of any island not yet touched by the missionary, who represent the Aneityumese as they used to be, we arrive at a tolerably correct conclusion as to the results—at least externally—of the missionaries' work. The difference is very apparent, even to the most superficial observer. On Aneityum, they are clothed, they are at peace, have given up all those heathen abominations—such as cannibalism, strangulation of widows, infanticide, and obscene dances—and they regularly attend church on Sunday. Life and property are as safe there, or perhaps more so, than in Great Britain. In fact, they are now a christian community.

Now, do not misunderstand me. I don't mean to assert that they are all upright, infallible persons—that none amongst them ever do wrong. There are thieves amongst them, and quarrelsome persons; and no doubt some who have still a hankering after old times and old habits. But what I mean to say is this—that heathenism has taken its departure from that island, that the young generation is growing up ignorant of all those abominable heathen customs once so common, and that they now deserve the name of a christian population as much as any of our communities do, where people are brought up every day for committing all sorts of crimes and offences.

Men often accuse missionaries of colouring their reports, and sending to their churches exaggerated statements of the progress of their work. Such accusations do not apply here. If anything, I find that the missionaries are apt to take rather a depreciatory view of their own work; and they are very cautious on all occasions to avoid making things appear better than they are. Here is what Mr. Copeland, of Fotuna, writes in one of the reports :—

"We cannot reasonably expect to see a people anywhere throw off heathenism in a month or a year. When real, the embracing of Christianity is not a mechanical process; it results from the use of certain means, and is the outcome of certain inward changes. Before any transformation can take place among a heathen people, light must be communicated, and a better way of life be unfolded; before that can be done, a new language has to be acquired, independent of grammars and dictionaries; some knowledge must also be gained of the habits, ideas, and prejudices of the natives—so very different from those of Europeans. Divided as his time and energies will be in the New Hebrides between secular and spiritual duties, a missionary will not communicate much effective knowledge under two years."

And again, speaking of the danger of overstating things above alluded to, he thus appeals to the friends of the mission:—

"By an inordinate desire for the bright and the pleasing, don't force us to exaggerate, to send you accounts of converts that exist very much only on paper—to give cheques which we shall not be able one day to meet fully. If we missionaries have at all a tendency to err in our letters, it is to overstate matters, and to give accounts of our work a touch of the *couleur de rose*. Our parental eyes are sometimes a little blind to the defects of our work and our converts. Take care when you read our letters. Remember whence they come, and the people they describe, and that it is perhaps the first flush of a new feeling on the part of the natives we are writing about. Don't add to our statement. Remember that words and phrases may not comprehend here all they do with you. Don't make much of little; don't put constructions on simple and trivial circumstances which they will not bear; don't draw a universal conclusion from a single premise; and don't form high anticipations from mere passing events and outward appearances, but rather wait till time shall develop their results and test their values. More particularly, I would say, when the natives shall embrace Christianity, don't expect among them a high civilisation. As a race they are low, physically and intellectually, and are not capable, meantime at least, of a civilisation such as yours and mine. A certain amount of it they appear to acquire very rapidly, but the after steps are taken very slowly indeed. Even were they capable of a high civilization, they do not possess the materials for it; and the too sudden change would prove, physically, very injurious to them."

Another accusation made against missionaries is that they go out, from motives of personal gain, with the idea of enriching themselves and living comfortable easy lives. If that is really the case, the New Hebridean missionaries are decidedly the most irrational set of men I ever came across. The New Hebrides is the last place any sane man or woman would go to in search of comfort, and a missionary's is certainly the last trade any sane man would take up that wanted to make his fortune. The idea is too absurd to talk seriously about. I have not the slightest hesitation in saying that every one of them might occupy a very much better position, pecuniarily, in a civilised land than they do at present, and that there is nothing in their present mode of life to counterbalance this—nothing save the consciousness that they are doing their duty towards God and their fellow-men.

Not only are the missionaries doing good to the natives; they are also benefitting Science. As educated men amongst new peoples and new forms of animal and vegetable life, their observations upon these subjects are of great value. I can quite understand and believe the remark "that the missionaries have done more to bring to light new languages than all the learned societies in the world."

Then they are opening up new fields for commerce; they are

teaching the natives *to want*—and when they want they will work to supply their wants—work, too, on their own islands.

Again, where the missionary has settled and laboured, other foreigners may safely follow; and though these men are not slow to take advantage of the result of the missionary's work, they but seldom give him the credit that is his due.

This struck me particularly in the case of the author of "South-Sea Bubbles." When on a quiet and civilised island, where not the slightest ghost of danger exists, he abuses the missionaries right and left, and bravely wishes that he only could have been on the island before these obnoxious individuals had tainted its primeval freedom. Looking at some women in church, he says, "I gazed sadly on them, thinking what much better fun I would have had if I had visited the island fifty years sooner." He takes very good care, however, not to risk his precious body upon islands which are still as savage as he wished that one was, and where he might have enjoyed the fun of being killed, and cooked, and eaten.

Aneityum being the island upon which missionaries first settled, is naturally the farthest advanced, and is the head-quarters of the mission in this group. The missionaries upon the other islands have not been idle however. Aniwa may be said to rank next to Aneityum. Its population of 240 have also as a body renounced heathenism, and gradually their characters are being formed and their principles elevated by the teachings of their missionary, Mr. Paton. On Tana, the missionaries' influence is being felt for some distance round the stations; but the progress on that island is slower than it otherwise might have been on account of the large mass of heathenism, the constant wars among the tribes, and the diversity of language. Along the coast between the two mission stations—a distance of fourteen miles—teachers are planted, and services are maintained on Sundays at several places, with good results.

On several occasions the missionaries have been able to prevent the outbreak of war, and have succeeded in suppressing many of the vile heathen customs. They are respected and looked up to by the natives in their neighbourhood; and if they are able to remain steadily at the stations they now occupy, will no doubt accomplish more than ever has been done yet on Tana. For although this island was one of the first on which missionaries settled, they were prevented by the fierce hostility of the natives from remaining long enough thoroughly to acquire the language or get acquainted with the customs of the people. The two missionaries now on the island have been longer there than any of their predecessors, and their influence is now beginning to tell in the manifest improvement of the natives in the vicinity of the mission stations. On Fotuna, Eramanga, and Efaté, churches have been formed; while on Nguna and Santo, the islands last settled, a footing has been gained.

A missionary cannot, like a clergyman, enter on his proper duties immediately on arriving at the sphere of operations. The language has to be learnt, and he has to get acquainted with the natives and their customs before he can expect them to benefit by his preaching. This may take a couple of years; but during that time he may be quietly paving his way for his future work; he may be disarming the suspicions and gaining the confidence and goodwill of the people. It is not to be supposed that the savage islanders will be found on the beach, anxiously waiting to welcome the missionary, or that they feel in themselves the slightest desire for moral or spiritual improvement. No; they love their heathen customs, and it is an act of great self-denial on their part to give them up. For the most part, at first, they do not wish a missionary to come among them; or if they do acquiesce in it, it is merely in the hope of getting calico and other goods from him by fair means or foul. When Mr. Neilson went to settle at Port Resolution, and the timber for his house was put on shore, the natives threw it back into the water; but as he persisted in landing it, they gave in, and he has been able to reside in safety on the island ever since.

The missionary's knowledge of medicine—though it may not in every case be very deep—gives him a hold upon the minds of his parishioners, and, not unfrequently, he now supersedes the disease-maker. Gunshot wounds, broken bones, sores, and fever and ague, come under his treatment. When the natives observe the good results, they gain confidence in his skill, and are not, I think, wanting in gratitude.

The progress of the work all over the group is slow certainly, but I do not think on that account the less sure. There are no startling accounts of wonderful conversions, or of whole islands turning from their evil ways in one day—such as we sometimes hear of taking place in other quarters of the globe. The tribes here being so small, and the chiefs having so little influence, such a thing cannot happen. Wholesale conversions cannot occur. Every man and woman has to be dealt with separately, and each has to be convinced of the truth for himself and herself. Therefore it must be a work of time; but then it ensures that what is done, is done well.

I am convinced that this work is going on steadily, and that these Christian missionaries are raising populations out of the fearful state of barbarism in which they have been living, are presenting to them the simple truths of Christianity, and are showing them that there is something to live for besides the mere gratification of the animal passions. They are doing this by the teachings of the church and of the school, and not less effectually by the example of consistent Christian lives.

Before dismissing this subject, I must say a word or two about that other agency which is at work in this group—a humble but none the less a useful one, viz., the native teachers.

It has been found that the natives of other groups of islands cannot stand the climate of the New Hebrides. Eastern Island natives have been tried, but many died; Loyalty islanders have been tried, but with the same result. Upon the advanced natives, then, of the New Hebrides the missionaries are dependent for teachers, that is to say, upon the Aneityumese Christians. There are about twenty of these men and their wives out at work on the various islands. They get £5 per annum, and are extremely useful. They act as servants, assistants, and right-hand men to the missionary, or are placed on separate stations under his superintendence. They quickly pick up the language, and their knowledge of the native customs generally and native forms of idiom, enables them to give great assistance to the missionary in the work of translation, as well as fits them for effectively addressing men of kindred natures.

If there is a mission worthy of hearty support, it is that of the New Hebrides. A good work is being done, but the missionaries feel sadly crippled by the want of men. Instead of eleven, they say there ought to be twenty at least. It is to be hoped that their appeals to the churches in this respect will be successful, and that many will be found willing to go to these islands, fully alive to all the difficulties and discomforts of the work, but resolved on carrying it out under the constraining power of the love of Christ, and in obedience to his last command.

## LETTER XV.

LEAVE TANA FOR ANEITYUM—THE HURRICANE—THE WRECK—A SALE BY AUCTION—LIFE OF THE SHIPWRECKED PARTY ASHORE—THE EARTHQUAKE.

*Anelcauhat, Aneityum,*
*February,* 1873.

ON Thursday, the 2nd January, I left Tana for Aneityum, in the "Dayspring," commencing my homeward voyage. The vessel having returned from the colonies, had made a trip round the islands, and was now on her way to Sydney *via* Aneityum and Fotuna. On Friday she anchored in Anelcauhat harbour. After our arrival, Captain Jenkins, who had taken the place of Captain Rae, resigned, went round to Anamé with the second mate and Mrs. Goodwill, who was proceeding to the colonies on account of her health. On Saturday I went ashore to spend Sunday and Monday with Mr. and Mrs. Murray, expecting to sail on Tuesday. Signs of a coming storm began to appear on Saturday afternoon—a heavy swell rolling into the harbour, without any wind to account for it. On Sunday matters looked still worse. Sharp squalls of rain and wind came from the N.E., while the glass was steadily sinking. The first mate, Mr. McArthur, who was in charge of the vessel, did not allow these portents of bad weather to pass unheeded, but took every precaution for the safety of the vessel: an additional anchor was let go, every inch of cable was paid out, and the fore-top-gallant mast and yard sent down on deck. On Monday morning we witnessed one of the most fearful hurricanes that has ever visited these islands.

At half-past four a.m. I suddenly awoke to find the roof of the building in which I was sleeping split open, the rain pouring in, and the whole place reeling before the furious blasts of the gale. The noise was something fearful, as the wind tore, shrieking, through the trees, breaking the palms like pipe stems, and carrying along with it showers of cocoanuts, leaves and bits of thatch. Quickly dressing, I made my way to Mr. Murray's quarters, and found both he and Mrs. M. up, and their rooms in a similar condition to mine. For about an hour we stood sheltering ourselves in the verandah in lee of the house, watching in the dim light the great trees blowing before the storm, or crashing to the ground if too stiff to bend; watching the hailstorm of nuts, branches, and leaves, as they whirled furiously by, listening to the booming and roaring of that mighty gale, and wishing for day. As it began to get light we strained our eyes eagerly towards the anchorage of the vessel, although we hardly hoped to see her again, and we were rather relieved to make her out at last, although from her position there was no doubt of her being stranded on the outer reef of the harbour. Soon we were able, with the aid of a glass, to make out figures on board, and could observe them cutting down the foremast, which quickly disappeared over the side; then the jib-boom went, and next the main topmast, after which a flag of distress was run up on the mainmast.

Along the beach, a short distance from the mission station, there lives an Eastern Islander—a whaler—who has several fine boats; and to him I went, to see what could be done. Nothing,—he said; no crew could pull against such a gale. For the wind had now veered from the N.N.E. to the N.W., and was blowing from that direction, into the harbour, almost as

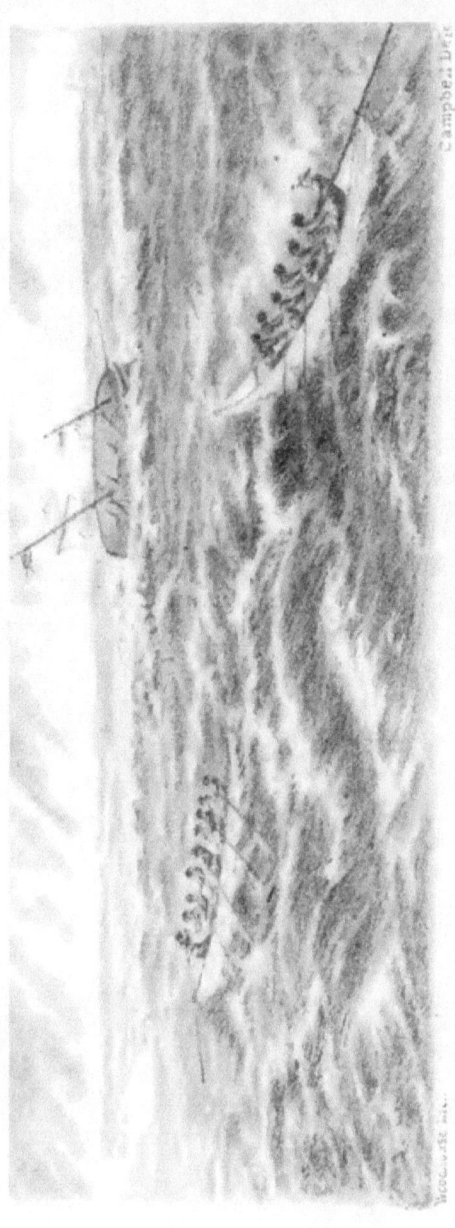

Wreck of the Brigantine "Dayspring" at Aneityum

hard as it had blown off the land. So for two hours or thereabouts, we had just to sit twirling our thumbs and watching the wreck through the glass. Another flag of distress went up on the forecastle, and as the wind had again veered—this time to the west—and was falling somewhat, I made another excursion to the whaler's. He consented, so, having secured crews, we started—he in one of his whaleboats, and I in Mr. Murray's boat. Soon after we left the shore we saw a boat pulling off from the islet of Inyug, which having a shorter distance to go than we, and having no head wind to pull against, reached her first. Notwithstanding the squalls of wind and rain, still heavy, and the nasty cross sea, we all made the trip to and from the vessel in safety, taking on shore the native teachers, who were passengers in her, the mate, crew, ship's papers, instruments, and some boxes. After this the wind quickly fell, and during the remainder of the day the boats were busily employed in taking passengers' luggage, stores, &c. on shore.

The following extract from a letter of Mr. Inglis to Dr. Steel of Sydney, will give an idea as to what those on board experienced at this time.

"About four o'clock on Monday morning the wind blew with such irresistible violence that both anchors were started, and the vessel, dragging her chains and anchors, ran out of the harbour as if she had been a mail steamer going at full speed. She was all but clear of the harbour, and out to the open sea, where she would have been safe, when the wind suddenly veering, or a cross sea coming up, or both, she was struck with such force on the broadside as, notwithstanding the breadth of her beam, all but capsized her; a tremendous sea at the same time bearing her along, pitched her right up on the edge of the reef. Here she was exposed to the full force of the breakers; and had she remained in that situation the probability is that she would soon have gone to pieces, and every one on board have perished. But a second tremendous sea came on, lifted her up, and carried her a considerable way on to the reef—as far, indeed, as the chains would permit, the anchors being caught by the coral. As soon as daylight enabled the sailors to see, they cut down the foremast, fearing lest the working of the mast would have split up the vessel. When the rain, mist, and spray had so far cleared off as that the vessel could be seen from the mission house, flags of distress were observed flying and men were noticed perched on the rigging. The ship's boats were smashed, and the people on board had no means of escape. But the storm rapidly subsided, and as soon as it was at all safe to go out to the vessel, Mr. Joseph Underwood, of the whaling establishment on Inyug, went out with his boat to render what assistance he could. Manhera, a Tahitian, belonging to the other whaling establishment, also went out in his boat; and Mr. F. A. Campbell, of Geelong—who was a passenger in the "Dayspring," but who had gone ashore when the vessel came into harbour—went out with Mr. Murray's boat. All on board—men, women, and children—were got safely on shore."

The captain and second mate then appeared on the scene having walked over from Anamé in the wind and rain, and being quite tired out by the time they reached this. The captain had heard of the wreck, by a messenger despatched by Mr. Murray in the morning. It was a sad blow to him, poor man; and though no fault of his, he must have been greatly distressed by it,—this being his first trip in charge of the vessel.

The effects of this hurricane upon the island were very fearful. Everywhere there was to be seen the same picture of desolation. There seemed to be more trees lying on the ground than standing upright, and not a green leaf was to be seen.

The wind had scorched them as a great bush fire would have done. The garden round the mission house was now a pitiable spectacle—strewed with thatch, broken trees, branches, and fences. But Anelcauhat was on the lee side of the island during this gale. At Anamé things were still worse. For there the sea came up to help in the general work of destruction; and rolling up far beyond its usual limits, smashed all the boats, sheds, and fences along the line of beach.

The hurricane reached its height between four and five in the morning, and during that time nearly all the damage was done. The barometer fell 1·60 inches, *i.e.*, to 28·28 just before the storm was at its highest, but rose quickly after that. This hurricane was felt very severely all over the group, also on New Caledonia, and, I believe, on Fiji. It evidently came from somewhere about the N.W., and had a circular motion, in the direction that the hands of a watch move.

For a few days after the wreck everyone was busy, getting goods from the wreck and storing them; and boats were busy plying to and fro with all sorts of cargoes, the whole scene being quite in the Swiss-family Robinson style. If there was anything that reconciled me to the wreck of the poor old "Dayspring" and of our hopes of getting speedily to the colonies, it was the signal triumph over our old enemies the cockroaches. They were conquered at last. They found a watery grave—every cockroach of them—and will torment the human species no more.

As the position of the vessel was somewhat precarious, the captain deemed it prudent to have her reported on by three carpenters, who pronounced her a total wreck, and advised her to be sold without delay, in case she might go to pieces. This was done. A public auction was held in the large schoolroom, which was quite large enough to hold all the bidders. I mounted the desk, and starting at £20, ran her up to £38, at which price she was knocked down to Mr. Underwood, of Inyug.

We now began to realise our position. We were a shipwrecked party—not, it is true, upon a heathen island, and for that we were thankful; but upon an out-of-the-way place, where we might be cooped up for months, on short rations perhaps. The beautiful scenery now had not much attraction for me, and time hung rather heavily on our hands.

The cabin table, and dishes, and the galley-stove, had been removed into a building at the back of the mission station; and this we used as a dining-hall, other buildings being kindly put at our disposal, by Mr. Murray, for sleeping apartments.

In order to get up a little excitement to vary the monotony of our existence, I arranged a day of sports, which on the whole came off very successfully. We had all the ship's bunting hung out from two cocoanut-palms, and we had a fine wide grassy road as the course. There were running flat races, walking races, sack races, and jumps, in which both whites and blacks competed. The blacks were nowhere. The great feature of the day, however, was a pulling match across the harbour, distance about one mile, between a white and black crew. Mr. Underwood acted as coxswain to the blackfellows, while I coached the whites. In this race we got unmercifully licked. For some time the boats kept very even, but the blacks rowed with a quicker stroke, kept it up all the way, and came in about twenty yards ahead of us. They were, however, a crack whaling crew, whereas my men were not much used to pulling steadily. The day's entertainment concluded with a grand display of fireworks, which included rockets, blue lights, &c., and rather astonished the natives. Another evening we had a select drawingroom entertainment in the schoolroom, consisting of a highly moral magic lantern, with slides, which I was called on to exhibit and explain. This was a very great success indeed. Another diversion we had was an earthquake. This was the greatest success of all—though, to tell the truth, we did not wish any more of it after we had experienced the first dose. It took place about three weeks after the wreck, at nine o'clock in the evening. I was in my room alone, with the lamp standing on the table. First there came a quick tremulous motion accompanied by a strange noise; then it changed to a fearful swaying to and fro, and the lamp fell over and went out. I had time to pick it up and light it before the motion ceased, from which I should judge that it lasted fully half a minute. It is a horrible sensation to have the solid earth swaying under your feet, and the thought presenting itself to your mind, that it may suddenly make an enormous gape right under you and swallow you up alive. I knew that the safest place was to remain where I was, for it was a small wooden house; but some of the crew—foolish fellows—when they felt it, bolted for the beach, intending to get into the boat, I suppose. Several walls were cracked during the shock, and, like the hurricane, it was much more severe than is usually experienced on these islands. The barometer was curiously affected by it, for it fell suddenly about half an inch as the shock came on, and rose again just as quickly, immediately after the shock had passed.

Besides these general diversions, I had various occupations of my own, such as drawing and writing. The result of the latter employment, or a portion of it at least, I shall give in the following letter.

## LETTER XVI.

THE LABOUR TRAFFIC—THE TWO GREAT EVILS CONNECTED WITH IT—THE MISCHIEF DONE BY THE PROCURERS OF LABOUR—THE BAD EFFECTS OF THEIR RESIDENCE ABROAD UPON THE NATIVES—DEPOPULATION OF THE ISLANDS.

*Anelcauhat, Aneityum,*
*February,* 1873.

I DO not know that there is any group in the Southern Pacific which supplies a greater number of natives for the plantations of Queensland and Fiji than does the New Hebrides. The labour vessel is a familiar sight to everyone living here; indeed, it is no rare thing to see several lying in harbour at one time. I have seen the ships sailing off to the distant plantations with their living freight, and I have seen them sailing back and discharging the returned labourers upon their native islands. I have met scores and scores of returned labourers and I know them well. What follows is the result of my observations.

I do not go the length of denouncing this traffic as always and necessarily a slave trade; I do not look upon every vessel engaged in it as a prowling slaver, and I do not consider that its master must be a villain of the deepest dye: but I do think that this traffic, as it is carried on at present, is an unmixed evil. It is productive of evil in two ways: in the first place it gives rise to those fearful atrocities which occasionally, and to a certain extent inevitably, are committed upon the natives; and in the second place it degrades and ruins nearly all those natives who are the subjects of it.

Lately a great deal has been said and written—and not too soon—upon this first point. The frightful revelations which from time to time have come before the public have been of too serious a nature to escape condemnation, even by those who formerly were staunch upholders of the traffic. The public mind has been thoroughly aroused, both in Great Britain and the colonies; an act has been passed constituting kidnapping a felony; and several gunboats have been ordered to cruise these seas for the purpose of suppressing these outrages.

I can hardly believe, however, that these measures, though right as far as they go, will do much permanent good. It appears to be an easy matter for the labour vessels to put on such an appearance of innocence when they are boarded, as will satisfy the inspecting officer—as witness the case of the "Carl," which, I understand, was boarded and examined, and passed by a British officer, not long after that frightful massacre took place. The gunboats will no doubt impose a partial restraint on the actions of the unprincipled villains who are working such mischief, and save some of the islanders from their horrid cruelty; while the representations of the masters of these vessels may lead to the adoption of more stringent measures, and finally to the abolition of the traffic, should the regulation of it be found impossible.

This first matter then having been so warmly taken up, so well exposed by competent authorities, and in a manner adjudicated upon for the present, I shall say nothing upon it, beyond a remark or two upon the following points:—

I. With the exception of those who have been abroad before, the natives, as a rule, do not and cannot understand what they are going away for, when they leave their islands for three years' service on a foreign plantation.

I have been led to this conclusion by the consideration of the very simple fact that there are no persons who can explain the terms of a contract to them. For firstly, the natives of the New Hebrides—as I have stated before—speak at least twenty different languages. Secondly, in very few cases can any of them understand two of these languages; and no white man—with the exception of the missionaries and other three men, I believe—can speak any one of them. Thirdly, the natives have no words in their own language to express years, wages, &c. Fourthly, the few that know any broken English would find their knowledge of no use to them in this particular matter. And fifthly, I am quite convinced that, even although they had a more extended knowledge of the words, they could not form the slightest conception of what three years' steady labour under plantation laws meant.

Of what use, under such circumstances, I would like to know, are Queensland enactments? Of what use is it to enact that the natives must comprehend the nature of the transaction before leaving the island or entering the plantation? Of what use is it to enact that there must be interpreters and agents in the labour vessels? If the Queensland Government were to make enactments steadily for the next hundred years at the rate of twenty per diem, do you think that they would produce one single interpreter capable of speaking the New Hebridean languages, or enable the poor, stupid, bewildered savage to comprehend what three years' absence from home means, when he has never been a couple of miles from his hut all his life long, or enable him to comprehend what three years' steady labour means, when his hardest work hitherto has been carrying his musket or leisurely attending to his yam plantation—leisurely that is compared with the way in which he will have to attend to his master's work? The idea is absurd.

II. You may ask then, why do the the natives leave their own islands? why do they go away if they do not know what they are going for? The following statement represents the matter, I believe, with tolerable accuracy. I give it in a tabulated form for the sake of clearness.

    10 per cent. are taken by force.

| | | |
|---|---|---|
| 20 | ,, | are obtained by deceit practised on the natives by masters of labour vessels or native agents. |
| 20 | ,, | are obliged to go by chiefs or relatives from whom they have been bought. |
| 10 | ,, | go because they are defeated in war and driven off their own lands. |
| 15 | ,, | are returned labourers, who finding their own plantations destroyed, wives gone, &c., ship off again in disgust. |
| 5 | ,, | accompany their chiefs when they go or are taken away. |
| 20 | ,, | go from curiosity, or from a desire to get muskets and other goods. |
| 100 | | |

From this statement it will be observed that I consider that about one-half of the labourers are obtained by what might be termed unfair means. The various ways of obtaining them unfairly are—1st, forcible abduction; 2nd, buying them from chiefs and relatives; aud 3rd, deceiving them.

With regard to the second method, whatever name the recruiters may call it by, there is no doubt but that the natives look upon it as buying and selling, inasmuch as the chiefs or relatives receive goods for the natives shipped. The chiefs, 'tis true, have no great influence over the people; but when they are tempted by the masters of labour vessels with goods which they have a wish for, they have enough of power, at least, to make it plain to certain natives that they had better ship off when they are ordered, or it will be the worse for them. This is the case especially with young lads, who are comparatively easily managed.

Then as to the deceptions which are practised on the natives, they are various, and often very successful. A native from one island will be shipped as agent on board the labour vessel, and going to a neighbouring island will invite natives to come with him and visit his friends. Unsuspectingly, they go on board, and when the vessel has got its complement in this way, she sails off for the plantations. These practices are, I am afraid, more common than is generally imagined.

I don't think that more than fifteen per cent. at the very outside are influenced by the motive which the upholders of this traffic declare to be the main one, viz., the desire of acquiring property. The remainder who are obtained fairly, are—first, those who go from curiosity to see new places; second, those who accompany their chief when he goes; thirdly, those who are driven from their homes in war, and take shelter in the labour vessel; and fourthly, those who have been away before, and on their return, finding their property destroyed, and having been unsettled in their habits, ship off again for a foreign plantation.

But now I hasten to the second division of the subject—the second great evil in connection with this traffic, viz., the bad effects which their sojourn in foreign lands has upon the natives.

This is a point which has been comparatively little noticed, the attention of the public having been entirely engrossed by the more glaring evils connected with the procuring of the natives. I question very much, however, whether the former is not as important as the latter, inasmuch as the latter may possibly be suppressed by the vigorous execution of the laws in force for that purpose, while the former would exist, even though the whole business was carried on in a lawful way.

I believe that the benefits arising from this labour traffic are entirely confined to the procurers and employers of the labour, while the labourers themselves lose in every way by the bargain—lose pecuniarily, bodily, mentally, spiritually.

Take the case of a native who is treated in a fair and lawful manner. He receives from £1 to £5 per annum for his three years' service, with which, in the shape of various goods, he returns to his own island. I have before alluded to the prevailing custom among the islanders of giving away everything anyone asks for. Hence it nearly always happens, that within a few hours after his arrival he distributes the most of his property to importunate friends, reserving some special articles, such as a musket and ammunition, for himself. A musket, ammunition, and an empty box frequently represent the three years' work on the plantation. Then over and against these acquisitions he has to place the serious loss he sustains in his own island property; he finds his plantations neglected, his pigs and fowls gone, and frequently his wives also : so that all the property he brought with him—even if he gave little or nothing away—would be swallowed up in restoring his plantations, rebuilding his hut, and buying pigs and fowls.

But if the man who is treated honestly does not reap pecuniary benefit from his labour—which those acquainted with the customs of the New Hebrideans know to be the fact—of course those who do not receive proper payment must be miserable losers by the transaction. They sometimes arrive at home with literally nothing, save, perhaps, a few shillings-worth of goods, as the fruit of their three or four, or even five, years' toil.

Then some of them come back broken down in health, while some never come back at all, but die on the plantation. As they are not naturally of a robust constitution, and are unaccustomed to steady labour, it tells on them severely, however well they may be treated; while those who are treated as no better than slaves, cannot be expected to return to their homes stronger and healthier men than they were when they left.

But, we are told, this trade improves them mentally—it elevates them as no other civilising agency has been able to accomplish

Mr. Trollope, in his work on Queensland, writes :—" The islanders who are brought to Queensland all return, and not a man of them returns without taking with him lessons of civilization. On the planters' grounds in Queensland they learn each other's languages, they have to live as white men live, they have to cook, to sow, dig, to plant, to hoe canes, to clothe themselves, and to be proud of their clothes—and they learn that continued work does produce accumulated property. These lessons they take back to the islands, and then they send their friends and return themselves, and so they are gradually being brought within the pale of civilization." The same author also writes of " the happy Polynesian, who is allowed to escape from the savage slavery of his island to the plenty and protected taskwork of a Queensland sugar plantation." Mr. Trollope politely refers to the arguments against this traffic as " buncombe ;" but if there ever was buncombe, it is contained in the paragraphs just quoted from his own writings. It sounds well, no doubt, all that about the natives taking back the lessons of useful industry to their islands, and of their thus being brought gradually within the pale of civilization; but it is as pure a lot of fiction as ever that distinguished novelist wrote—at least as far as the New Hebrideans are concerned, and they represent a large proportion of the labourers, as well as fair specimens of all the rest.

The returned labourer is not civilized a bit by his sojourn abroad—that is my experience. He may wear clothing, and may appear quiet and steady when on the plantation, for there he cannot help himself. But no one can judge from his appearance and behaviour there what he will do afterwards, and no one who was not remarkably shortsighted would think for a moment of doing so. Let those who write and speak after the manner of the novelist accompany the natives back to their island homes, and watch their behaviour there; then, but not till then, will their observations and statements be worthy of credit. How inexpressibly shocked would the good Mr. Trollope be to see his civilized native, his model reclaimed savage—who has learnt to plant, and dig, and wear clothes, and be proud of them, moreover — contemptuously fling aside the cherished garment, plaster himself with horrid paint, resume with eager delight the heathen abominations of which he has so long been deprived, and speedily appear again in his primitive condition. And yet this is the custom with the returned labourers here.

The only accomplishment I know which they bring back, and of which they are proud, is the facility of swearing in the English language. The fact is, that they not only relapse at once into their old barbarous ways, but I believe that they are actually worse men after their return—more degraded, if that be possible, and certainly more vicious—than before. The plantations are finishing schools of a high order, for they turn out some of the most accomplished specimens of savage scoundrelism imaginable—men who have engrafted on their original depraved nature the vices of civilization, but none of its virtues.

Some people seem to fancy that those who go to Queensland, being hedged in with enactments, must be better off than those who go elsewhere. But I never could see any difference in them after their return. They are all alike.

The only man I ever knew who derived any real benefit from his foreign service, had been in Fiji; but that benefit he owed to the missionaries there, and not to the plantation.

Lastly, the labour traffic is depopulating these islands to a deplorable extent. Mr. Inglis, of Aneityum, who is well qualified to speak upon the subject, says—" The population of Tana may be eight thousand. This gives four thousand males of all ages, or two thousand males above seventeen years of age. Now, as nearly as can be estimated, there are not fewer than twelve hundred of these in Queensland, Fiji, New Caledonia, and elsewhere." This drain of their population must of course have a most disastrous effect upon the islands, breaking up society, and reducing the quantity of food raised, and hastening the extinction of the race. If it goes on much longer, the whole of the young and able-bodied men will be carried off, and the islands be left barren and desolate; whereas were the people left alone, and brought under the influence of Christian civilization, these beautiful islands would be open to the planter, and, in course of time, labourers would be found on the spot, able and willing to do such light work as the growth of the cotton and coffee require.

## LETTER XVII.

LEAVE ANEITYUM FOR NEW CALEDONIA IN THE "SEA WITCH"
—APPEARANCE OF THE SHORES OF THAT ISLAND—A
BRIEF ACCOUNT OF ITS CHARACTERISTICS — LIFE AT
NOUMEA—LEAVE FOR SYDNEY.

*Sydney*,
March, 1873.

FROM the heading of this letter you will see that I have got back to the white man's world. The last letter was from Aneityum; and I shall now fill up the gap by telling you what happened to us on our way from the islands to the colonies.

We were detained more than five weeks on Aneityum, before any vessel came to our assistance; but we thought ourselves fortunate in getting away as soon as we did. Few vessels are to be seen amongst the islands during the hurricane months; and we imagined that if any vessels had been in the vicinity of the group, they must have met the same fate as the "Dayspring." Nor were we far wrong in our conjectures, for several other ships were wrecked in that hurricane, and the vessel which appeared to help us— though it had been lying in one of the best-protected harbours which the group affords, viz., Fili Harbour, Efaté—narrowly escaped being driven on shore.

I had gone round to Anamé to spend some of the time with

Mr. and Mrs. Inglis, the rest of the party remaining at the harbour. One morning I was awakened by the cry of "Sail ho!" and dressing hastily and rushing out, I observed a schooner sailing along the coast as if for Anelcauhat harbour. A boat was immediately got ready, and on reaching the harbour I had the pleasure of seeing the vessel lying safely there at anchor. She proved to be the "Sea Witch,"—a fore-and-aft schooner of eighty tons, from the northern New Hebrides to Fiji, with natives. An arrangement was made with the owner to convey us and our baggage to New Caledonia for a consideration; the natives to be landed on the islet of Inyug, and await the return of the vessel. The party comprised Mrs. Goodwill and child, Captain and Mrs. Jenkins and myself, aft; and the two mates, crew, and native teachers, for'ard. We sailed on Wednesday, the 12th of February.

It was about ten months since I first saw the scene which was now fading from our view. Then it was morning; the newly-risen sun was casting a brilliant light upon the hills, and the walls of the great white church: now it was evening; and the darkness, as well as the ever-increasing distance, blended all things into one neutral grey; but as long as we could see anything, our eyes rested on the gleaming white hull of the old "Dayspring" as she lay dismasted and doomed on her rocky bed.

The two scenes were quite appropriate to the occasions, and would form studies for an artist. SCENE I.—*The first sight of the tropics:* Bright morning, fine breeze rippling the surface of the ocean, the lovely island resting on its bosom, with the vessel careering merrily towards it; passengers all on the alert, gazing eagerly and joyously on the beautiful and unwonted prospect, ever growing more and more distinct. SCENE II.—*The last sight of the tropics:* Dull evening, strong breeze, island in shadow, vessel plunging sullenly away from it, and the passengers gazing pensively back at the scene of their detention, and at the shattered hull of their old vessel now disappearing in the distance.

On Friday we reached Maré, and there landed the teachers, and next morning sighted the great island of New Caledonia. It appeared as a long range of blue mountains extending far across the line of vision, getting fainter towards the extremities until it disappeared on either side. All that day we sailed towards it, and when evening came were near enough to make out the cocoanut palms and pine trees which fringed the coast. The hills were generally of a reddish hue, and had rather a barren appearance. Altogether the land had a very different look from the islands of the New Hebrides, the vegetation being much less luxuriant. Next morning (Sunday) we were off Havannah Pass—an entrance through the long line of reef, opposite the south end of the island; and with a man at the masthead to direct the steersman, we ran through into the still water of an extensive reef-enclosed lagoon. As we coasted along the shores, making for Noumea, which lies on the south-east side of the island, we caught a glimpse of the Isle of Pines away towards the south, rising dimly on the horizon, like a pale blue haystack. Several small islands, thickly covered with pines, dotted the surface of the lagoon, and the varying depths gave a multitude of colours and shades of colour to the water, from the lightest green to the deepest blue. The shores of the island sometimes appeared as gentle grassy slopes, clad with pines and other timber; sometimes as great black beetling cliffs, over which small streams burst in white spray.

> "A land of streams! some, like a downward smoke,
> Slow dropping veils of thinnest lawn, did go."

Then we sailed through a narrow passage between the mainland and a high island; gliding down its twisted course, under the force of the current rather than of the wind, which had almost died away. Here and there we passed lagoons that ran

far into the land, bearing on their bosoms many fair islets;
then, through openings in the sea-front, we would get a glimpse
of the distant ranges of the interior, or, sweeping round some
rocky point, would discover a native village nestling in a se-
cluded bay. It is a lovely place, and only wants the addition
of a few fine villas on the hill-sides, gardens, boats, and people,
to make its beauty perfect. By the time we reached the other
end of this pass, it was almost dark, and we saw the twinkling
rays of the lighthouse of Amedee, on the reef opposite
Noumea. It was a pleasant sight, being the first sign of our
return to civilization. Next morning we were at anchor in the
harbour of that town. But before proceeding further with my
narrative, I shall say something of the characteristics and the
population of this fine island of La Nouvelle Calédonia.

New Caledonia is 200 miles long, by twenty or thirty broad.
It is completely encircled by a coral reef, which extends for a
long way to the north, and to the south as far as the Isle of
Pines. It lies at a distance from the shores varying from two
to twelve miles. There are several openings easy of traverse,
and inside the water is deep enough for vessels to cruise, and
shallow enough for them to anchor. The northern stretch of
reef is beautifully dotted with wooded islets.

This island occupies a most important position, since it commands the communication of the Australian colonies with
India, China, and America. It is a sad pity that Britain let it
slip through its hands. It was discovered by Captain Cook
immediately after his discovery of the southern New Hebrides
in 1774. He gives a very good account of the place and its
inhabitants, considering the short time he was there, a few extracts from which may be interesting. Speaking of the inhabitants, he says, "They are strong, robust, active, well-made
people; courteous and friendly, and not in the least addicted
to pilfering—which is more than can be said of any other na-

tion in this sea. Their houses, or at least most of them, are circular, something like a beehive, and full as close and warm; the entrance is by a small door, or long square hole just big enough to admit a man bent double; the side walls are about four feet and a half high, but the roof is lofty and peaked to a point at the top, above which is a post or stick of wood, which is generally ornamented with carving or shells, or both. Some houses have two floors, one above the other. Land birds, indeed, are not numerous, but several are new. One of these is a kind of crow—at least so we called it, though it is not half so big, and its feathers are tinged with blue. They also have some very beautiful turtle-doves, and other small birds such as I never saw before." Speaking of the appearance of the country, he says, " The plain or flat land which lies along the shore appeared from the hills to a great advantage. The winding streams which ran through it, the plantations, the little straggling villages, the variety in the woods and the shoals on the coasts so variegating the scene, that the whole might afford a picture for romance.—The mountains and other high places are, for the most part, incapable of cultivation, consisting chiefly of rocks, many of which are full of mundicks; the little soil which is upon them is scorched and burnt up with the sun; it is, nevertheless, coated with coarse grass and other plants, and here and there trees and shrubs."

The natives of New Caledonia are superior in some respects to those of the New Hebrides. Their huts are better, and their canoes much larger. They have also the art of making that pottery, which is found on Santo alone of all the New Hebrides. They somewhat resemble the Tanamen, only, I should imagine, have more of the Papuan blood in them. They cultivate the yam and banana, and sugarcane, for food, as the New Hebrideans do, and they have pigs and fowls. The pigs Cook did not find on the island, as he did on the neighbouring group, and so he left several with them—

which are the ancestors, I suppose, of the present generation—those they now have.

This island, together with the Isle of Pines, was taken possession of by the French in the year 1853, and the Loyalty Islands were shortly afterwards annexed. Since that time they have been occupying it as a penal settlement and military station, but doing little in the way of colonizing it. I have no doubt, however, but that it will eventually become a very important place. It has all the necessary requisites: a commanding position; a fine healthy climate; soil fit for cultivation and for grazing; minerals in great variety and abundance; and splendid harbours. At present, cattle breeding and sugar growing are the chief industries. Sheep don't feed well, as the grass is too coarse; but cattle seem to thrive splendidly, and must pay the breeder handsomely, as there is a great demand for fresh meat for the supply of the military and penal establishments and men-of-war.

The French Government are inclined, I believe, to favour the settlement of colonists of other nations on New Caledonia—giving them land at a nominal rental, with option of purchase after a certain number of years. There are several young men on the island now who went from the colonies; how they are getting on I am not in a position to say.

The minerals are as yet almost entirely undeveloped. There is a gold-mine at the northern end of the island, which is said to be paying well: but besides gold, copper and iron abound, and are waiting to be extracted from the mother earth.

The harbours which New Caledonia possesses can hardly be surpassed: there is first the outer encircling reef, and then innumerable well-protected bays along the coast inside of it. The bay upon which Noumea stands is one of the best, having the shelter of two islands, which lie in front of it.

But to return to the "Sea Witch" and her passengers. On the morning of our arrival an English gentleman boarded us, and introduced himself as Her Brittanic Majesty's vice-consul. He was very kind and attentive, and by his advice we took possession of a furnished cottage belonging to a friend of his at that time in the country. Of course if the hotels had been suitable for our party, we should have gone to one of them; but they had no accommodation fit for a lady: so we thankfully entered the cottage, and commenced housekeeping on our own account. It was rather a strange experience. After the island life among the savages, it was a novel thing to be able to go to a shop and get what you wanted, and it was a novel thing to pay for it; but the novelty was much increased by our being in a strange town, amongst a lot of foreigners. Fortunately, in most of the shops some of the assistants could speak English, otherwise we should have fared badly indeed, my French being of the most threadbare description. The captain and I used occasionally to sally forth, under cover of darkness, and forage for our supplies, returning loaded with sundry queer parcels.

We found housekeeping in Noumea rather expensive on the whole, everything being dear, except claret, cigars, and eau de Cologne: so, by way of economy, we endeavoured to live as much as possible on these luxuries—at least I did. The consul was a friend in need, supplying the place of interpreter and general entertainer on all occasions, and rendering the three weeks spent at Noumea much more pleasant than otherwise they would have been. Several times I went out riding with him, to get a look at the surroundings of the town. There are some beautiful spots near the coast, and fine views from the hills; one of the prettiest is obtained from the rising ground at the back of the town, by looking across an islet-dotted bay towards Mont D'Or and the ranges lying behind and to the left of it.

You have all the shades and tints requisite for a lovely picture—distant range, light blue; Mont D'Or, red, brown, and yellow; the foreground green, brown, &c., and the sea and sky deep blue.

Mont D'Or, New Caledonia.

The roads which run out from Noumea are capital and numerous, all being the work of the convicts. Going out in one direction we visited the racecourse one day, while on another occasion we went by another road, eight or ten miles out to an *auberge*, and there, sitting under a shady tree, tried the French drink *absinthe*. Sickly stuff I thought it, and resolved to taste it no more. Every here and there along these roads we passed bands of convicts at work, well guarded by armed sentries—all of whom, the prisoners as well as soldiers, saluted us with truly French politeness.

The country has in many places a most striking resemblance to some parts of Victoria, a tree which grows plentifully in the bush, being very like the stringy-bark of that colony. The vegetation is not at all luxuriant, in fact, upon the hillsides there seems almost nothing at all.

Noumea, the capital—in fact, the only town in the island, has a population of 4000 or 5000 I should think, independently of the prisoners and military force. The streets are straight, laid out at right angles to one another, and are well made. The houses are mostly wooden, with an occasional brick one here and there. There are a few very respectable wholesale stores, one or two indifferent hotels, a good number of shops, a printing office—which produces a weekly paper, a museum, government house, one or two other public offices, a R.C. church, and two immense barracks a little way out of the town; the remainder being private dwellings. The town is, as I said before, situated on a bay, and is at the foot of a steep hill, 300 or 400 feet high, on the top of which is a tower, used as a semaphore station. It commands a splendid view across the reef, and far away out to sea. When a vessel is observed in the offing, the signal is made and the little pilot-schooner starts off to pilot her through the reefs. The bay on which the town lies has generally a very lively appearance. When we were there, five men-of-war were lying in harbour at one time, besides sundry other crafts. Looking from the bay, the barracks at once attract attention, on account of their size and commanding position. There are two buildings—one for infantry, the other for artillery. The convicts live upon an island on the opposite side of the bay from Noumea; and as there are several thousands of them, their quarters form quite a town. Every morning they cross over, and march through the town in gangs to work. They make roads, embankments, fortifications, buildings, &c. There is no want of cheap labour in these quarters; in fact, there seems to be a difficulty in employing them usefully, for I noticed that they have commenced to cut a road through a great hill—a road to nowhere. As amongst such a number of men there must naturally be some musicians, the authorities have provided instruments, and allowed them to form themselves into a band. This band plays every Thursday and Sunday afternoons—plays high-class music, and plays it well too. Some of the convicts employ their leisure hours in carving nautilus and cocoanut shells, producing very pretty results, and selling them at very moderate prices.

The communists, of whom there are now a large number, are kept quite separate from the convicts, their quarters being on a peninsula of the main island. They have there comparatively comfortable habitations, are not made to work, and have plenty of food to eat and plenty of time for reflection. Altogether they are not badly off.

About a fortnight after our arrival in Noumea, we were obliged to flit. As we were sitting at dinner one day, a gentleman appeared with a servant and portmanteau, and proved to be, as I could see at a glance, the owner of the cottage returned from the country. He seemed greatly taken aback at the sight of a company of strangers seated comfortably in his house, for he had received no notice of our occupation. Of course, we were in rather a fix too; but after explaining to him how matters stood, he very considerately gave us the use of the house until his lease was up—this, however, was in two days' time, so that we did not receive very much benefit from his kindness. We commenced then to look about for other quarters, and would probably have experienced considerable difficulty, had not a gentleman come forward and put at our disposal a store and offices which he had just built, and which were still standing empty. We occupied these buildings as our sleeping apartments, and went to a hotel for our meals. We now were obliged to fall in with French customs. Two meals a day—breakfast at ten a.m. and dinner at six p.m. The latter meal could be prolonged over most of the evening if we felt inclined; and, as we had nothing to do, generally we felt so inclined. Innumerable little courses of meat, &c., dressed in various fashions, and *vin ordinaire*, followed by small cups of thick black coffee, constituted the usual bill of fare. One day, as a great treat, we had grapes—not in great bunches, however, as we eat them in Victoria, but a few on a plate, previously extracted from a bottle of brandy in which they had been preserved.

Nothing worthy of notice occurred until the sailing of the steamer for Sydney, unless I except the fact of my meeting a historical character in the streets one day. I refer to the son of John Adams, of the "Bounty" mutiny celebrity—the governor, schoolmaster, and minister of the Pitcairn islanders. His son is now an elderly man. He had come across from Norfolk island (where the Pitcairn islanders are now living) to Noumea, for the purpose of consulting the French doctors regarding some failing in the eyesight of his little daughter, whom he brought over with him.

On the 7th of March we packed up bag and baggage, and went on board the steamer. My baggage now amounted to something considerable. In the way of curiosities collected amongst the islands, I had native weapons, dresses, bags, baskets, cloth, shells, coral, a collection of dried plants and ferns, two bottled snakes,* a few carved ornaments from Noumea, &c.

The day after we boarded the steamer she sailed for Sydney, the whole of Noumea turning out to say good-bye to friends and witness our departure. After a very fair passage of six days, we passed the Heads on Thursday, the 13th.

---

* One of these snakes was a blue and black banded sea-snake, the Platyurus Fischeri, killed by myself on Tana; whilst the other was a brown viper, which Professor McCoy states is unknown to him, and is probably altogether a new species. This last I got from Mr. Hebblewhite, who killed it on Efate. Both these snakes are poisonous.

## Letter XVII.

A few days having been very agreeably spent in seeing the lions of Sydney, the blue mountains and the zig-zag, I took steamer for Melbourne; and on the 25th of March, with no little thankfulness of heart, entered once again its busy streets, and speedily was lost to view in the crowd.

# CONTRIBUTIONS

## TO THE

# Phytography of the New Hebrides

### AND LOYALTY ISLANDS,

#### FROM

#### MR. F. A. CAMPBELL'S COLLECTIONS.

BY

BARON FERD. VON MUELLER,
C.M.G., M.D., PH.D., F.R.S.

"Quaerite et invenietis."—EVANGEL MATH. Cap. vii., 7;
et EVANGEL LUC., Cap. xi., 9.

# APPENDIX.

# Phytography
## OF THE
# New Hebrides and Loyalty Islands.

The notes of the following pages arose from various considerations. The writer wished to place connectedly on record his observations on a series of plants from some of the Pacific Islands, gathered, in ready response to his request, by a young friend during the past year. It seemed likely, also, that the narrative of this itineration, while it would be scattered through the mission settlements, might animate others, to add likewise to our store of phytographic material from these and other island groups, if a special chapter was devoted to the plants collected on this occasion. More particularly this might be expected if it could be shown that, even during the very transitory visit of places discovered fully a century ago, a search among the constituents of their rich vegetation had still brought to light a proportionately large share of plants, either imperfectly understood, or perhaps utterly unknown before; and this from a collection necessarily limited. Furthermore, it appeared manifest that, by promoting a gradual scientific disclosure of the vegetation of any part of Polynesia, while civilization proceeds on its glorious path, new natural treasures would also become early scrutinised, the value of the indigenous resources of many a remote and lonely spot would be enhanced, and even intellectual enjoyment be increased in perhaps some distant solitudes.

To these general reasons for appending the subsequent unpretensive Notes to Mr. Campbell's work, one may be added, emanating from direct wishes of the writer. It is felt that the important works of the venerable Dr. Asa Gray and of the lamented Dr. Berthold Seemann, which form already a solid foundation for our knowledge of the plants of the Polynesian groups, should be extended, not only to the vegetation of numerous Pacific islands almost totally unexplored, but also to the plants of many inland recesses, to which heathen barbarism formerly gave no access, although the littoral skirts of these interior regions, on numerous islands, were brought long since under the benign influence of Christendom.

Since almost the middle of the last century, naval discoveries have rendered the world gradually acquainted with the almost endless number of isles—many almost of a paradisaic nature—dispersed through the Pacific ocean; but it yet remains a startling fact, that of their vegetation far less has become elucidated than of the flora of many other wide spaces of the globe, in regions discovered, occupied, or colonised since a much more recent date.

Vicinity and commerce necessarily must bring most of the Pacific islands prominently in contact with the Australian colonies, and, as a sequence, these beautiful groups will be connected also with us most easily for scientific communion.

Thus, ever since the untimely death of his friend Berthold Seemann, in the latter part of 1871, the writer has ventured to nourish a hope that a work on the whole vegetation of Polynesia might most readily be promoted from a centre of phytographic research, such as, in Australia, he endeavoured to form.

If, then, the many educated inhabitants located in the various groups, as well as scientifically inclined travellers, would aid in securing material of any kind for extended researches in the direction indicated, new sources of delight would arise to the writer, by affording not merely special information to the Senders, but also by obtaining gradually, the material for an universal work.

Moreover, the vegetation of the South-Sea islands stands in manifold bearings to that of Australia; so much so, that even the elucidation of the plants of the Australian continent, which has engaged extensively the writer's attention during more than a quarter of a century, would receive much collateral support from a closer insight into the whole vegetable empire of Polynesia.

Our unacquaintance with much of the vegetation of the Pacific islets may be largely traced to the fact, that the generality of the inhabitants or travellers, even if imbued with any desire to turn easy opportunities to scientific account, become attracted, during any of their searches for plants, mainly by the gracefulness or lovely delicacy of the ferns, which Nature, with a prodigious and marvellous lavishness, has strewed over these islands. Or the Searcher's predilections and exertions are limited to efforts of obtaining the more gorgeous forms of plants which present themselves to his view. Thus a modest herb, though of medicinal virtue—thus a plain-looking grass, though of nutritive importance—thus a concealed moss, though of microscopic beauty—or thus a delicate seaweed, though of charming structural perfection—are left alike unregarded. Need I speak of blossoms at first sight unshowy, or of fruits perhaps still less attractive, though the produce of trees both utilitarian and stately? to say nothing of the unwieldy flowers and bulky fruits of many a graceful palm, or of numerous succulents, ever so useful, but less readily amenable to any preparation for museum or study purposes.

But since Divine wisdom has called forth all these vegetable beings by a godly design, to be subservient to our earthly wants, we ought to recognise it as a duty, while we wish to enjoy and utilise all these gifts of providence, to draw them also from thoughtless disregard and hidden obscurity into the cyclus of rational reflection, into the precincts of experimental tests, and into the reach of the full light of natural science.

---o---

## PITTOSPOREAE.
### *Pittosporum Campbelli.*

Arborescent; leaves broadly lanceolate, thickly chartaceous, somewhat acuminate, glabrous, like the peduncles verticillate crowded; pedicels several or rather numerous, slightly downy; calyces minute, almost bell-shaped, only to about one-third of their length cleft into five rounded teeth; corolla white, exceeding the calyx several times in length; petals narrow, cuneate—oblong, disconnected; filaments somewhat dilated, twice as long as the slightly pointed anthers; style extremely short; capsule bivalved, many-seeded; valves thick, almost oval, narrowed at the extremities, especially at the summit; uneven yet not wrinkled on the outside; seeds dark—or blackish-brown, turgid, angular, wingless.

Found on TANA, on wooded places. Seen about fifteen feet high. Leaves 3 to 5 inches long, 1 to 1½ inches broad, paler beneath; veins and lateral nerves exceedingly thin. Petioles ¼ to ⅜ inch long. Primary peduncles varying in length from ½ to 1½ inches, terminal or in the axis of the upper leaves. Pedicels 2 to 3 lines long, rather crowded. Calyces only one line long, glabrous. Petals about 4 lines long, blunt. Anthers measuring about one line. Pistil smooth. Ovary very slender. Valves of the capsule about ⅔ of an inch long, sometimes verging into a rhomboid form, but always longer than broad, and often considerably so; outside turning blackish, inside orange-yellow, not viscid. Seeds generally almost 1½ line long, not sticky. Funicles almost obliterated.

The flowers are delightfully odorous, like those of most congeners. The species is dedicated to the young gentleman, who thoughtfully and kindly provided the material for this essay. It is the first Pittosporum from the New Hebrides, and bears some alliance to P. rhytidocarpum (Asa Gray, *Botany of Wilkes's Exploring Expedition*, p. 228, tab. 18.) The differences, however, are obvious; for P. rhytidocarpum has sessile umbels, free sepals (though not so shown in the plate,) a downy sessile ovary, a longer style, larger capsules outside warty or tubercular and deeply wrinkled, and finally larger and more compressed seeds.

P. glabratum (Lindley, in the *Journal of the London Horticultural Society*, vol. 1, p. 230) differs already in its deeply divided slightly ciliated calyces, connate petals, thinner and broader valves, which are three in number, also larger seeds. P. ferrugineum (W. T. Aiton, *Hort. Kew*, sec. edit., II., 27) is still more widely distinct.

Pittosporum Brakenridgei (Asa Gray, *l. c.*, p. 225, tab. 17) accord- to Seemann's Feegee-plant numbered 56, presents, like the following, a short-lobed calyx, but is dissimilar in many other respects.

P. ramiflorum (Zollinger, in *Miquel Flor. Ind. Batav.*, vol. 1, part II., p. 122) is to be distinguished already in its entirely lateral inflorescence, smaller and connate petals. This species again is closely allied to P. Richii (A. Gr., *l. c.*,) and both have the short-lobed calyx of P. Campbellii, while the fruit of P. Richii is broader than long.

P. Timorense (Blume, *Mus. Bot. Lugd.*, I., 160) is described as having short and only dentated calyces. The only specimens of any Pittosporum which I possess from Timor (in fruit only) have roundish capsules, ¼ to ⅔ of an inch long, strongly compressed, outside almost even. None of the described species of Pittosporum from New Caledonia (Brogniart and Gris, in *Annales des Scien. Nat.* 1865, p. 143—147) is closely allied to Mr. Campbell's plant.

# RUTACEAE.

MICROMELUM PUBESCENS (Blume, *Bijdragen*, vol. 1, p. 137.)
M. minutum (Seemann's *Rep. on Mis. to the Viti Islands*, p. 434.)

EFATE. Recently detected. also, in the Samoan group, by the Rev. S. T. Whitmee, F.L.S., F.G.S., F.R.G.S.

MURRAYA EXOTICA (Kœnig, in *Linn. Mantiss. Alt. Plant.* p. 554.)

SANTO. There only four feet high, when in flower. The older and restorable name, Chalcas paniculata (*Lin. Mantiss.*, p. 68; Chalcas cammuneng, Burmann's *Flor. Ind.*, p. 104) is referable to this plant. Known also from New Caledonia.

CLAUSENIA CRENULATA; Murraya crenulata (Oliver, in the *Proceed. of the Linn. Soc.* vol. 5, sup. p. 29.)

TANA. A tree attaining a height of thirty feet, and perhaps more. Leaflets chartaceous, the lower ones sometimes hardly above an inch in length; all often only very faintly crenulate. Cymes forming a dense corymbose terminal panicle. Peduncles and pedicels thinly downy; the latter when flower-bearing about one line long, when fruit-bearing lengthened to three or four lines. Calyces five—cleft, hardly above half a line high, nearly one line wide; its lobes deltoid—semi-orbicular. Petals almost oblong, overlapping at the lateral margins, white, sessile, nearly a quarter of an inch long. Stamens ten; five alternately somewhat shorter; the longer filaments about two lines long, downward more dilated than the others; all nearly subulate. Anthers one-third of a line long, erect, with two parallel oval cells. Pistil glabrous. Style about one line long, deciduous, rather thick. Stigma visibly exceeding the width of the style. Berry depressed—globular, slightly raised on an extremely short stipes, about two-thirds of an inch broad, four celled, not rarely perfecting all its seeds. Pericarp thin. Septa membranous. Seeds smooth, ovate—trigonous. Cotyledons plan—convex, not folded.

This plant connects the genera Clausena and Murraya, which eventually might be united, should even no additional members of the genera hereafter be discovered. Clausenia claims antecedence as being published in 1768 (Burmann, *Flor. Ind.*, p. 87); whereas Murraya, or, as it was originally written, Murraea, became promulgated in 1771. But, with still greater justice, Burmann's generic name would have to give way to that of Calchas, established by Linné in 1767 (both in his first *Mantiss.* pag. num. 1261; and in the twelfth edition of the *Syst. Nat.* vol. 2, p. 293,) Chalcas paniculata being referable to Murraya exotica.

Mr. Campbell's plant agrees with that from Queensland, at least as far as foliage and fruit are concerned, the flowers of the East Australian congener having as yet not been collected. Those of the Tana plant accord, however, with the short description given by Oliver of the original species from the Phillippine Islands. The corymbosely depressed inflorescence separates Clausenia or Chalcas crenulata already from all other species of that genus known to me. In the shape of its berries it differs, likewise, from most, if not all, of its congeners. This is a new plant for Polynesian records.

EUODIA HORTENSIS (R. and G. Forster, *Charact. Gener.*, p. 14, tab. 7.)

SANTO, EFATE, and TANA. Flowering already at a height of two feet. Both the narrow and broad-leaved varieties were collected by Mr. Campbell.

## TILIACEAE.

TRIUMFETTA ANGULATA (La Marck, *Encyclop. Méthod.*, III., p. 421.)

ANEITYUM and TANA. Abundant on clear flats. Height, two to three feet. Not previously recorded from any of the islands of the Pacific ocean, nor from Australia. Sepals conspicuously hairy. Stamens, twelve to sixteen. Fruit-awns sometimes beset with minute bristles.

GREWIA MALLOCOCCA (Linné fil. *Supplem. Plant.*, p. 402.)

SANTO and TANA, in forests. Height to twenty feet, and perhaps more. Leaves attaining a length of eight inches. Peduncles one to three-flowered, solitary or two together. Flower-buds first globular, soon egg-shaped. Bracts two to three lines long, ovate lanceolate, very early deciduous. Sepals four to six lines long, white inside, not distinctly nerved. Petals acute. This species approaches in many respects to G. orientalis (L., *Sp. Pl.* 964) and to G. laevigata (Vahl, *Symbol*, 434.) Irrespective of some other differences, its longer leaves with deeper indentations distinguish it.

It may here passingly be observed, that Trichospermum Richii (Seemann, in *Bonplandia*, p. 254) has been found also in the Samoan group by the Rev. S. T. Whitmee. The leaves of this remarkable tree attain a length of over six inches.

## MALVACEAE.

SIDA RHOMBIFOLIA (Linné, *Sp. Plant*, 961.)

SANTO. This herb might be utilised for the sake of its beautiful fibre—especially as the plant is perennial, and occurs probably in abundance on all the islands of the group, Captain Cook himself (as recorded by Dr. Seemann) having gathered it already at Tana. The leaves are more frequently lanceolar than rhombiformed, and on the specimens transmitted from Santo, they are scarcely paler beneath. The sides of the fruitlets are distinctly reticular to above the middle.

HIBISCUS ABELMOSCHUS (Linné, *sp. pl.*, 980.)

SANTO. A purple-flowered variety, according to Mr. Campbell's note. In respect to colour, the flowers of this plant seem to be variable; although in no instance this capability of variation among Malvaceae is as great as in the Hollyhock, while in most species of this extensive order no play of colours seems to occur.

HIBISCUS ROSA SINENSIS (Linné, *sp. pl.*, 977.)

ERAMANGA. The number of segments of the surrounding bracteal involucre varies from six to ten.

## STERCULIACEAE.

### KLEIHOVIA HOSPITA (Linné *sp. pl.*, 1365.)

ANEITYUM. New for the group. The transmitted flowering and fruiting specimens came from a shrub only four or five feet high; whereas in age this plant assumes the dimensions of a stately tree. Hasskarl's description (*Pl. Jav. Rar.*, 313) is from the tree in its living state. The Rev. S. T. Whitmee found it in Samoa.

### MELOCHIA ODORATA (Linné, fil. *suppl. pl.* p. 302.)

EFATE; originally described from TANA. Attains a height of twenty-five feet, as observed by Mr. Campbell. Bark light-coloured. Lower leaves orbicular-cordata, measuring about five inches; uppermost leaves only one to one and a-half inches long, and lanceolate, all chartaceous. Petals much longer than the stamens. Anthers broadly ovate, dorsifixed. Fruitlets separating in age. Seeds not conspicuously winged. This species occurs also in Dr. Veillard's collection of New Caledonian plants.

## SAPINDACEAE.

### CARDIOSPERMUM HALICACABUM (Linné, *sp. pl.* 925.)

ANEITYUM. Occurs also in the Samoan Islands, according to collections from the Rev. S. T. Whitmee.

## LEGUMINOSAE.

### SOPHORA TOMENTOSA (Linné, *sp. pl.* 533.)

EFATE.

### CANAVALIA OBTUSIFOLIA (De Candolle, *Prodr.* II., 404.)

TANA, along the sea-shore.

### DOLICHOS LABLAB (Linné, *sp. pl.* 1019.)

ANIWA, on open ground. The white flowering variety collected. Brief notes on the uses of this bean are given in the volume of the Acclimitisation Society of Victoria for 1872.

### DESMODIUM POLYCARPUM (De Candolle, *Prodr.* II., 334.)

TANA, in open places. The upper leaves consist sometimes of a single leaflet only. Found also in Samoa by the Rev. S. T. Whitmee and Rev. S. Powell.

### DESMODIUM UMBELLATUM (De Candolle, *Prodr.* II., 325.)

ERAMANGA. Pod sometimes five-seeded, sometimes reduced to a single article.

### DESMODIUM PENDULUM.

TANA; abundant in the forests. A shrub; according to Mr. Campbell's notes attaining a height of fifteen feet. Racemes pendent, with white flowers.

This plant, according to an imperfect specimen from the museum of the Botanic Garden of Calcutta, communicated under the above name and collected by Mr. Tyesmann, seems identical with a species from the island of Ternate. It differs from D. ormocarpoides (De Candolle, *Prodr.* II., 327) so far as the material before me allows me to judge, already in narrower stipules, short-toothed calyces and long-stalked pods. The latter, in a half-ripe state, resemble those of D. laburnifolium (De Candolle, *Prodr.* II., 337,) but are not sessile, and the articulations are still deeper. In the simplicity and form of the foliage, the Tana plant agrees with D. ormocarpoides. The expanded upper petal is beyond its base almost orbicular. The tenth stamen is free. Ripe fruit is unknown to me. The racemes attain a length of one foot. The large leaflets are sparingly beset with short appressed hair; but this would not be a positive characteristic of the species, inasmuch as D. ormocarpoides occurs in Ceylon with leaflets copiously downy beneath, including therefore, probably, D. zonatum (Miquel, *Flor. Ind. Bat.*, I., 250.)

TEPHROSIA PISCATORIA (*Pers. Enchir.*, II., 329.)

ERAMANGA and EFATE. About two feet high. Flowers white. Dr. Veillard's plant from New Caledonia, distributed under the above name, appears to represent a distinct species.

ACACIA FARNESIANA (Willdenow, *sp. pl.*, 1083.)

MARE, Loyalty Islands, where it grows to the height of twelve feet. Pinnæ sometimes reduced to two pairs. Peduncles not rarely solitary. Calyces and corolla occasionally six-cleft.

## MYRTACEAE.

EUGENIA RICHII (Asa Gray, in Wilkes's *Unit. Stat. Explor. Exped. Bot.*, p. 510, pl. 58.)

TANA, where it grows to a height of forty feet. This evidently stately tree, with large leaves and globular fruits above an inch in size, either belongs to the above-indicated species, or must be regarded as botanically new. It has the characteristic winged-angular branchlets, and the round or cordate based-leaves of E. Richii, and it may thus be easily discriminated in comparison with E. Malaccensis, (Linné, *sp. pl.* 672,) but the flowers seem somewhat smaller than those delineated by Sprague, the calyx-tube is more turgid, the calyx-lobes are conspicuously unequal; and for the comparison of the ripe fruits of the Tana species with that from Fiji and Tonga, no opportunity has as yet been afforded.

BARRINGTONIA RACEMOSA (Blumé, in *De Cand. Prod.* III., 288.)

TANA, inland in forests. A tree, forty feet high. Petals and stamens white. Fruit greenish. Kernels, according to Mr. Campbell's note, eatable. This appears to be the most widely-spread of all congeners, extending even to East Africa, but in Australia it has as yet only been found on Rockingham's Bay. The racemes are sometimes fully four feet long on trees of the last-mentioned locality. The allied B. Samoensis (Asa Gray, *Bot. Wilk. Explor. Exped.*, 508) has much smaller flowers, with a calyx cup-shaped in bud, but not closed, while the fruit is much larger—one-and-a-half to two inches long, and so much impressed around the pedicel as to form four turgid prominences. In Upola, where it is frequent, it passes by the name of "Falaga," according to the Rev. S. T. Whitmee. Barringtonia speciosa (R. & G. Forster, *Charact. Gener.*, p. 76, tab. 38) occurs, doubtless, also in the New Hebrides and adjoining islets, it having been traced to Rockingham's Bay and some other shores of North Queensland. Some of the other Indian species of Barringtonia may be looked for in the Pacific archipelago as well as in tropical Australia. The sections Butonica and Stravadium of Barringtonia hold, in reference to the forms of their calyx, almost the same relation to each other as Busbeckia to Eucapparis in the genus Capparis.

## MELASTOMACEAE.

MELASTOMA MALABATHRICUM (Linné, *sp. pl.*, 559; M. velutinum, Seemann., *Flor. Vit.*, p. 90.)

ANEITYUM; there a bush five feet high. Petals white, as in the variety described as M. Taitense (*De Cand. prod.* III., 144.)

The allied order of Lythraceæ, by an oversight, is passed unnoticed in Dr. Seemann's work, so rich in original observations. The following plants of that order are known to exist in the Pacific islands:—Pemphis acidula (R. & G. Forster, *Charact. Gener.*, p. 68, tab. 34); Lythrum maritimum (Humboldt, *Bonpl. et Kunth. nov. gen. et spec. Amer.*, VI., 193); Sonneratia acida (Linné, fil. *suppl. pl.*, 252); and to these are probably to be added, Lythrum hyssopifolium, Lawsonia alba and several species of Ammannia. Cupheanthus Neo-Caledonicus (Seemann, *Flor. Vit.*, p. 76) requires to be moved from Myrtaceæ also to Lythraceæ, as suggested by its author.

## EUPHORBIACEAE.

CODIÆUM VARIEGATUM (Blumé, *Bijdrag.*, p. 606.)

TANA, in the woods, where it attains a height of fifteen feet. The generic name, established by Rumpt (*Herbar. Amboin*, IV., 65-66) already 120 years ago, should be adopted also in horticultural appellations for this plant, as it is not a Croton in the scientific meaning of that extensive genus.

EUPHORBIA HIRTA (Linné, *Amoen. Academ.*, III., 114.)

SANTO; frequent near the sea-shore. The above specific name is far preferable to that of E. pilulifera, first given on the same page of the work quoted.

ACALYPHA FOSTERIANA (J. Mueller, in *De Cand. prodr.* XVI., pars II., 870.)

EFATE, and other islands of the New Hebrides; abundant in woods. A shrub up to six feet high. Another species exists in Tana, growing in woody localities to the height of twenty feet. It requires further examination from more extensive material.

CARUMBIUM PEDICELLATUM (Miquel, *Flor. Ind. Batav.*, vol. I., part II., page 414.)

TANA, where it forms a shrub about five feet high. Easily distinguished from C. populifolium (Reinwardt in Blume's Catalogues, Van Gervassen, Buitenzorg, p. 105) a plant also extending to some of the Pacific isles, in having its staminiferous racemes provided with minute gland-like bracts, which generally occupy the middle of the more elongated and singly dispersed pedicels, in having the calyces far less conspicuous, the stamens more numerous, and the basal glands of the leaves arising from the lower page. Moreover, the fruit is pointed at the base and apex, though it is not longer than broad. The Rev. S. T. Whitmee has found the identical species in Samoa, where the large-fruited C. acuminatum also exists.

## URTICACEAE.

TREMA CANNABINA (Loureiro, *Flor. Cochinchinens*, ed. Willd., 689.)

Abundant in TANA. A lithogram of this plant has been issued in my work, "The Plants of the Colony of Victoria," plate xc. This bush has shown itself poisonous to pastoral animals, who in dry seasons will eat it with avidity, but die (according to Mr. T. Maitland's observations) a few hours afterwards. The specific name is derived from the textile bast, which might yet be drawn into extensive use on localities where the plant spontaneously vegetates. Sent from Samoa by the Rev. S. T. Whitmee.

PIPTURUS ARGENTEUS (Weddell in *Candolle prodr.* xvi., 235)

TANA, on hill-sides in woods. The bast-fibre resembles that of the Ramee, according to experiments in my laboratory. Mr. Campbell found this plant to attain a height of about twenty-five feet, and the fruit to be white and watery-succulent.

BOEHMERIA SPICATA (Thunberg in the *Transact. of the Linn. Soc. of Lond.*, II., 330.)

SANTO. Frequent in forestland. A bush about five feet high. Mr. Campbell's collection contains a small branchlet without fruits, which does not admit of specific recognition; but the very variable B. spicata is recorded as occurring in the New Hebrides. Moreover, it was desirable that this plant should not be passed altogether on this occasion, especially as it yields a fibre similar to that of the Rhea or Rhamee. The fibre of the Santo-Boehmeria would likely become an article of extensive export, if its value was once recognised by the native inhabitants, and it would probably be obtainable also as an indigenous product from many of the adjoining isles. This plant requires still comparison with B. acuminata (Weddell in *De Candolle*, prodr. xvi., 209) from New Caledonia. It is identical with a species from Wagap, in Dr. Veillard's collection, distributed under number 1226, so far as, in the absence of fruit, it is possible to judge.

## UMBELLIFERAE.

TRACHYMENE AUSTRO-CALEDONIA (Bentham and Hooker, *Gener. Plantar.*, I, 873; *Didiscus Austro-Caledonicus*, Brogniart and Gris, in *Annal. des Scienc. naturell., cinquième série, Botanique*, tom. III., p. 235.)

NEW HEBRIDES. Previously only gathered in New Caledonia and the isle of pines.

## COMPOSITAE.

VERNONIA CINEREA (Lessing, in *Sehlechtendal's Linnaea*, p. 291; *Chrysocoma purpurea*, G. Forster, prodr. p. 54.)

ERAMANGA and EFATE. Not mentioned in Dr. Seemann's work; perhaps therefore not extending eastward through the Pacific isles, but occurring in New Caledonia also, according to Mons. Pancher's and Dr. Veillard's collections.

## RUBIACEAE.

HEDYOTIS FOETIDA (Sprengel, *Pugillus plantar.*, II., 28, non Dalzell.)

TANA, along the sea-shores. About two feet high. Corolla white. Not before gathered in the New Hebrides. This plant is very closely allied to H. racemosa (La Marck, *Encyclop. méthodique*, III., 76) which is shown by Mr. Whitmee to exist also in Samoa, while Mr. Campbell found it in the island Espiritu Santo. It is now also known to occur in North Queensland.

CALYCOSIA MILNEI (Asa Gray, in the *Proceed. of the Americ. Acad. of Scienc.*, IV., 48.)

ANEITYUM, in woodlands. Attains a height of six feet. The limb of the calyces is rather herbaceous than membraneous, and in a dry state yellowish; like the leaves and corollas also, the calyces are densely beset with black dots, reminding of those of many primulaceous plants.

IXORA PAVETTA (Roxburgh, *Flor. Ind.*, I., 385.)

EFATE, abounding in woods near the sea, and attaining a height of six feet. Not previously recorded from Polynesia.

## GOODENIACEAE.

SCAEVOLA KOENIGII (Vahl, *Symbol*, III., 36.)

ANEITYUM, TANA and EFATE; abounding on the sea-shore. Native name, Nanatto.

## LOGANIACEAE.

GENIOSTOMA RUPESTRE (R. & G. Forster, *Charact. gener.*, p. 24, tab. 12.)

TANA: there discovered already in Captain Cook's second expedition.

On wooded ridges. Height to about fifteen feet. Corolla white. Style glabrous. It varies with leaves rounded at the base, and also with rounded capsules. The Rev. S. T. Whitmee has sent the same plant from Samoa.

## ACANTHACEAE.

### ERANTHEMUM REPANDUM (R. Brown, according to Roemer and Schultes' *Systema Vegetabilium*, I., 175.)

MARE, Loyalty Islands. To the brief definition published in 1786, by George Forster (*Justicia repanda, Flor. Insul. Austral., prodr.*, page 3) which appears as yet to be the only record of this species, the Maré-plant sufficiently responds. Tana being about 150 geographical miles distant from Maré, it may very readily be assumed that Forster's original Tana-species extends also to the Loyalty Islands. Mr. Campbell's plant forms a bush about three feet high. The leaves are two inches long, or less, ovate or verging into a rhomboid form, chartaceous, lightly or imperfectly repand, not acuminate, but provided with conspicuous petioles. The number of flowers on the short axillary peduncles is either three or it is reduced to two, or even occasionally one. The bracteoles at the base of the short pedicels are only two-thirds line long and cymbeo-semilanceolar. Segments of the calyx subulate-semilanceolate, hardly one and a-half lines long. Corolla white, fragrant, its tube nearly or fully one and a-half inches long, slender, slightly curved; lobes broadly oval, blunt, one-third to one and a-half inches long. Anthers enclosed within the summit of the tube. Style with its upper part exserted. Stigma distinctly two-lobed. Fruit unknown.

This Eranthemum may have a cyclus of forms as wide as that of E. variabile. The precise relation of two other congeneric plants of Mr. Campbell's collection to E. repandum remains to be investigated. One of these from Eramanga has narrower oblong or lanceolar leaves, with not distinctly repand margin, the tube of the corolla shorter in respect to the lobes and the anthers exserted. The other Eranthemum alluded to came from Santo, where it forms a shrub five feet high, with showy white flowers sprinkled with red. The leaves are almost membraneous, the lower ones about four inches long, ovate-lanceolate, acuminate, on comparatively short petioles, repand at the margin; the upper leaves are almost sessile, broadly ovate, gradually narrowed into the pointed apex and not repand; the lower peduncles are usually only one-flowered, while the flowers of the summit form a small corymb; the bracteoles are longer and so also the segments of the calyces; the tube of the corolla is hardly one inch long. Fruit-capsules of none of these three plants are extant for comparison, and it may thus on this occasion be passingly remarked, that on carpologic characteristic in most in most instances the safe limitation of specified forms of plants can be perfected, when floral characters fail to effect an exact discrimination. Indeed, the truth of the Bible words, "A fructibus eorum cognoscetis eos," (*Evangelium Matthaei*, caput VI., 16) is also here significant.

Beyond the species recorded by the late Dr. Seemann as Polynesian, the writer is acquainted with Eranthemum variabile (R. Brown, *Prodr.*

*Flor. Nov. Holl.*, p. 47) from New Caledonia, out of Pancher's collection; further, with a large leaved densely downy species, producing terminal somewhat racemose flowers from the Society Islands. This handsome plant seems to have hitherto remained phytographically unnoticed; but the material before me is not really sufficient for absolute diagnostic definition, especially as we are aware that the genus Eranthemum contains numerous closely allied forms, of which several have unduly been raised already to a specific rank.

RUELLIA REPTANS (G. Forster, *Flor. Insul. Austral., Prodr.*, p. 44.)

SANTO. This plant was seen by Mr. Campbell to attain a height of five feet. He noticed the corolla to be whitish. Peduncles not rarely solitary. Flowers very few in terminal, almost fascicular cymes. Seeds about fourteen, dark brown, obicular-ovate, smooth, slightly turgid, about two-thirds line long.

SOLANUM MILNEI (Seemann's *Journal of Botany*, 1863, page 210.)

ERAMANGA. The specimens collected represent a small leaved variety.

## ASPERIFOLIAE.

CORDIA MYXA, (Linné, *spec. plant*, 273.)

TANA, on hills. Height to fifteen feet. Flowers white. Not previously recorded from the New Hebrides—thus, like many others of Mr. Campbell's plants, new from there.

## LABIATAE.

OCIMUM SANCTUM (Linné, *Mantiss.*, p. 85.)

SANTO. Three feet high. Flowers purplish, according to Mr. Campbell. This is the first record of this and the following plant from Polynesia.

OCIMUM BASILICUM (Linné, *spec. plant.* 883.)

SANTO and EFATE. This species has also been found in Feegee by Dr. Seemann, but is mentioned in his work as O. gratissimum. Probably the latter occurs in Feegee also, along with O. Basilicum, like in many parts of India, and both may have been mixed in Seemann's collection. A small flowered variety was gathered in Madagascar by Dr. Meller, according to specimens communicated by Sir Henry Barkly. The limits of most species of Ocimum have not yet been accurately ascertained.

COLEUS SCUTELLAROIDES (Bentham in *Wallich plant. Asiat. rarior.*, II., 16.)

SANTO.

TEUCRIUM INFLATUM (Swartz, *Prodr Flor. Ind. Occid.*, page 88.)
TANA, near the sea-shores. Three feet high. Corolla purple.

## VERBENACEAE.

LIPPIA NODIFLORA (Cl. Richard, in *Michaux Flor. Boreal Americ.*, II., 15.)
TANA. Frequent in swampy places. Mr. Campbell records it two feet high. Peduncles not rarely opposite, such as may be observed also in specimens from other parts of the globe.

VITEX TRIFOLIA (Linné, *fil. suppl. pl.*, 293.)
TANA and ANEITYUM. From the latter island with five leaflets, representing apparently Vitex bicolor (Willdenow, *Enumerat. Plant. Hort. Berolin*, p. 606.) Leaflets sessile or conspicuously stalked.

PREMNA OBTUSIFOLIA (R. Brown, *Prodr. Flor. Nov. Holland*, 512.)
ANIWA, in woods. Five feet high. Flowers white. Fruit black. The seemingly identical species occurs in New Caledonia and Samoa, according to the collections of Dr. Veillard and the Rev. S. T. Whitmee, but the distinctions between P. integrifolia (Linné, *Mantiss.* 252) P. Taitensis (J. C. Schauer, in *De Candolle, Prodr.* xi., 638) and P. latifolia (Roxburgh, *Flor. Ind.*, III., 76) have never yet been set forth with clearness. Roxburgh designates the flowers of the last mentioned plant as yellow. The length of the petioles of P. obtusifolia is variable, and the leaves verge more or less into an oval or orbicular or cordate form.

## MYRSINEAE.

MAESA BAEOBOTRYS (Roemer et Schultes, *Syst. Vegetab.*, v. 226.)
TANA, on sides of hills. Height up to about fifteen feet. Leaves charactaceous, verging sometimes into an almost orbicular form. Bracteoles rhomboid-orbicular. Lobes of the calyx almost deltoid; those of the corolla about as long as the tube, roundish semiovate, white.

The opposite leaves of some species of Ardisia on the one hand, and the almost woody stem of several Lysimachiae on the other hand, obliterate still more the physiognomic differences between Myrsineae and Primulaceae.

Mr. Campbell's collection from Tana contains also a branchlet with flower buds only of a sapotaceous tree, evidently distinct from the likewise yet obscure Bassia obovata (G. Forst., *Prodr.*, p. 35) from the same island. The sap of this tree should be subjected to experiments for ascertaining whether it could be converted into gutta-percha; it being now well known that many very different kinds of sapotaceous trees yield this substance, now so extensively in demand for commerce and manufactures.

## PRIMULACEAE.

LYSIMACHIA DECURRENS (G. Forster, *Flor. Insul. Anstral. prodr.* p. 12; L. Javanica, Blume, *Bijdragen tot de Flora van Nederlandsch, Indie*, p. 736; L. multiflora, Wallich in *Candolle prodr.* VIII., 62, non Klatt, fide Miquel *Annal. Mus. Bot. Lugdun, Batav.*, IV., 145; L. sinica, Miquel in *Journ. de Botan., Ne'erland*, I., 110.)

Herbaceous, glabrous; leaves scattered, membranous, almost lanceolate, acuminate, narrowed into a conspicuous and decurrent petiole, mainly towards the margin glandulous; racemes terminal, many-flowered; bracts subulate-linear, shorter than the pedicels; flowers small; corolla white, little longer than the lanceolate segments of the calyx; its lobes twice as long as the tube, blunt, entire, almost oblong; stamens disconnected, exserted; anthers almost oval, many times shorter than the capillary filaments; staminodia none; style rather long, filiform; capsule globose, valveless, slightly excelling the calyx in length; seeds smooth, almost tetrahedrous, numerous, wingless.

In open flats of TANA. A herb, about one foot high, not much branched. Stems fistulose, prominently angular. Leaves, when fully developed, from two to three inches long, entire, somewhat paler beneath. Racemes attaining a length of eight inches, but occasionally few-flowered, and then hardly above one inch long. Pedicels thin, very spreading, at first about two lines, subsequently four lines long, angular, beset with exceedingly minute glands. Calyces about one and a-half lines long; the segments broadly or oftener narrowly lanceolate, at the inner side marked with four streaks. Corolla, chiefly in its lower part, dotted with minute dark glands; its lobes overlapping in bud. Stamens inserted on the base of the lobes of the corolla. Filaments one and a-half to two lines long, downward beset with minute black prominent glands. Anthers versatile, about one-fourth of a line long. Style also glabrous, thinly filiform, slightly thickened upwards, about two lines long, persistent. Stigma depressed, exceedingly minute. Capsule extensively surrounded by the appressed calyx, thinly cartilagineous or slightly crustaceous, measuring one and a-half to two lines, breaking at last irregularly, outside opaque, inside very shining. Placenta thinly and conspicuously stalked, globular, densely covered with the seeds. The latter dark brown or black, smooth, of about a quarter line measurement, flat at the vertex, thus forming, with the placenta, an even globular mass.

From the material, brought by Mr. Campbell, I am now enabled to bring this plant, which was buried in obscurity for almost a century, anew into fuller light; and therefore I offer now a somewhat extensive description of it. The two Forsters discovered it in Tana during Cook's second voyage, and the younger Forster gave, in 1786, the first and hitherto only description of the Tana plant, in the work above quoted, with the customary briefness of the time. Blume, not having access to Forsters' plant, was prevented from recognising it, when he discovered the identical species in Java; but I find original specimens from Blume in my collection, precisely agreeing with the plant from the New Hebrides. Dr. Klatt, in his elaborate and profusely illustrated monography of the genus Lysimachia, published in 1866 (*Abhandlungen aus dem Gebiete der Natur-wissenschaften*, Hamburg,) passes Lysimachia decurrens, as then almost unknown. My late friend, Dr. Berthold Seemann, in his highly meritorious work on the Fiji plants, just completed, and in its concluding portions posthumous, alludes passingly (*Flora Vitiensis*, p. 147) to the original plant of Forster's, which he had the advantage of re-examining in the British Museum, and identified with it Macgillivray's Lysimachia from the isle of Pines. I possess L. decurrens also from New Caledonia, where Mons. Pancher found it in "prairies humides," the specific identity not having been established before.

Since the issue of Klatt's monography, many new localities have been additionally recorded for the species then enumerated. On this occasion it would lead too far to dwell on that particular subject; but it may here be observed that the following species have since been defined :—

LYSIMACHIA COUSINIANA, Cosson. On the river Zhour, near Collo in Algeria.

LYSIMACHIA KEISKEANA, Miquel, *Annal. Mus. Bot., Lugdun, Batav.*, III., 120. (L. acroadenia, Maxim. *Mélang. Biolog.*, VI., 272; L. multiflora, Klatt in Hamburg *Abhandlungen*, 1866, part IV., p. 14, non Wallich,) Japan.

LYSIMACHIA SIKOKIANA, Miquel, *l. c.*, III., 121. Japan.

LYSIMACHIA INCONSPICUA, Miquel, *Journ. de Botaniq., Neerland.* I., 110, South China.

LYSIMACHIA SALICIFOLIA, F. von Mueller in Bentham's *Flor. Austral.*, IV., 269. New England (N. S. Wales); Gippsland.

LYSIMACHIA CHRISTINÆ, Hance in Trimen's *Journal of Botany*, 1873, p. 167. North-east China.

LYSIMACHIA SAMOLINA, Hance. North-east China.

LYSIMACHIA HILLEBRANDI, J. Hook, according to Seemann's *Flora Vitiens.* p. 147. Sandwich Islands.

LYSIMACHIA PACIFICA. Lubinia pacifica, Seemann, *l. c.*, p. 147. Isle of Pines.

It might still be added, that L. deltoidea, Wight, *Illustrat. of Indian Bot.*, II., 137, tab. 144, has been reduced to L. Japonica by Dr. Thwaites (euumeration of *Ceylon Plants*, p. 172); further, that L. quadriflora (Sims in *Botan. Magaz.*, tab. 660) by priority should take precedence of L. longifolia (Pursh *Flora of North America*, I., 135,) although the excellent Dr. Asa Gray still upholds the latter appellation. (See *Manual of Botany of the Northern United States*, fifth edition, 1870, p. 316.)

L. decurrens is nearest allied to L. lobelioides (Wallich in *Roxb. Flor. Ind.*, II., 22) which, according to Himalaian specimens from Dr. Falconer, differs already in its capsules valved towards the summit. L. Leschenaultii, (Duby in *Candolle prodr.* VIII., 68,) also from upper India, of which I have no authentic museum-plants for comparison, is distinguished, according to the illustrations given by Wight and Klatt, in more distinctly denticulated leaves, and in a more general and conspicuous glandular pubesence. It requires closer comparison.

## ASCLEPIADEAE.

ASCLEPIAS CURASSAVICA (Linné, *System. Veget.*, 289 ; *spec. plant*, I., 314.)

ANEITYUM; frequent now, though originally immigrated from tropical America.

HOYA AUSTRALIS (R. Brown in the *Transactions of the Horticultural Society of London*, VII., 28.)

TANA, the original place of discovery of this plant; Dr. Seemann having identified it with Asclepias volubilis (G. Forster, prodr. p. 21.) In Tana it grows on rocks along the sea.

## APOCYNEAE.

CERBERA LACTARIA (Hamilton in *De Candolle, prodr.* VIII., 253.)

TANA, frequent; there a tree about twenty feet high. Mr. Campbell's specimens are without fruit, and imperfectly in flower, but seem to belong to the above noted species. He describes the fruits egg-shaped, green, and abont two inches long. The same species appears to occur in Queensland and New Caledonia. It differs from C. Odollam (Gaertner, *de fructibus*, II., 193, tab. 124) in shorter less acute lobes of the calyx, and in smaller and blunter lobes of the corolla, which are almost as broad as long, further in smaller fruits.

TABERNAEMONTANA ORIENTALIS (R. Brown, *Prodr. Flor. Nov., Holland*, 468.)

EFATE, together with Ixora Pavetta. Only the fruit gathered.

## CONVOLVULACEAE.

CONVOLVULUS PARVIFLORUS (Vahl, *Symbol*, III., 29.)

EFATE. Mr. Campbell notes the flowers as light-yellow. R. & G. Forster originally found this plant in New Caledonia already during Captain Cook's second great discovery voyage; but it had hitherto not been brought from any part of Polynesia, although it is known to be amply dispersed over continental and insular India and the more littoral parts of tropical Australia.

## CASUARINEAE.

CASUARINA EQUISETIFOLIA (R. & G. Forster, *Charact. Gen.* p. 103, fig. 52.)

ANIWA.

## CONIFERAE.

NAGEIA CUPRESSINA (Podocarpus cupressina, R. Brown in *Memoir. du Musée*, XIII., 75.)

NEW HEBRIDES. L'Heritier's genus Podocarpus was first publicly noticed in 1806, by La Billardiere (*Nov. Holl. plant spec.* II., 11) in a note referring to the South-African Podocarpus elongata, and republished by Persoon in 1807 (*Synops. Plantar.*, II., 580,) whereas Gaertner's genus Nageia was clearly rendered known already in 1788 (*De Fructib. et Seminib.*, I, 191, tab. 49.)

## SCITAMINEAE.

GUILLAINA NOVO-EBUDICA.

Flowers solitary in the axil of the thinly chartaceous very obtuse slightly distant bracts, without any special cylindrical bracteole; lobes of the corolla as well as the labellum small and short.

Santo, somewhat inland, in open places of the forests.

The finder noticed only one individual plant, which was six feet high. Well developed leaves, long lanceolar, one to one and a-half feet long, about two inches broad, paler beneath; clasping portion of the petiole fissured longitudinally, terminated by a semi-ovate firm ligula; free portion of the petiole very short. Spike one and a-half feet long, proliferous at the base, the offshoots bearing leaves one to two inches long. Bracts red, not crowded, oblong or oval, somewhat cuneate, moderately spreading, one to one and a-half inches long, and a third to a half inch broad, or the lower ones still larger. Calyces very slender, one-half to two-thirds of an inch long, tubular, with three short acute teeth, not conspicuously slit downward. Corolla half exserted; its tube gradually widening at the summit, its lobes narrow and acute. Labellum roundish, measuring hardly two lines. crisp, above bearing two raised lines and some short downs; its length hardly exceeding that of the limb of the corolla. Filament linear, channelled, on the surface towards the summit finely silky. Anther cells contiguous, parallel, about one and a-half line long; the apex of the anther protracted into a minute roundish membrane. Style capillary, glabrous. Stigma small, obconic, truncate. Fruit unknown.

This plant, impressingly beautiful through its long red spikes, is placed here provisionally into the genus Guillaina, the identification resting ou the examination of the remnants of a few shrivelled flowers. Genericly this plant, as well as the original G. purpurata (Veillard, *Notes sur quelques Plantes interessantes de la Nouvelle Calédonie*, p. 4) recedes materially from Globba, in the completely three-celled ovary, the ovules being attached to the parietal part of the septa. So far as observations could be instituted on existing material, the New Caledonian typical plant diverges from that of Santo in thicker leaves and bracts, in longer lobes of the flowers, and especially in the presence of an accessory tubular bract, which frequently embraces two flowers, and is sometimes binerved and bilobed, thus indicating a confluence of two bracteoles. The only specimen of Dr. Veillard's plant, which could be compared, was presented with numerous other New Caledonian plants to the Melbourne Phytagraphic Museum by Madame Lénormand, of Vire, Calvados—a lady who for many years has most generously and enthusiastically promoted the progress of the scientific knowledge of plants, and especially those of the marine Floras.

CANNA INDICA (Linné, *spec. pl.*, 1.)

TANA. The variety with red flowers.

## ORCHIDEAE.

SPATHOGLOTTIS PACIFICA (G. Reichenbach in Seemann's *Flor. Vitiens.*, p. 300.)

ERAMANGA. Only a few flowers occur in Mr. Campbell's collection; these seem not to differ from those of the Fiji-plant above.

named. S. plicata (G. Reichenbach, *l. c.*,) from New Caledonia, according to Turpin's delineation (La Billardiére, *sert. Nov. Caled.*, t. 25) has the labellum saccate at the base. Two other allied plants of the genus are: S. plicata (Blumé, *Bijdragen*, p. 400) from India, and S. Paulinæ (F. Mueller, *Fragmenta Phytographiæ Australiæ*, vol. 6, p. 95) from Queensland.

## PERISTYLUS NOVO-EBUDARUM (*Habenaria Novo-Ebudarum*, F. V. M.)

Glabrous; leaves several, lanceolate, membraneous; spike slender; bracts semi-lanceolate, acuminate, almost as long as the flowers; sepals very small, lanceolate-oblong, the inner two hardly shorter; labellum nearly as long as the inner sepals, broadly unguiculate, the upper part rhombiform in outline, with two shallow sinus in front, thus three-toothed, the teeth blunt, the middle one slightly longer; spur globular-ovate, gibbous, attenuated upwards, hardly half as long as the calyx; column extremely short.

ANEITYUM, on hilly and bushy timberland.

The whole plant about one foot high. Tuber narrow, ellipsoid-cylindrical, measuring about one inch in length. Petioles tubular, except the summit, the lower ones leafless and blunt; free part of the upper ones very short. Lowest leaves only about one inch long; all others attaining a length generally from two to four inches, and a width of one-fourth to three-fourths of an inch; apex acute. Spike a few inches long. Bracts three to five lines long. Flowers, according to the discoverer of the plant, brownish-yellow. Sepals about one and a-half line long, the upper one almost oval, all bluntish and undivided. Labellum slightly downy on the surface, only crenated in front, the lateral teeth or lobes roundish; cilia or conspicuous appendages none. Spur less than a line long, blunt at the base, turgid in front. Anther bluntly bilobed. Pollen masses, consisting of minute granules. Ovary slender, gradually attenuated to the summit, sessile.

Peristylus Lawii (Wight, *Icon. Plantar. Ind Orient.*, tab. 1695) from Malabar, shows the nearest affinity. The flowers of the Aneityum plant are still smaller, and the teeth of the labellum are still shorter and not acute. P. brevilobus (Thwaites, *Enumer Plant. Zeilan.*, 311) differs already in its short and dense spike, and in the minuteness of the middle tooth of the labellum. The genus Habenaria, in its normal type, extends to Samoa, one long-spurred species having been discovered there by the Rev. S. J. Whitmee. Dendrobium Tokai exists there also.

## GASTRODIA OROBANCHOIDES.

Racemes few-flowered, slightly hairy; bracts lanceolate, acuminate; pedicels extremely short; calyces small, their lobes much shorter than

the undivided tube ; labellum nearly half exserted, **cleft to the middle
into** two rhomboid-cuneate in front and outward irregularly **denticulated** lobes, slightly thickened but not cristate towards the **middle;
column exceedingly short ; anther very minutely rostrate, also terminated by two narrow-spathulate transparent** appendages, **and
furthermore produced on both sides into two** linear-subulate **laciniae.**

ERAMANGA ; discovered by the Rev. Hugh Fraser.

Two raceme exstant in Mr. Campbell's collections. Bract below
the raceme empty, about two-thirds of an inch long, tubular towards
the base, like the floral bracts, membraneous. Flowers crowded almost into a corymb. Their bracts three to five lines long, one-nerved,
beset with but few hairs. Calyces membraneous, more or less bluntly
or acutely five-toothed, oblique at the broad base, there rounded on
the outer side, and almost gibbous on the inner one, only about three
lines long ; the petaline lobes still more delicately tender than the
sepaline ones ; the tube not separated into two labia as in the section
Leucorchis. Labellum four to five lines long, membranous ; the
sinus between the two lobes forming an acute angle ; the lower portion of the labellum broad-linear, canalicular-bent. Appendages of
the anther less than one line long. Pollen-masses oblique ovate,
granular. Young fruit obovate, somewhat pear-shaped, conspicuously
constricted at the junction of the floral parts. Fruit-pedicels hardly
one line long.

This very remarkable species accords in the size of its flowers
and their paucity with G. verucosa (Blume, *Mus. Bot. Lugdun.* II., 173)
and G. pallens (Epiphanes pallens, G. Reichenbach, in Seemann's
*Flor. Vit.*, 296 ; Didymoplexis pallens, Griffith in McClelland's
*Calcutta Journ. of Nat. Hist.*, 1844, p. 17 ; Apetalon minutum, Wight,
*Icon. Plant. Ind. Orient.*, v., tab. 1758 ;) while it agrees in the short-
ness of the column, and also in the very abbreviated pedicels, with
G. Cunninghami (J. Hooker, *Flor. Nov. Zeel.*, I., 251,) but it differs
not only from these three congeners, but also from all others hitherto
known, namely, G. sesamoides (R. Brown, *prodr.* 330) G. gracilis,
G. elata, G. Hasseltii (Blume, *l. c.*) G. silvatica (Leucorchis sylvatica,
Blume, *l. c.*, vol. I., 31) and G. Javanica (Endlicher *Genera Plant.*, 212)
in the deeply bilobed and partly exserted labellum.

CORYMBORCHIS VERATRIFOLIA (Blume, *Les Orchidées de
Archipel. Indien. et du Japon*, p. 125, planch. 32 and 43.)

SANTO, in dense forests. Attains a height of six feet.

## LILIACEAE.

DIANELLA INTERMEDIA (Endlicher, *Prodr. Flor. Norfolk*,
page 28.)

ANEITYUM and ERAMANGA. The fibre of all Dianella species is of remarkable strength. The Pacific plants of this genus require yet a fuller description from ampler material.

## FLAGELLARIEAE.

JOINVILLEA ELEGANS (Gaudichaud, *Voyage autour du Monde sur la Bonite, Botanique, Atlas,* pl. 39, fig. 7, 26.

ANEITYUM; very abundant on flat open ground. Mr. Campbell observes that the plant is up to ten feet high, and very useful to the natives, it being used for trellises, thatches, fences and other requirements. The material before me consists of a flowering panicle, and another with unripe fruits. I note some discrepancies from the descriptions given by Jos. Hooker (*Kew Miscellany*, 1855, p. 200, pl. 6) The anthers are attached to the filament near their base, and the latter are not as long as or even longer than the anthers, but so short as to render the anthers almost sessile. Brogniart and Gris (*Annales des Scienc. Natur.*, 1864, p. 332) also found the "filets assez courts." These diversities of structure, in all probability, may be reconciled to dimorphism; or perhaps the stamens become elongated in advancing age. The sepals are more or less acuminate, and the three inner ones are sometimes hardly shorter than the rest. In Fiji specimens, recorded by Seemenn (*Flor. Viti.*, p. 315) the stigmata are mostly yet persistent in the ripe fruit, while the berries of the Aneityum plant are generally deprived of the stigmata already in a young state. When not all three seeds are ripening, then the berry becomes oblique.

This stately somewhat palm-like plant would probably prove hardy here, like the allied Flagellaria Indica, and would for scenic effect be valuable in our gardens.

## CYPERACEAE.

RHYNCHOSPORA AUREA (Vahl, *Enumer. Plant.* II., 291.)
ANEITYUM; also in Samoa. Whitmee.

SCLERIA MARGARITIFERA (Willdenow, *Sp. Pl.*, IV., 321.)
SANTO, on open flats. Found by Mr. C. H. Walter, during the Victorian Eclipse Expedition on Fitzroy Island.

The brown disk, divided into three acute deltoid lobes, protrated downward and encircling the thus hollow base of the fruit, distinguishes this species from Scleria laevis (Retzius, *Observ. Bot.*, IV., 13) and from Scleria Sumatrensis (Retzius, *Observ.*, v., 19.)

FILIBRISTYLIS COMMUNIS (Kunth, *Enumerat. Plantar.*, II., 234.)
ANEITYUM, on hill-sides near the coast. Farvensis (Vahl, *Enumer.*,

II, 201) is likely to exist also in the New Hebrides, it having been found in New Caledonia and the Fiji Islands. It has shorter leaves, and almost smooth fruits.

CYPERUS DISTANS (Linné, fil., *Suppl. Plant.*, 103.)

ANEITYUM. A variety with larger and less distant florets. In Samoa also, according to the Rev. S. J. Whitmee.

## GRAMINEAE.

COIX LACRYMA (Linné, *Spec. Plant.*, 1378.)

TANA, on the sides of streams. The natives use the seeds as beads.

CENTOTHECA LAPPACEA (Desvaux in *Journ. de Botanique* 1813, p. 70.)

ANEITYUM and TANA.

PANICUM COMPOSITUM (Linné, *Spec. Plant.*, 84.)

SANTO, near the sea-shores; also in Aneityum. Several of the numerous forms of this excedingly variable species occur on these islands.

PANICUM SANGUINALE (Linné, *Spec. Plant*, 84.)

ANEITYUM, near the coast.

THUAREA SARMENTOSA (Persoon, *Synops. Plant.*, I., 110.)

ANEITYUM; frequent on the sandy sea-shores. The spikes sometimes above an inch long.

CENCHRUS ANOMOPLEXIS (La Billardière, *Sertum Austro-Caledon.*, vol. I., p. 14, tab. 19.)

SANTO, on open hill-sides. The specific validity of this grass as distinct from Cenchrus Australis (R. Brown, *Prodr.* 196) requires yet to be further demonstrated. Sprengel (*Systema Vegetabilium, Curæ posteriores*, page 33) regarded LA Billardière's plant merely as a variety of that of R. Brown. Its destination seems to rest mainly on larger size, particularly of leaves and flowers. The segments of the inner involucellum are more densely bearded than shown in the analytic figure of the plate above quoted. Comparisons with C. calyculatus (Cavan., *Icon.*, v., 39, t. 463; C. Fainsis, Steud. *glum.*, I., 419) are needed.

ERIANTHUS JAPONICUS (Beauvois, *Agrostographie*, p. 14; Eulalia Japonica, *Trinius Acta Societ. Petropolit.* 1833, page 333.)

ANEITYUM, near the sea-shores. The stalks attain a length of five feet. Steudel (*Synopsis Plantarum glumacearum*, I., 412) and Seemann (*Flora Vitiensis*, p. 321) describe the leaves as linear-filiform, and Bentham also (*Flora of Hong Kong*, p. 420) calls them narrow. This applies, however, scarcely even to the uppermost leaves, and almost prevents the recognition of this species from description alone; inasmuch as the lower leaves, not only of specimens from the New Hebrides, but also from the Fiji Islands and from Whampoa (the latter from Dr. Hance's collection) are over half an inch or even fully one inch broad. Such, indeed, are shown likewise in Turpin's plate 18 of La Billardière's *Sertum Austro-Caledonicum.*

APLUDA MUTICA (Linné, *Spec. Plant*, 1486.)

ANEITYUM. One of the two lateral peduncles bears not rarely a two-flowered spikelet, articulated with it, one of its flowers being staminiferous, the other separately pistilliferous; but the latter seems not to perfect any grain. The ultimate peduncles or pedicels are at the base laterally dilated, to form a receptacle for the sessile fertile spikelet. The flowers of the latter are not always advancing to their normal development. A. geniculata (Roxburgh, *Flor. Ind.*, I., 327) seems not specifically distinct from A. mutica. This is the first record of Apluda in Polynesia; nor is this genus found hitherto represented in Australia. As a whole the grassflora of the South-Sea Islands seems remarkably scanty. Beside the few gramineæ alluded to in Dr. Seemann's work, and those mentioned in these pages, our museum collections here contain only Lepturus acutiglumis (Steudel, *Glumac.*, I., 359) from the almost unexplored Gilbert's group, procured there by the Rev. S. J. Whitmee; Setaria glauca (Beauvois, *Essai d'une nouvelle Agrostographie*, p. 51) from New Caledonia; Aira sabulorum (La Bill., *Sert. Austro-Caled.*, p. 51, tab. 21,) Andropogon cortortus (L., *Spec. Plant*, 1480) both from the same island; Andropogon pertusus (Willd., *Spec. Plant*, IV., 22) in its efoveolate form from Fiji, where it was gathered by Mr. Swanston, and two other Andropogons, are allied to A. fragilis (R. Br., 202) from New Caledonia, the other belongin gto the section Spodiopogon, and from the Loyalty Islands.

## LYCOPODIACEAE.

LYCOPODIUM CERNUUM (Linné, *Spec. Plant.* 1566.)
NEW HEBRIDES.

## FILICES.

SELAGINELLA WALLICHII (Spring, *Monograph. Lycopod.*, page 86.)
NEW HEBRIDES. Lycopodium phlegmaria (Linné, *Spec. Plant,*

1564) as well as L. squarrosum (G. Forster. *Prodr.*, p. 86) were some years ago collected in the same group of islands by Mr. H. Richards, of Sydney, who communicated to the author besides many other ferns from these islands. The same zealous collector discovered there the Lycopodium serratum (Thunb., *Flor. Japon.*, p. 341, tab. 38) the most lovely of all species; it was found also in Honolulu by Dr. Hillebrand, an early contributor to our museum. Like the last-mentioned species also L. laterale (R. Brown, *Prodr.*, 165,) noted in 1824 as New Caledonian already by La Billardière (*Sert. Nov. Caled.*, p. 10., tab. 15,) remained unrecorded in Dr. Seemann's work.

ACROSTICHUM REPANDUM (Blume, *Flor. Javæ*, 39, tab. 14 and 15.)

NEW HEBRIDES. F. Campbell, Esq. In the fifth volume of the *Fragmenta Phytographiæ Australiæ*, p. 139, I referred at some length to the characteristics of this fern from Bishop Patteson's Eramanga collection.

SCHIZAEA FORSTERI (Sprengel, *Anleitung zur Kenntniss der Gewaechse*, III., 175.)

ANEITYUM. This species is often misunderstood and confused with S. dichotoma (Smith, *Act. Turin*, 1791, p. 419,) from which it differs in the more regularly flabellar disposition of the frond-segments, and also in the proportionately but not always absolutely greater width of the latter, by which means the aspect of the plant becomes very distinct when compared with the outline given by the unequal heights of the ramifications of S. dichotoma, the sori of that species not being placed into an almost equal radius. But a still more important distinction between these two plants consists in the arrangemeut of the sori, which are strictly pinnate in S. dichotoma, though the lower ones may occasionally be bifid or trifid; whereas in S. Fosteri the disposition of the sori is fascicular, almost in the manner of that of S. digitata, (Swartz, *Synopsis Filicum*, p. 150, t. 4,) although their length is very much less. The sori of S. Fosteri are sometimes reduced to two or three in total number, and generally less numerous than those of S. dichotoma, which however vary from eight to about sixty, with a length from one and a-half to five lines.

Specimens of S. Forsteri have on this occasion been compared from New Caledonia, Fiji, various islands of the New Hebrides, also from Lify (Allan Hughan.) Dr. Seemann records it from Tahiti, but of the occurrence of this plant anywhere in Australia I am not aware, although this, as well as S. digitata, may be expected to occur in Queensland.

Schizaea bifida (Swartz, *Synops. Filic.*, p. 151) embraces merely such forms of S. dichotoma, as are reduced from the typical very multifid state to but few divisions of the frond; and this reduction may even proceed so far as to render the plant utterly branchless, when it assumes closely the appearance of the South-African S. pectinata (Sm.. *l.c.*, from which S.

tenella, Kaulfuss, *Enumer Filic.*, t. 1, fig. 7, may not be specifically distinct) S. dichotoma is found sparingly from the southern extreme of Australia through the littoral eastern regions quite to the remotest northern points of the Australian continent; it occurs also in New Caledonia, Fiji, and Samoa, and likewise in Mauritius, according to Lady Barkly's collections. It may exceptionally be seen fruit-bearing when hardly two inches high.

### LYGODIUM RETICULATUM (Schkuhr, *Farren Kraeuter*, tab. 139.)

NEW HEBRIDES. The fronds membraneous, as in plants of this species from N. E. Australia.

### ANGIOPTERIS EVECTA (Hoffmann in *Comment. Soc. Reg. Gœtting*, XII., p. 29, tab. 5.)

NEW HEBRIDES.

### ALSOPHILA LUNULATA (R. Brown, *Prodr.* 158.)

NEW HEBRIDES. A. decurrens (Hooker, *Spec. Filic.*, I., 51, and Cyathea propinqua, Mettenius in Miquel, *Annal. Mus. Bot. Lugd. Batav.*, I., 56) occur in a collection of ferns kindly gathered and communicated by Captain Fraser, the commander of the mission ship "Dayspring." Several other tree ferns are known already from these isles, and others remain likely to be discovered. The characteristics, however, of the stems, generally very distinctive, are ascertained in but few cases.

### POLYPODIUM ACROSTICHOIDES (G. Forster, *Flor. Insul. Austr. Prodr.* p. 81.)

NEW HEBRIDES.

### POLYPODIUM PHYMATODES (Linné, *Mantiss. Plant*, 306.)

NEW HEBRIDES.

### POLYPODIUM RIGIDULUM (Swartz, *Synops. Filic.*, p. 34.)

NEW HEBRIDES. The magnificent P. conjugatum (Kaulfuss, *Das Wesen der Farn. Kraeuter*, p. 104) was found in the group by Capt. Fraser.

### ASPIDIUM EXALTATUM (Swartz, *Synops. Filic.*, p. 45.)

NEW HEBRIDES.

ASPIDIUM ACULEATUM (Swartz in Schrader's *Journal fuer die Botanik*, 1800, II., 37.)

NEW HEBRIDES. This fern, though regarded as almost cosmopolitan is absent from most parts of Australia, being there restricted, as far as hitherto ascertained, to the south-eastern and eastern regions.

ASPLENIUM FALCATUM (La Marck, *Encyclopædie method.*, II., 306.)

NEW HEBRIDES. Under the above specific name A. polyodon and A. caudatum (G. Forster, *Flor. Insul. Austr., Prodr.* p. 80) are to be combined.

ASPLENIUM NIDUS (Linné, *Spec. Plantar.*, 1537.)

NEW HEBRIDES.

ASPLENIUM VULCANICUM (Blume, *Enumerat. Plânt. Jav. Filic.*, 176.)

NEW HEBRIDES, from whence this stately fern was not recorded before.

PTERIS LONGIFOLIA (Linné, *Spec. Plant.*, p. 1047.)

NEW HEBRIDES. F. Campbell. Collected in Eramanga already by Bishop Patteson, the martyr of Santa Cruz, who, amidst the arduous duties devolving on his high office, set also an example for zealous and devoted appreciation of Divine revelation, as afforded us in the works of nature. So, through the personal exertions of this unfortunate prelate, we became early acquainted with numerous plants from the islands then under his Lordship's ecclesiastical care.

The marginal serratures of the pinnæ of P. longifolia are at times very conspicuous; the auricular protrusion of the anterior basal angle measures occasionally fully a quarter of an inch.

PTERIS CRENATA (Swartz, *Synops. Filic.*, p. 96 and 290.)

ANEITYUM, F. Campbell; ERAMANGA, Bishop Patteson.

PTERIS COMANS (G. Forster, *Flor. Insul. Austral., Prodr.* p. 79.)

ERAMANGA. Collected by Bishop Patteson, Captain Fraser, and Mr. F. Campbell. The lateral pinnæ attain a length of one and a half feet; also the upper segments are sometimes lobed.

PTERIS QUADRIAURITA (Retzius, *Observat.*, VI., 38.)

NEW HEBRIDES.

PTERIS AQUILINA (Linné, *Spec. Plant.* 1074.)
NEW HEBRIDES.

VITTARIA ELONGATA (Swartz, *Synops. Filic.*, 109.)
NEW HEBRIDES.

LINDSAEA NITENS (Blume, *Enum. Plant. Jav. Filices,*
217.)
NEW HEBRIDES.

ADIANTUM CAUDATUM (Linné, *Mantiss. Plant.*, p. 308.)
NEW HEBRIDES. Seemingly not known before from any of the Polynesian groups.

ADIANTUM DIAPHANUM (Blume, *Enum. Plant. Jav. Filic.*, 215.)

NEW HEBRIDES. Many observations, bearing also on the ferns of Polynesia, are recorded in the writer's "Vegetation of the Chatham Islands (1864) p. 62-74; and in his "Fragmenta Phytographiæ Australiæ," vol. v. (1866) p. 111-142.

Mr. Campbell's collection contains also a few mosses of the genera Hypnum, Spiridens and Leucobryum, and likewise several algae referable to the following genera:—Halimeda, Galaxaura, Turbinaria, and Sargassum.

Printed by George Mercer, Malop Street West, Geelong.

www.ingramcontent.com/pod-product-compliance
Lightning Source LLC
Chambersburg PA
CBHW032058220426
**43664CB00008B/1052**